The Complete Guide to

COMPANION PLANTING:

Everything You Need to Know to Make Your Garden Successful

By Dale Mayer

24.95

THE COMPLETE GUIDE TO COMPANION PLANTING: EVERYTHING YOU NEED
TO KNOW TO MAKE YOUR GARDEN SUCCESSFUL

Copyright © 2011 Atlantic Publishing Group, Inc.
1405 SW 6th Avenue • Ocala, Florida 34471 • Phone 800-814-1132 • Fax 352-622-1875
Web site: www.atlantic-pub.com • E-mail: sales@atlantic-pub.com
SAN Number: 268-1250

Library of Congress Cataloging-in-Publication Data

Mayer, Dale, 1961-
  The complete guide to companion planting : everything you need to know
to make your garden successful / by Dale Mayer.
     p. cm.
  Includes bibliographical references and index.
  ISBN-13: 978-1-60138-345-7 (alk. paper)
  ISBN-10: 1-60138-345-2 (alk. paper)
  1. Companion planting. I. Title.
  SB453.6.M36 2010
  635'.048--dc22
                              2010016795

PROJECT MANAGER: Amy Moczynski   •   amoczynski@atlantic-pub.com
PEER REVIEWER: Marilee Griffin   •   INTERIOR DESIGN: Samantha Martin
FRONT COVER DESIGN: Meg Buchner   •   meg@megbuchner.com
BACK COVER DESIGN: Jackie Miller   •   millerjackiej@gmail.com

Printed on Recycled Paper

Printed in the United States

We recently lost our beloved pet "Bear," who was not only our best and dearest friend but also the "Vice President of Sunshine" here at Atlantic Publishing. He did not receive a salary but worked tirelessly 24 hours a day to please his parents. Bear was a rescue dog that turned around and showered myself, my wife, Sherri, his grandparents Jean, Bob, and Nancy, and every person and animal he met (maybe not rabbits) with friendship and love. He made a lot of people smile every day.

We wanted you to know that a portion of the profits of this book will be donated to The Humane Society of the United States. *–Douglas & Sherri Brown*

The human-animal bond is as old as human history. We cherish our animal companions for their unconditional affection and acceptance. We feel a thrill when we glimpse wild creatures in their natural habitat or in our own backyard.

Unfortunately, the human-animal bond has at times been weakened. Humans have exploited some animal species to the point of extinction.

The Humane Society of the United States makes a difference in the lives of animals here at home and worldwide. The HSUS is dedicated to creating a world where our relationship with animals is guided by compassion. We seek a truly humane society in which animals are respected for their intrinsic value, and where the human-animal bond is strong.

Want to help animals? We have plenty of suggestions. Adopt a pet from a local shelter, join The Humane Society and be a part of our work to help companion animals and wildlife. You will be funding our educational, legislative, investigative and outreach projects in the U.S. and across the globe.

Or perhaps you'd like to make a memorial donation in honor of a pet, friend or relative? You can through our Kindred Spirits program. And if you'd like to contribute in a more structured way, our Planned Giving Office has suggestions about estate planning, annuities, and even gifts of stock that avoid capital gains taxes.

Maybe you have land that you would like to preserve as a lasting habitat for wildlife. Our Wildlife Land Trust can help you. Perhaps the land you want to share is a backyard— that's enough. Our Urban Wildlife Sanctuary Program will show you how to create a habitat for your wild neighbors.

So you see, it's easy to help animals. And The HSUS is here to help.

2100 L Street NW • Washington, DC 20037 • 202-452-1100
www.hsus.org

· DEDICATION ·

A book is not written in a day and a writing career is not built overnight. Along the way, there are many bumps and turns that cause havoc in the process. It is during these times that you realize who your supporters truly are. In this area, I have been blessed more than most. I have several good friends who do not judge or criticize me. They love me and honor my choices. Then there is my family. It is easy to say they support me because that is what families do, but I'd like to think their support is based on their belief in me. My four children have always been my strongest supporters, firmly believing in their mother's ability to make it. Without these special people in my life, that long and twisted road would have been very lonely. Thank you to all those that walked by my side.

·TABLE OF CONTENTS·

Companion planting is a phrase that has taken on many meanings for today's gardeners. Within the scientific community, companion planting is also called **intercropping** and is a form of **polyculture**, which describes a method of planting species of plants together for mutual benefit, usually in agricultural situations.

For the layman, **companion planting** is best described as the practice of planting two or more plants together to enhance the growth and quality of nearby plants; to provide maximum ground cover; and, when possible, to improve the soil. This approach to gardening offers many benefits, with the trade-off being that more thought needs to go into the garden planning stage when deciding which plants should go where. Although there is no scientific explanation as to how or why the plants benefit one another, when planted in "companionable ways," much has been learned over the years — with a great deal of success.

Some of the successful companion planting relationships are due to the release of chemical secretions at the roots, which may affect other plants or have an effect on organisms in the soil. It has been theorized that companion planting benefits may result from the plant releasing certain gases or odors that can repel pests from either the roots or the above-ground parts of the plant. With certain predators (notably insects that damage the plants) out of the way, the plants can flourish. The same goes for other potential pairings. One plant may have the ability to do something like provide structure, add nitrogen to the soil, or offer shade in such a way that makes another plant flourish without hurting itself.

There have been lab studies where scientists have tried to replicate the results of companion planting — with mixed results. By adding the juices of pairs of plants to a 5 percent copper chloride solution and allowing it to crystallize slowly on a glass plate, Dr. Ehrenfried E. Pfeiffer and Dr. Erica Sabarth of the Bio-Dynamic Association were able to predict which plants would be companions and which would be antagonistic from the resulting crystallization patterns. Their findings, along with the trial and error of numerous gardeners, were summarized in a pamphlet by Richard Gregg in 1943 called *Companion Plants and How to Use Them*. Today, similar studies use paper chromatography techniques for related tests.

The companion planting suggestions in this book should be used as a basis for your own experimentation, not as a proven guide to success. One of the most important considerations when you look at choosing your own companion plants is to not lock yourself in by this book's information. Try some of the combinations out for yourself, experiment with new ones, but also play around with the spacing between the plants and the ratio of one plant to another. For example, there are suggestions that bush beans are most beneficial to celery and cucumbers in the ratio of one bean plant to six celery or cucumber plants. This means if you plant a large cucumber patch, you may only need to plant one or two bean plants to keep them happy.

As you become more familiar with the subject, you will eventually realize there is conflicting information — partly due to everyone's individual experiences based on geographical location, climate, and garden conditions. Therefore, the rule to companion gardening is simple: Try it out for yourself. Keep a record of your attempts and have fun with it. Plant basil in among your tomatoes and watch them grow like mad. Try basil in with the peppers for a similar result. Or, try adding in parsley as it can help tomatoes grow strong and healthy.

Companion planting requires a gardener to shake off his or her idea of traditional gardening and make room for new concepts. You will need to let go of concepts that define what a weed is and consider the fact that the weed could have value. Are there stinging nettles, a common weed across the United States, in your area? Have you spent hours trying to eradicate this weed that can grow up to 10 feet tall? Well, stop because they have value. If you grow them close to aromatic herbs, they are supposed to increase the aromatic oils in these herbs by as much as 75 percent. Stinging nettles, like foxglove and lily of the valley, are reported to improve the length of time the fruit from their companion plants can be kept once picked, particularly tomatoes.

Scientific research supports companion planting in the agriculture industry in terms of intercropping and crop rotation, the process of rotating crops for healthier soil and plants *(see Chapter 2 for more information on crop rotation)*. Companion planting applies to prevention or protection from pests and diseases, as well as attracting the right type of insects for pollination and for soil improvement. It is important to note that just as some plants will benefit from being close together, other plants will suffer from the pairing.

There are a few rights and wrongs to take note of, such as realizing that not much will grow under the black walnut tree, which it found across most of the United States and Canada. This tree releases a chemical into the soil that ensures nothing near it can compete with the nutrients and moisture that it needs, making it an undesirable plant to choose in companion planting. Marigolds are planted all over the world to repel all kinds of pests. If you take the dead marigold plants and **dig them under** in the fall (meaning, leave the plant in the ground and turn the dirt and soil over, chopping the plant and roots as you do so), almost nothing will grow where they grew, and as the plant pieces decay, they will kill anything you plant. But by spring, the soil is safe for planting again. Companion planting allows you to take advantage of the systems already in place in nature to make the most of your garden.

Companion planting can increase your yield of vegetables and even enhance the flavor of some if planted with specific herbs. Beneficial plants to have in your vegetable garden are wild rose, elderberry, buddleia, privet, golden rod, and mustard. With this type of system, it is easy to combine flowers, shrubs, trees, and vegetables for larger and better-tasting yields. If you are short on space, consider planting to maximize the space available such as by planting runner beans with dahlias or pairing curly parsley with cosmos. Another combination that can work well are clematis flowers with apple trees as the clematis can climb the trees and utilize the space under the tree that is often wasted.

While companion planting is a lot of fun, it also makes the vegetable garden more attractive, both to the eye and to the nose, and offers practical solutions to common gardening problems.

It can intensify the beauty of flowers by combining them with plants of contrasting shapes, color, and height. This type of system can be used to provide practical needs like shelter from wind, shade, or help prevent soil erosion. It allows a gardener to combine all the elements of a backyard garden into a small space without sacrificing yields or beauty.

Companion planting has guidelines but no rules. It offers suggestions, but ultimately allows you to create a garden that will work for you in the space you have available. This type of system will work for any level of gardener, who takes the time and put in the effort to find what works best for their area.

This book will take you through the required steps to establish your garden and how to begin companion planting. You will learn about the insect army already living in your garden, what plants to grow to keep out the wrong insects, and what plants will attract the right insects. There is special section on feeding your garden properly to ensure it grows big and healthy. The second half of the book goes into detail about how to companion plant with herbs, vegetables, annuals, perennials, wildflowers, bulbs, shrubs, and fruits. The book finishes with a list of resources to help you learn more about companion planting.

Happy planting!

B efore you begin analyzing your garden's needs and how you would like to begin companion planting, you should learn a little about the history and practice behind companion planting.

History

Historically, there is no one point where we can say that companion planting actually started or at what geographical location in the world it originated. Many agricultural practices have been used for centuries with the origins lost – companion planting is just one of them.

In North America, the search for the origin of companion planting leads us back to American Indians and their companion planting practice called "Three Sisters." The Iroquois of the Northeastern United States and Canada primarily used this practice and it involved planting corn, beans, and squash. These crops were the mainstay of the Iroquois' diet and were believed to be special gifts from the Great Spirit; as such, they were under the protection by the spirits called the Three Sisters. They were planted as a mainstay crop for the people and their system of planting was revered.

The Iroquois planted the three crops together. Corn gave structure and support for the bean plants to climb up; the beans replenished the soil with nutrients for both the corn and squash; and the large multiple leaves of the squash vines offered a protective mulch that helped the plants conserve water while providing weed control for all three plants. When planted in this special way, the plants thrive in a small space and are capable of producing high-quality yields with minimal to no environmental impact.

Over time, many other companion planting combinations were tried, with varied results. Much of this knowledge was handed down from generation to generation, and some of it today may be found to be folklore of other cultures.

Plants and their identifications have changed over time, as have horticultural methods, climates, and soil content. There has also been the introduction of chemically based pesticides and fertilizers and advancement in seeds, propagation, and cultivation. All of these affected the basics of gardening but the premise of companion planting remains the same.

Companion Planting Pairs

Companion planting is the process of putting together plants with contrasting and/or complementary properties. Common examples include:

- Sun-loving plants offering shade to shade-loving ones

- Plants with deep roots paired together with those that have shallow roots

- Slow-growing plants matched with fast-growing plants as the plants will have different space and nutrient requirements

- Heavy-feeding plants are intermixed with light-feeding plants or crops that incorporate nitrogen into the soil

- Aromatic plants, which often repel pests, are planted with non-aromatic plants

- Plants that produce early flowers that provide pollen and nectar are paired with plants that do not flower until closer to the end of the season

Companion planting can involve all different types of plants and shrubs. Throughout the years, companion planting has involved almost every type of plant. As various plants have become more popular in home gardens, they have been incorporated into companion gardens. When considering what species of plants to incorporate, here are the types of plants you should consider:

- **Perennials** — plants that live longer than two years
- **Annuals** — plants that complete their life cycle in one year or less
- **Ornamental shrubs** — shrubs grown purely for looks
- **Herbs** — small, seed-bearing plants that are most noted for their aromatic, medicinal, healthful, and cooking qualities
- **Vegetables** — plants that are either edible or part of the plant is edible
- **Fruit bushes/trees** — trees and/or shrubs that bear edible fruit
- **Grasses** — plants that have jointed stems, leaves, and produce seed-like grains
- **Roses** — a particularly well-loved and long-living flowering plant
- **Dwarf trees** — variations of trees that through horticulture practice have been kept artificially small
- **Flowering shrubs** — shrubs that are grown primarily for their flowery show
- **Nut bushes** — bushes grown for the nuts they produce
- **Crop plants** — plants grown primarily for human food and animal feed

Having a garden in the right location is essential to successful gardening, allowing you to select the perfect location for the types of plants you want to grow: roses drenched in sun, ferns in the shade, or a mixed border that takes advantage of both. Most people like to have the gardens somewhat close to their house so they can see it through their windows.

Finding a Place for Your Garden

Before deciding where to place your garden, you need to consider what type of garden you want to have. Here are some questions you should consider when deciding what type of garden to plant:

- What are the goals of your garden?
- Are you simply trying to enhance a shrubby border that already exists?
- Are you interested in adding herbs and other foods to your perennial border?
- Are you starting with a clean slate on new ground, or are you hoping to improve the appearance of your home and lawn?

Once you determine the basics of what you want to achieve, it is important to understand that each plant has specific requirements in which it will survive. There are conditions in which the plant may survive but you will not get the yield or growth from it the same as you would under ideal conditions.

In order to work well, a garden must balance what is already there with what is going to be planted. The following should be taken into consideration in order to properly analyze the site:

- Existing structures
- Existing plants
- The soil's pH, the amount of acidity or alkalinity in the soil

- Microclimate
- Hours of sunlight per day

The ideal soil will be loose, somewhat well-drained, and loamy, meaning a mixture of sand, clay, and organic matter. However, if all the other factors work except for the soil, it is possible to improve the soil so it should not be the deciding factor in where to position the garden. City residents are often limited in their choices, but if there is an option available, avoid planting the garden over rocks or in a poorly draining area. It is also best to avoid areas that are heavily infested with Johnson grass or weeds because these will require a lot more work to eradicate for the first year or two.

Also consider the rainfall and how it manages to reach the garden area. If your bed is planted directly against a house, an overhang or gutter system may prevent your garden from receiving water. If it is on a slope, water may drain off too quickly to provide moisture for the plants. And regardless of whether rain is available, watering is normally necessary at least once every week if not more, so plan for easy access to water.

All vegetables bearing fruit or seeds must have full-sun. Avoid planting in the vicinity of large trees as their roots can extend as far out as two times the size of the tree's canopy. Also avoid trees that have a shallow root system, like the weeping willow tree, because they will compete with your garden for water and nutrients.

Here are a few considerations to help you decide the perfect location for your garden:

- The more level the area, the better
- Full or near-full sunlight is best, unless your plan calls for a shade garden
- Well-drained, fertile soil is best
- A water supply should be within reach

- Avoid large trees or shrubs that might compete for sunlight and nutrients
- Avoid planting near black walnut trees

Every garden should have plants of various shapes and sizes to make it interesting. In fact, planting is often opposite of what you would expect; for example, a tiny garden filled with dwarf plants will only emphasize how small garden is. Instead, use a very tall plant like the juniper or a bamboo to draw the eye upward and make the garden appear taller. Likewise, many 12- to 24-inch plants in a row will seem flat and boring. Consider adding emphasis by using grasses, plumed poppy, small shrubs, and climbers.

Start by drawing a map of your garden. Include your home and any other structures or large trees that exist on your property and that you intend to keep. Make sure you emphasize the natural characteristics of your land like slopes or hollows. If there are terraces, decks, patios, or water features close by, also mark them in their position.

Next you will draw in all the other **hardscape** factors, which are features in the garden that are not growing; for example, paths, driveways, parking areas, and any other structures in the garden. If you are planning to incorporate a new path into the garden (it should be at least 3 feet wide and have a hard surface), draw that, too. Compost bins and other utility areas should be near the major garden area or near the garage. If you do not like the looks of these utilities, you can screen them off by using a fence or a hedge. Consider the best location for each plant in relation to the house and exposure to the elements.

Full-sun garden

Full-sun gardens with the right plants for the space are the easiest to grow. This type of garden requires plants that can tolerate the hottest summer days and the dry conditions in your area. If you are choosing perennials, after becoming established they will need little care other than **deadhead-ing**, which is the process of plucking off the dead blooms. Spring bulbs can tolerate full-sun conditions, as can many perennials and annuals. By planting some of each, you will have blooms all season long.

The following are just a few ideas for easy full-sun growth. When visiting the nursery, you can find hundreds more.

Perennials

- Purple coneflowers
- Black-eyed Susan
- Threadleaf coreopsis
- Catmint

- Yarrow
- Siberian iris
- Stonecrop

Annuals

- Petunia
- Marigold
- Moss rose
- Verbena

- Dianthus
- Butterfly bush
- Phlox
- Salvia

Vegetables

Nearly all vegetables like full sun, but the following can be grown for beauty as well as for production:

- Sweet pepper
- Rhubarb
- Artichoke

- Asparagus pea
- Cabbage "Ruby Perfection"

Herbs

- Basil
- Many varieties of parsley (use several for interest)

- Rosemary
- Sage

The full-sun garden lends itself well to a variety of fruit trees, vines, and shrubs. Consider mixing up the selection to ensure color and interest all year round.

Pros and cons of full-sun gardens	
Pros	*Cons*
Able to grow sun-loving plants	Unable to grow shade-loving plants
Colors are bright and vibrant	Too much sun can make some flowers look washed out
Offer year-round color options	Gardener is forced to work in the heat
Ideal for drought-tolerant plants	Requires more water

Shade garden

The shade garden is much more restful in appearance than the full-sun garden. Full-sun gardens have a strong, bright look to them where as a shade garden offers a cooler, more subdued appearance. Shade gardens can be harder to work with than full-sun gardens if the shade is produced by a deciduous tree, a tree that loses its leaves comes winter, that is competing with the plants for nourishment or there is improper soil preparation. Before planting, be sure that the ground has been properly dug over and compost has been added in. Occasionally, plants that did well a few years ago begin to dwindle and fade as a tree in the garden grows taller and thicker. If this happens, prune back the tree branches high above the garden to let in more light. Filtered sunlight or dappled light that comes through the leaves of the trees is beneficial and still considered **light shade**. **Full-shade** is when no direct sunlight reaches the ground at any time of the day. However, this does not mean locations such as under decks or other structures as some natural light must reach these areas.

When designing the shade garden, mix fine-textured plants like ferns with stronger, glossy-leaved plants. Plants with darker-colored leaves can give the feeling of a more spacious garden, and should be used often. Some cool season vegetables, like lettuce, spinach, and radishes, can grow in light shade. Others like peas, potatoes, turnips, and cabbage will grow in light shade, but will not yield as large a crop as they would in full sun.

The following plants mix well into the shade garden:

Perennials

- Variegated hydrangea
- Hostas, many varieties
- Western Spirea
- Canyon Sunflower
- Ferns (try Japanese tassel fern or cinnamon fern)
- Ivy
- California strawberry
- Sierra Iris
- Foxglove
- Wild petunia
- Snowberry
- Foam flower
- Periwinkle

Annuals – *light shade*

- Curly parsley
- Lettuce and other CCA crops

When looking to grow vegetables, people are often surprised to hear that many varieties are happy in the shade or in partial-shade. If you plant tall plants with mid-sized or short plants, the tall plants receive the full sun and the others receive either partial shade or full shade, making them happy.

Here are samples of combinations to consider planting together to maximize limited space and to maximize the growing preference of various plants.

Tall Plants	
Corn	You should plant one of the taller plants and mid-sized and/or short plants beside it. The tall, sun-happy plant provides shade and the other plants are happy in the tall plant's shadow.
Sunflowers	
Trellised climbers	
Tomatoes	
Mid-sized plants	
Broccoli	Some plants do not do well in the hot summer heat. Broccoli and lettuce race through their life cycle to produce to seeds before the vegetables can be eaten if it is too hot.
Cauliflower	
Celery	
Peppers	
Small plants	
Carrots	Lots of water can help cool the plants, but can cause other problems if the watering is too heavy. Planting tall plants with short plants provides an easy mainte-nance solution to the problem.
Lettuce	
Swiss chard	
Cucumbers	

Pros and cons of shade gardens	
Pros	Cons
Ability to grow shade plants like ferns	Moss has a tendency to flourish in shade
The gardener can work and enjoy the cooler conditions for longer during the summer months	Cooler space attracts more insects – not necessarily the ones you want
White and silver plants shine instead of looking washed out	Needs large shade-creating trees or structures to keep garden in shade
Require less water	Cannot plant sun-loving plants

Container garden

Container gardening, or growing plants in containers instead of in a garden, is the most forgiving style of planting for garden plans, because if the plant is not growing well in its current location, you can simply relocate it. It is also easy to swap the plants around so that the one in bloom is always front and center.

Another advantage of container gardening is that plants can be enjoyed nearly anywhere — even in locations where there is no room for a flower bed or where the soil is too rocky or too desert-like for a traditional garden. Try placing containers on the roof, balcony, porch, front stoop, or even in the outdoor garden for variety and change. They can be moved as weather changes or the sun shifts, and they can be rearranged if pests become a problem. Planting difficult plants in containers and then placing them in the garden will help control plants that tend to grow rampant; simply bury them into the garden and lift them out again after the growing season has passed.

Nearly any type of container can be used, so this is a great area to let your creativity loose. In addition to the traditional ceramic or clay pots, there are planter boxes, hanging baskets, wooden barrels, and many other non-traditional containers that can be used. Consider planting in kitchen bowls that are no longer in use, or other items from the garage and home.

Containers at the front door, around the pool, or on the deck make a great focal point and offer strong impact for homes and gardens. Use tubs, half barrels, or large urns and fill them with wonderful combinations of herbs, vegetables, and flowers, or consider filling them with tall tomatoes, citrus trees, morning glories, or scented geraniums.

Troughs are a good choice for shorter gardens, salad crops, herbs, and shorter flowers. Be sure that the troughs are built from pressure-treated lumber (they should be labeled as such). These can be stained or left bare, in which case they will weather to a beautiful silver shade. Another idea is the special compost-filled plastic bags designed for growing crops, petunias, impatiens, and other annuals. The bags can be found in most garden centers and provide a quick and easy way to brighten up areas around your home. If you select plants that spread, they will grow to hide the plastic and resemble regular hanging baskets.

For best results, use containers with wide openings so that you can get your hands in and out easily for planting. Avoid terra cotta pots if your summers are very hot as they will dry out too quickly and the plants may die. Instead, select ceramic pots that have been glazed. Use large containers if you are growing deep-rooted vegetables. Most plants have root systems that are a bit larger than the top growth that you see, so choose a container that holds enough potting material to slightly outsize the plant at maturity.

Make sure any pot that you purchase has holes in the bottom at least ½-inch wide to allow for drainage. Do not set the containers directly on the ground, but instead place them on bricks or blocks so that they can drain. To use hanging baskets during hot summer days, hang the baskets where they will not catch the afternoon sun. To help retain water during the long summer days, line the pots with moss carpet and fill with a special water-retaining potting soil, both of which can be found at your local garden supply store.

Container plants tend to dry out quickly because they cannot access the moist dirt in a garden, so they must be watered almost daily. Rather than carrying water back and forth to these plants, if you can, set the planters close together and lay a soaker hose (a hose that has small holes throughout the tubing) across them to water them all at once. These soakers could even be set up on automatic timer so that the plants are watered regularly. Another option is glass garden bulbs for small planters. These bulbs will give the plants a steady supply of water for a couple of days depending on the heat and the size of the bulb. However, they will not supply sufficient water for large planters. Another valuable way to retain moisture is by using mulch. Bark mulch is popular, but gravel can be a better choice because it stays cool and it will help deter slugs. There is also a product called a Spanish water ring that comes in two sizes. They reduce the need to water the plants as they store water at the root level for up to ten days. They have absorbent granules built into the organic matting so when you water the plants, these granules swell with water and retain it. The rings last one season then break down in the soil. The organic matting goes at the bottom of the pot before it is planted.

Container gardens also require a great deal of fertilizer to perform their best. Mix a slow-release fertilizer in the compost or soil before planting the container in your garden. Once a year, work a few more fertilizer pellets into the top few inches of the compost or soil. For fast-growing crops or flowers, add a weekly dose of liquid fertilizer. Remember to keep all container plants deadheaded at all times.

Watering issues

The most common problem when attempting a container garden is water balance. Too much water can cause:

- Wilting
- Stunted growth
- Small roots
- Root rot
- Fungal infestation

Too little water causes wilting and **scorching**, which is when leaves burn and they become brown and dried up. This is detrimental to the growth of the plant because allowing the plants to dry out repeatedly will eventually stunt their growth. The best container garden will be watered when soil is dry to the touch. At that time, water the plants slowly and thoroughly. The container must have drainage holes for excess water to drain out because you do not want plants sitting in water. Use saucers under the container to prevent water and dirt from washing over your patio or pavement. If drainage is not a problem, it is better to not use a saucer so the pot can drain thoroughly after watering.

Annuals suitable for containers

- Geraniums
- Lantana
- Thunberia – Black-eyed Susan vine
- Pansy
- Petunia
- Snapdragon
- Baccopa

Vegetables suitable for containers

Containers are versatile, so try out combinations of some of your favorite flowers and vegetables. The following vegetables can be grown in 5 gallon-sized containers or a window box:

- Snap beans
- Broccoli
- Onion
- Pepper
- Spinach
- Squash
- Tomatoes

Herbs for container gardens

Herbs are easily grown in pots, even small ones. For easy kitchen access, keep the pots on the deck or stairs. Herbs do require a lot of sunlight and will produce better yields when grown in a sunny site. However, areas with late afternoon and evening shade are fine.

Harvesting herb leaves regularly is healthy for the plant and encourages more growth. By constantly using the herbs, you avoid them outgrowing their container. Another advantage of growing herbs in containers is that in the fall, they can be moved indoors for the winter.

The following herbs do well in garden containers:

- Basil
- Catmint
- German chamomile
- Chives
- Cilantro
- Lemon balm
- Nasturtium
- Parsley
- Thyme

Trees for container gardening

Container gardening is versatile enough to grow small fruit trees, like lemon trees. Dwarf varieties do well in containers, but make sure you select an appropriate-sized container. Trees are easy to prune and harvest when planted in a container. You will find that younger trees bear fruit faster this way than they would if they were grown in an orchard. In general, fruit trees grow best in full sunlight, but some can also grow in shade or a mix of both. These trees are pruned during their dormant season, which is late in winter. There are new cultivars available that offer more than one variety of fruit grafted together on one tree. (Grafting, or attaching a plant from a different type of fruit onto the main tree, is normally done at the nursery.)

Some varieties are cultivated especially for container gardening; anything labeled "Ultra Dwarf," meaning the plant will stay small when compared to non-dwarf varieties, can be used in container gardening. Read the label for height information.

The overall weight of the container should be taken into consideration when growing trees. The container should be large enough to accommodate the tree at maturity, and containers should be selected that are as tall as they are wide. A container full of potting soil can be heavy, so remember to take this into consideration when using them in areas like balconies, patio stones, or lawns were the weight could make a difference. Lightweight plastic pots are a good choice unless windy conditions will cause small pots to overturn. If the container is going to be left in place year-round, a heavier clay or terra cotta pot is a good choice. If you need to move the container from place to place, consider purchasing a small **dolly**, a stand on wheels, especially designed to fit and stay under large plant pots to move them from one place to another.

When selecting trees for containers, be sure to consider the hardiness of the tree to see if it will survive the normal winter temperatures in your area. Choose those that are hardy enough to withstand the most extreme temperatures where you live. In nature, the soil helps insulate tree roots from extreme cold. In pots, the plant does not have the same level of insulation. If the soil temperature drops below freezing, the roots will not be able to store water. Tree roots can also die if the soil temperature becomes too hot, which is why it is important to check the label to see if the tree will grow in your area and if you are planning on leaving it outdoors over winter. You can use mulch to somewhat compensate for freezing and overheating, but only if the hardiness zone is for your area. *More about hardiness zones will be explained in Chapter 2.* Heat from asphalt and concrete can quickly burn roots and dry out soil.

Small trees to consider for container planting include:

- Dwarf Meyer lemons
- Dwarf kumquat
- Dwarf apple
- Avocado
- Banana
- Pineapple
- Papaya
- Lime
- Orange

- Fig
- Dwarf stone fruit
- Boxwood
- Dwarf camellia
- Holly
- Dwarf Alberta spruce
- Japanese maple
- Star magnolia

Pros and cons of container gardening	
Pros	*Cons*
Good for limited space	Initial container purchase can be expensive, depending on what you end up choosing
Plants can be moved to change the landscape	Large containers may be too heavy to move easily
Easy to respond to different water requirements	No way to provide automatic watering system; may take longer to water and must be watered often
Weed and pest control are easy	Soil often dries out quickly
Can use plants that are not native to your region	Pots may become root bound
Can be placed where soil is poor and no garden would grow	The pot must be filled with good soil, mulch, and have fertilizer added to provide the essential nutrients for the plants to grow

Window box garden

Nothing makes a statement like a garden at window height overflowing with beautiful flowers. The plantings can be formal or a casual mix of fruits (for example strawberries), herbs (parsley), and flowers (alyssum). Choose plants that are drought tolerant and resistant to wind. If they are placed near kitchen windows, they offer easy watering. Consider the plants' watering needs when you place the window boxes on second story windows as you will need to carry watering cans from box to box during the summer. You can purchase an indoor/outdoor coiled hose to attach to an indoor sink tap that you can use to water indoor plants and window box gardens.

Some plants that thrive in a window box environment include the following annuals:

- Sage
- Alyssum
- Nasturtium
- French marigolds
- Trailing bush tomatoes
- Thyme

- Wild crocus bulb (will need to be pulled and kept indoors over winter)
- Curly parsley
- Impatiens
- Trailing strawberries

Pros and cons of window box gardens	
Pros	*Cons*
Good for limited space	Initial container purchase can be expensive, depending on what you end up choosing
Plants can be moved to change the landscape	Large containers may be too heavy to move easily
Easy to respond to differing water requirements	No way to provide automatic watering system; may take longer to water and must be watered often
Weed and pest control are easy	Soil dries out quickly
Can use plants that are not native	Pots may become root bound
Offers easy access and easy viewing of the plants and flowers	The window box must be filled with good soil, mulch, and have fertilizer added to provide the essential nutrients for the plants to grow

Small corner or mini-garden

Many people think that a garden has to be a huge sweeping space, but this is not true. Even a small area can be used for a corner or mini-garden. Most people do not have the physical space or the time to give to a large garden so growing a mini-garden is a fun way to get started. Plants grown in a small garden receive more attention because you are more able to maintain your garden and truly enjoy what you have planted. It is a great way to transform a mailbox area, an ugly corner, or even a strangely shaped entryway into a beautiful focal point.

Due to the limited space, you will need to pay particular attention to the size the plants will be at maturity. Watch out for the temptation to buy plants that are going to grow too large for your mini-garden, thinking that you will replace them later or that they probably will not reach the size suggested. Plants have a way of taking off and growing well once planted in the garden. Instead, choose small varieties or dwarf plants that will fit there for years. Knowing space is at a premium, do not try to grow too many plants or mix in too many colors. Focus instead on one or two colors, adding in different textures for an interesting look. Selecting interesting colors will help the garden appear larger, and mixing tall plants with short ones will make the garden more spacious. Usually with small gardens, the entire area can be seen at once so it must be cohesive. Every plant will need to have a purpose, and everything needs to count.

When gardens are small, all the parts must work together as a whole. Do this by creating changes in height and color, repeating plants, and making use of a limited color palette. Avoid using too many different kinds of plants or too many types of landscaping materials. This is a good place to remember that less is more. Continuing with a particular material also used in window boxes, edgings, or walkways can also help create a feeling of unity.

Do not be tempted to skip over the garden planning stage. Even though your garden is small, drawing it out on paper to scale will help you visualize what you are working with and will help ensure that you achieve your goals. Make layers for different trees, shrubs, flowers, and grasses. Make notes of the features you want to be able to view and the ones you want to block out. Try several different designs before you make the final drawing to be sure you have a combination that is most pleasing.

Keep in mind that with a small garden, overfilling the space with plants can create a canopy of shade that can cause problems. It is important to not have one plant that will overwhelm another. Careful diligence will maintain a good balance between sizes. Having said that, encourage plants to grow as a mix, not in rows. You can accomplish this by allowing them to spread together naturally, with stems growing loose and occasionally intertwining. If one becomes too dominant, simply trim it back.

Having a focal point will draw the eye and help create unity. In small gardens, the focal point has to be scaled to size so that it does not overwhelm the other plants. The focal point can be a dwarf shrub or tree, an ornament like a small statue or birdbath, a water feature, a large or unusual plant, or even a thick grouping of plants. The focal point should be decided on first with the balance of the garden designed around it. Soften the effect of the focal point by adding birdhouses, butterfly houses, or a small trellis for flowering vines.

Rather than placing your focal point in the center of your garden, try to have it off-center and plant around it. Consider the rule of thirds, placing the focal point one-third or two-thirds of the way across the garden. The design and dramatic effect are easy to follow this way. Try to select plants that will last more than one season for color and interest throughout the year. Immediately discard those plants that are not performing well because there is no room to waste in a mini-garden.

Using mirrors around the garden on trellises, fences, and rocks will create the illusion of more space and will reflect sunlight onto shady parts of the garden. Outdoor mirrors must be weather resistant so they need to have plastic or wood frames that can age over time. You can purchase mirrors of all sizes but try adding in only one or two, depending on what structures you have available to support them. They will not overheat the plants and if you place them against something instead of leaving them hanging in the wind, birds will be less likely to fly into them. If the mini-garden is surrounded by walls or fences, consider painting them a light color to open up the space that they surround. Do not forget about exterior lighting because the garden will really pop if you include lights. Simple solar lights can help create an interesting evening look.

Small corner gardens are easy to enclose and you might want to install stone edging or even a stone wall. Using a taller hedge can give the feeling of a secret or private garden. Use low boxwood edging to give the garden a more formal appearance.

Incorporating vertical space into the garden can help define areas, support more plants, and also provide privacy. Vertical structures like fences, walls, or arbors are a great way to do this. **Vertical gardening** refers to incorporating plants that will climb, like snap beans or kiwi, so the picking is done at a higher level. Alternately, use hanging planters for crops like strawberries and cherry tomatoes where the plants hang down. This is great for people who have difficulty bending down to tend to an in-ground garden. If the small garden is going to contain crops, utilizing vertical space is crucial for the garden to show much yield. You can grow runner beans on fences and attach them to the structure with wire. Grapes or cane fruits can also grow on the sides of the house or on a trellis or fence. If these are not available, a cylinder of plastic- or zinc-coated wire will even serve as a support. There are many dwarf and column-like fruit trees that are available. Cherries, peaches, and even apples are all attractive and offer early flowers, summer fruit, and even autumn color.

Mini-gardens are easier to protect against wildlife, particularly persistent rabbits and squirrels, because it is much easier to discourage them when you are only concentrating on a small part of the yard. They will also be less likely to come around if the garden is in a small, enclosed area close to the house and if there are lights shining constantly.

If drainage is a problem, prevent ground saturation by creating raised beds or by heaping up the dirt into a hill or small raised portion of the space. Perhaps the back corner of the garden (where you are planting a dwarf tree) could be the highest point, with the rest of the garden sloping away from it. Be careful to guide the water away from structures, including the residence, or you could end up with a flooded basement after watering your garden.

Plants to consider for your mini-garden include the following annuals:

- Cherry tomatoes
- Cosmos daisies
- Baby's breath (gypsophila)
- Red lettuce
- Herbs of all kinds
- Runner bean "painted lady"
- Peppers
- Flowering ground covers like alyssum

Pros and cons of a mini-garden	
Pros	*Cons*
Easy design	Plants can be easily overwhelmed
Low maintenance	It is tempting to put in too many varieties
Good for a first-time gardener	More consideration is required in choosing the best plants

Raised bed garden

Raised beds are one of the most productive ways of companion gardening as more plants can be grown together in the same space, and they can also be one of the most attractive gardens. Traditionally in raised bed gardens, crops are grown in rectangular beds that are no more than 4 feet wide so the gardener can reach throughout the garden comfortably from either side. However, it is easier to mow around curves, so consider making your beds something other than square or rectangular if it suits your garden better. Many gardeners recommend that the edging is at least 6 inches high for a raised bed because this appears to be the best height to keep pets and people from walking on and into the garden.

Most raised beds are edged with some structural support like pressure-treated timber set on edge or stacked concrete made just for this purpose. Bricks, stone, synthetic stone, and logs are also suitable for edging a raised bed. The edging of a raised bed is often simple 6-inch wide boards placed on their sides to create a rectangle. Stained boards or logroll (strips of short logs placed on their narrow ends) are also attractive. There are many interesting materials to use for the edging and they can add a lot of interest to your bed.

If you are going to make beds, they do take some work to get ready. The good news is that once they are built, filled with quality soil, and planted, there is minimum maintenance required and they are less work than other garden styles as you move through the seasons. The advantage shows up year after year because the beds are already built.

First, the site must be prepared by removing weeds and rocks. Then, the boundaries need to be marked as you consider the size of your beds. If you make the beds too long, people will walk in them rather than go around them. If you make them too wide, it is hard to reach the plants in the center and the temptation is then to step inside the bed to work, which is bad because you will pack down the dirt and possibly crush your plants. One way around this is to use stepping stones, but these will take up some of the valuable growing space. If there is going to be more than one bed, leave a 3-foot pathway between them. If you can afford the materials and the space, four beds make for a good layout and allow for easy crop rotation *(crop rotation will be explained in Chapter 2)*. Once you have determined the size and location for your garden, lay out the timbers or whatever materials you have decided to use as edging and secure them into their final shape.

Next, secure heavy plastic along all the inside walls, folding it over to cover a few inches of the soil below. A generous helping of organic matter (compost, mulch, or a combination of the two) is placed inside the plastic-covered frame along with soil that was either in place when you started or topsoil purchased from garden supply house. This organic matter is then worked deeply into the soil. If you do not have a compost heap, use well-rotted manure, potting compost, or soil improvers available from your local garden supply house.

If you are planning to use soaker hoses on your raised bed, now is the time to lay them out on the soil surface. Give the soil a final raking and cover the hoses with mulch. (If you are going to use sprinklers or hand water your plants, do not worry about the hoses at this time.) The next step is to fill the garden in with vegetables, herbs, fruit, flowers, small trees, or shrubs. Because the organic matter that has been deeply worked into the soil has increased the amount of nutrients available to the roots, the plants can be grown more closely together than in a regular bed. If the bed is rich in nutrients, you might be able to grow twice as many plants in the space. Remember to make allowances for the full-grown size of the plant and try to plant above-ground growing plants, like spinach, with underground-growing plants, like carrots, to better utilize the nutrients at different levels. The more organic material you dig in, the more nutrients available and the more plants you can grow.

The raised bed can be planted in rows or patches. If you choose to plant in rows, consider planting alternating rows of flowers for cutting with rows of attractive vegetables for food. As you can grow many plants together, you can also plant cover crops to hug the ground and offer an interesting contrast. Sweet alyssum is a good annual as it offers continuous small flowers and it attracts beneficial insects. Buckwheat grain plant is another useful cover crop that is inexpensive, flowers quickly, and is easy to till into the soil by hand.

The more carefully a raised bed is prepared, the better the growth of the plants will be and the less maintenance will be required. Depending on the shape of the beds, you can easily grow plants in creative patterns such as zigzags, triangles, and other geometric shapes.

Trees can be present in raised bed gardens, but they usually are not because of their tendency to spread roots throughout the garden, causing problems to nearby plants. Because of this, it is better to use small trees behind the garden as a backdrop.

If the raised bed is going to contain crops that tend to run to seed in hot sun (meaning mature too quickly and produce seed before they can be eaten), consider planting them beneath a taller plant that offers them shade. Try spinach beneath the tallest varieties of dahlias, or lettuce beside nasturtiums. Cabbage can be both attractive and useful in the raised bed, and can benefit from taller plants. Avoid putting the cabbage beside tomatoes and pole beans as they do not grow well together. Onions, potatoes, sage, and peppermint are all good companions for cabbage. Onions are especially useful because they will repel rabbits from the cabbage patch. If you are planting carrots in the raised bed, mix in some parsley to repel carrot flies. Parsley will also give a boost to tomatoes and asparagus. Edge the bed with herbs and edible flowers such as dill, basil, nasturtiums, parsley, Sweet William, daylilies, and chives.

A raised bed salad garden

A few suggestions of easy-to-grow salad plants for your garden bed include:

- Spinach
- Cherry tomatoes
- Basil
- Radishes
- Romaine lettuce
- Leaf lettuce
- Johnny jump-ups

A raised bed flower garden:

The following flowers are easy to grow alone or together in a raised bed flower garden.

- Buckwheat
- Calendula
- Cleome
- Climbing rose
- Cosmos
- Honeysuckle
- Hollyhock
- Marigold
- Nasturtiums
- Sweet alyssum
- Zinnias

A raised bed kitchen garden

A few suggestions for plants to use in a raised garden bed that can produce herbs for your kitchen include:

- Chives
- Feverfew
- Thyme
- Dill
- Varied basils; try lemon, cinnamon, anise, and Thai
- Borage

This type of garden is a nice additional garden or a great way to start gardening. It will give you quick results, allowing you to harvest salads and herbs within weeks of planting.

| Pros and cons of a raised bed garden ||
Pros	Cons
Can build a plant-specific, fertile soil	Higher initial start-up cost for supplies
Good drainage	Some plants not suited to close growing
Fewer weeds	More work to set up initially
Less bending for the gardener	Limits garden to within the bed

Pros and cons of a raised bed garden (continued)	
Pros	*Cons*
Plants can be started earlier in the season	Cannot be easily changed
Soil can remain loose because no one walks on it	Needs more natural compost to keep plants nutritionally healthy
Easier to maintain than traditional garden	More permanent

Border garden

A border garden is a good choice where there is a limited area in which to plant, usually along the side of a path and backed against a fence, hedge, or wall. You will want the garden to be less than 5 feet deep. You can include only one type of plant, such as shaped boxwoods or stately roses, in your border garden for a more formal look. For the mixed border, the more traditional English border garden, there will be a combination of annuals, perennials, in the form of shrubs, vine, and bulbs. By mixing the various types of plants, along with a small tree or a climbing plant, you can extend the growing season from early spring into the fall or even the winter, providing color and interest for all seasons.

For a mixed border garden, the soil and water requirements become more important because with this style of garden, you are planning for the long-term and generally the lush look requires many plants placed closer together than normal. Many of the plants will be difficult to move once they have been put into place, especially if you incorporate many trees or shrubs into the plan. It is also important to consider the rate of growth for each plant so that they do not outgrow or overshadow the others. Mixed border gardens are great for companion planting as they can incorporate the slower growing, long-term plants like trees with seasonal flowers and vegetable that can be changed each year to allow for the change in growth of the bigger plants.

If this type of garden is planned carefully enough, it can break up a long, straight area of the garden or hedge line. It should feature plants that peak at different times of the year so that even as one begins to fade, another is blooming. For example, one plant in the back of the garden may flower during the spring, while another puts on a show in the middle of summer. This requires you to pay careful attention to the flower season, and also requires placing certain plants closer than usual to one another so as one fades, the one beside it can take over.

The rhythm of the design can easily be broken up by adding in elements later and by not keeping the heights terribly regimented. Taller shrubs work well in the mixed border garden because their small leaves offer a less dense look, meaning you can plant them further forward in this type of garden than in other gardens. Also, using evergreens as a focal point provides not only color through the year, but a background for the rose hips in the winter, and a natural shape for the overall plan.

Mixed borders should be developed with the following concepts in mind — in addition to your site analysis, of course:

• Planting the garden in layers

• Retaining existing plants, if possible

• Charting peak bloom or showy times for the plants included in the garden to ensure that a plant is blooming in each season

• Presenting a wide variation of foliage texture and color

• A definite color scheme, whether monochromatic or based around several contrasting colors

A mixed border is a good choice for someone who has less time to spend in the garden or someone who has never gardened before. It can be as big or as small, as simple or as complex as you would like to make it. There are no set plants you should include in this type of garden – most will work well.

Pros and cons of a border garden styles	
Pros	*Cons*
Mixed - requires less work than other gardens	A formal style will require more work
Accommodates all kinds of plants and trees	Permanent style of garden
Good style for new gardeners	Plants are harder to choose for location
Plants have time to mature in one place	

CASE STUDY: DAVID BEAULIEU

Landscaping guide for the Web site
www.about.com
landscaping.guide@about.com
www.landscaping.about.com

Plants have always been an integral part of David Beaulieu's life in one form or another. He has eight years of experience writing about land-scaping, which has encompassed most aspects of gardening in one way or another. David believes one of the biggest problems people have with establishing a garden is getting started. Here is the most simple and effective way to create a garden where only weeds or lawn exists without all the hard work.

"Starting a garden from scratch does not need to be the dry, labor-intensive job most people would assume. There are a few tricks and hints to help the process move forward faster and smoother. The first problem with establishing a new garden is getting rid of the old lawn. The easiest way to do this is to mark off your planned space and cover the entire area with newspapers. Make sure the newspaper layer is at least ten sheets thick and have each page overlapping the adjacent one by several inches. You do not want any of the grass below to show. You can mow the grass but this is not required. The newspaper sheets do not need to be laid down one by one; as long as a section is ten pages, lay it down as one.

The next stage is to lay mulch, 5 to 6 inches deep, down on the newspaper. This helps stop the papers from flying away plus it adds in nutrients to the eventual garden. Organic mulches of choice include compost, shredded leaves, and straw. Now water your 'garden' and wait. It takes several months for the newspapers and mulch to kill the grass. The sod will eventually break down along with the newspapers and the mulch, giving you a nutrient-rich beginning for your garden.

If your potential garden is not lawn but weeds, the problem is much bigger, but transforming the land can still be done. It involves a process called soil solarization, and is best done in June or July. Cut all weeds as low as possible with a lawn mower or even a sickle. Next, rent a powerful tiller to dig through the hard soil to loosen the weed roots. Then, use a large steel rake and rake out the bulk of the weeks. Rake it again to level off. You might think you are done at this point, but in fact, the weed killing has just begun. Next, water down the area and cover it with a clear polyethylene sheet. Use rocks, blocks, or logs to hold the plastic down, but be sure to not puncture any holes in the plastic. Keep the plastic stretched out over the area for four to six weeks during which time the sun is 'cooking' the weeds before they can sprout. Any pathogens in the soil will be killed as well. When the time is up, remove the plastic and you have a 'clean slate' to plant your garden."

Companion planting is a system that lends itself to trial and error. Over the centuries, gardeners have planted certain plants in close proximity and they have noticed the end results. Plants naturally take in air and minerals and release chemicals through their own secretions or root excretions. For example, a plant that excretes nitrogen into the ground can make this element available to others that need a nitrogen-rich soil.

Some plants are found to lift many trace minerals from the soil in which they grow. Plants like these can be especially useful when turned into compost or mulch because they will then feed other plants with these valuable minerals. Allow the plants to grow to a mature size, then turn them under for green mulch or harvest them and bury them in the compost pile.

Biological Benefits of Combining Plants

There are specific biological effects of combining plants, such as:

- **Nitrogen Fixation** – plants that increase nitrogen in the soil
- **Pest control** – plants that repel "bad" pests or attract in "good" insects to the garden

- **Enhancing flavors** – the plants that can subtly enhance the flavors of other plants

- **Level interaction** – plants that grow on different levels to provide ground cover or work as a climbing trellis

- **Pest trapping** – plants that can attract certain pests in order to keep them away from other plants

- **Shelter plants** – plants that provide windbreaks, shade, and prevent soil erosion

- **Crop rotation** – plants can be grown and tilled into the ground to provide nutrients for the next crops or rotated from bed to bed to minimize problems

Nitrogen fixation

"Nitrogen fixation" may sound odd, but it is the term for plants such as peas, beans, and clover that can "fix" or excrete atmospheric nitrogen for their own use and for any close neighboring plants thanks to their relationship with the bacteria in the ground. This relationship increases the nutrients in the soil, making it available to other plants that are growing beside it – a perfect relationship for companion planting – one plant "helping" another. The nutrients are also available to plants grown in the soil after the legumes are pulled.

Plants that have the bacteria that can convert the nitrogen in the air into nitrogen compounds and bind them to the soil include alfalfa, red clover, and bluebonnets. These last plants are intended to be turned under at the end of the season as a **green manure**, or organic compost for the benefit of the garden.

Forage legumes are commonly planted with grasses to minimize the use of nitrogen fertilizer. Another example takes us back to the American Indians and their system of planting beans with corn. The beans helped the corn receive enough nutrients by "fixing" the nitrogen that allows it to grow and produce excellent yields.

Pest control

Companion planting is often considered part of the organic gardening philosophy as it avoids using chemicals and pesticides. Controlling pests through natural means can have many positive effects on the garden such as:

- Preventing the spread of disease through your garden
- Decreasing the damage pests cause
- Reducing the effect of chemicals you may have been using in the past

Keeping away pests can help your plants grow and flourish in ways you never thought possible. For example, planting catnip in the garden deters aphids, ants, Japanese beetles, and weevils. Mice also do not like the plant and will not stay in a garden where catnip is planted. As the plant is bushy with a light green leaf and dark purple flowers, it is an attractive yet functional addition to any garden.

This type of planting can take some time for the results to show. If you have planted marigolds to deter nematodes, the effect is not going to show itself instantly or even in the next month. Instead, it may take a full year's cycle before the marigolds have done their job. Gardeners who claim the system has failed often have not given the plants time to work. The plants need time to take hold and the life cycle of the pests need time to die out.

Companion planting can also attract the "pests" you do want. Why would you want any pests? Some insects are helpful in the garden. Wasps, for example, are an asset for most gardens because they eat grubs. Some insects are also pollinators. Some plants require pollination because they cannot reproduce on their own or bear fruit unless the pollen is delivered from one plant to the next. The fastest and most efficient way to do this is to have the right insects in the garden. A few beneficial pests are bees, wasps, birds, and dragonflies. *Chapter 3 covers this topic in greater detail.*

Enhancing flavor

Companion planting is not an exact science; it is a natural science. However, some combinations have proven themselves over and over again. A prime example is basil, which goes great with tomatoes in the kitchen and can also enhance the flavor of the tomato if it is grown beside it in the garden.

Most herbs have been found to enhance the flavor or fruits and vegetables that are grown in close proximity, and basil grown beside tomatoes is a prime example. Bee balm is also known to improve the growth and flavor of tomatoes. German chamomile, also called wild chamomile, has a strong aromatic odor and is believed to improve the growth and flavor of cabbages, cucumbers, and onions when grown beside them. Whether that is due to the increase in nutrients or because the plants share the common soil where nutrients and by-products are expelled and mixed, gardeners swear by the practice. *See Chapter 6 for more information about planting herbs together to enhance growth and flavor.*

Level interactions

Level interactions, also known as **physical space interactions**, involves planting tall plants with short plants to provide shade and even structure. Tall, sun-loving plants will shelter short, shade-tolerant plants, which results in better production and can even offer pest control. A good example of this type of relationship involves the popular corn planted with squash in the Three Sisters example. The tall corn throws shade for the lower squash but also the corn appears to stop an insect called the squash vine borer beetle. Another added benefit is the prickly vines of the squash deter the raccoons from stripping the corncobs.

When planting this way, you can plant two or even three different levels of plants, including a ground cover crop at the base. If the soil has sufficient nutrients, then the plants can thrive.

Pest trapping

Another term for this type of companion planting is **trap cropping**. With this system, a specific plant will be placed in the garden for its ability to attract a pest, thus keeping the pest away from the rest of the crops. The trapped insects on the plants can be disposed of in another way, such as bending the branch or stalk of the plant in a bucket of soapy water to kill the insects. Or, if you prefer, you can leave the plant, now full of bugs, alone for the season because the bugs will remain there.

A prime example of a pest is the diamondback moth, which can destroy a cabbage crop. Plant collard greens close by to attract the moth, keeping it away from the cabbage. Rose plants are another example — to keep the Japanese beetle out of your roses, plant old-fashioned four o'clocks, a beautiful perennial aptly named because the flowers only open after the sun has gone down.

The mustard plant is a big contender in this category as well because it will attract cabbage worms and harlequin bugs. Cabbage worms refer to several species of caterpillars but the main one in North America is small, fuzzy, bright green, and feeds on cabbages, broccoli, and cauliflower. The harlequin bug, indigenous to the southern United States, looks like an orange and black stink bug and can destroy an entire crop of cabbage, Brussels sprouts, turnips, kohlrabi, or radish. In fact, if they cannot find any of these, they will move on to potatoes, okra, beans, beets, and even fruit trees and field crops. However, if you plant the mustard plant in a separate area of the garden early in the spring, the bugs will gather on it. You cannot get rid of them by pulling up the plants because the bugs will scatter and will simply find another plant to latch onto. Instead, you can dunk the leaves or bend the stems into a bucket of soapy water to drown the insects, or spray it with insecticidal soap. Even better, consider planting the mustard plants with some of the plants that attract parasitic wasps or tachinidae flies, such as tansy, clover, and dill, as they are both predators of the harlequin bug.

Shelter planting

One of the most helpful benefits of combining plants is the ability to provide natural windbreaks, shade, and trellises. Some plants can grow to different heights while occupying the same space. The example of planting corn and beans together applies here again; the cornstalk serves as a trellis for the beans to climb, while the beans do not harm the corn stalk or the corn and they help by adding nutrients to the soil.

Heavy winds can damage gardens by removing mulch, topsoil, and eroding packed beds and hillsides. Rain and hail can also cause severe damage by beating down young seedlings and tightly packing a new soil covering that has just been laid. This is where a tight ground cover can help. By carefully selecting the right type of ground cover, the gardener can help prevent soil erosion without harming nearby plants. The best groundcover plants are usually those that prefer shade. For example, **cut-and-come-again salads**, meaning salad greens that do not need to reach maturity before harvesting and can be cut to grow again, are easy to grow, and all they need is a narrow band beneath other rows of plants. They create a beautiful groundcover while taking advantage of a space that is not very useable for other plants. Clover is another example of a ground cover that likes shade and will help keep the soil covered against wind, rain, and hail.

Crop rotation

History has shown the problems of not utilizing crop rotation – think of the Irish Potato Famine problem of the mid-1800s. In this case, blight, a fungus, destroyed three-fourths of all the potato crops for years, creating widespread famine and eventual death for much of the population. Potato was the main crop of the country and the most widely consumed food of the middle- to lower-class people. The people starved when the potato crop failed because they had no secondary crops to succeed as food or cash crops. When only one crop is planted, this is called **monoculture**. Planting potatoes, sunflower, or safflower in the same place year after year can lead to an extensive spread of Verticillium fungus and kill off the entire crop for the season and even affect future crops.

Crop rotation means relocating the crops to a different part of the garden every year. When companion planting, you need to ensure succeeding crops are always a completely different genus or species than the previous year's crop to minimize disease. The rotation sequence is usually at least two years, but it may be longer. For example, if you plant potatoes in one spot, do not plant them in that spot again for at least three or even four years. The reason you want to rotate your crops is to accomplish the following:

- Minimize disease
- Discourage insect infestations
- Deter weeds
- Improve soil fertility
- Reduce erosion
- Reduce the use of chemicals

Number of beds to rotate

The number of crops you want to grow will determine the number of beds that you rotate. If this is your first attempt at establishing a vegetable garden, it is best to start small. A 10 foot by 15 foot plot will be large enough for someone just starting out. It does not have to be a square so consider a round, rectangular, or even an oval-shaped garden.

You will need to decide whether you will be companion gardening at ground level or in raised beds. Raised beds allow for more intensive planting and can provide just as many vegetables as their larger counterparts. When considering crop rotation with raised beds, you will take the crop from Bed 1 of this year and move it to Bed 2 next year, then to Bed 3 in the year after, and so on. If you are not sure how many beds to create, try for four. You can plant in three beds while allowing the fourth to rest as you build it up with compost and green manure.

Most people group beds by classification; others group them with "like" qualities. For example, you could divide crops by the nutritional requirements:

- *Group 1:* Leafy plants that thrive on oxygen — lettuces and salad greens, broccoli, cabbage, cauliflower, and kale

- *Group 2:* Fruits that need phosphorus — squash, melon, pumpkin, tomatoes, peppers, and cucumbers

- *Group 3:* Roots that love potassium — onions, shallots, garlic, leeks, carrots, turnips, and radishes

- *Group 4:* Soil replenishers — legumes, corn, potatoes, beans, and peas

Another way to divide crops is by these classifications:

- **Cultivated row crops** — corn and potatoes
- **Close-growing grains** — wheat and oats
- **Cover crops** — clover and grasses

There have been many studies showing that certain crops should (or should not) follow others for the best yield. Beets will yield best when they follow barley or wheat; soybeans should follow beets; and potatoes should never follow tomatoes.

For more information on crop rotation, here are some online resources you can reference:

- Manitoba Agriculture, Food, and Rural Initiatives' Web site offers extensive information on crop rotation research and the inherent benefits of this type of program — **www.gov.mb.ca/agriculture/ crops/forages/bjb00s43.html**.

- Ontario Ministry of Agriculture Food & Rural Affairs' Web site offers information on crop rotation for agricultural purposes — **www.omafra.gov.on.ca/english/crops/field/news/croptalk/2002/ ct_1102a6.htm**.

- North Dakota State University's Web site offers information and charts on the crop rotation for various agriculture crops and the benefits each type of crop provides — **www.ag.ndsu.edu/pubs/ plantsci/crops/eb48-1.htm**.

To decide how to rotate your own crops:

- Make a list of the crops you want to grow

- Fertilize and mulch the current bed for the crop it contains

- If you are growing legumes, always plant them after grains to replenish the nitrogen in the soil taken by the grain crops

- Incorporate as much compost or green manure into your garden as possible at all times

- Keep careful notes of your crop rotations so you know from year to year what was planted in what location

Another consideration after crop rotation is how to maximize your yield. Because each plant requires different nutrients and is also used as a food source for different destructive pests, planting a different crop in the space each season can both reduce the presence of pests and replenish the soil, giving the gardener the best chance of increasing yield.

Beans and corn once again offer an easy example. Corn requires a great deal of nitrogen in order to produce a good yield, and beans fix additional nitrogen into the soil. So by following beans with corn, you will have a greater production of corn.

Cover crops

Cover crops are a second crop planted to improve the production of the primary plant. This is an important concept of companion planting where one plant can help others. Examples of this type of crop include grasses that are grown in orchards or legumes grown during the winter season to improve the crops. Some plants like rye and clover can be planted immediately after a crop is harvested to protect and nourish the soil. In some instances, the secondary plant is grown immediately to absorb any nitrogen left in the soil after the fall harvest that would otherwise escape into the groundwater.

The home gardener needs to understand that some plants help build soil, and others leach the nutrients out of it. Most cover crops help build the soil and can:

- Provide protection from sun and weeds
- Give food for beneficial insects
- Provide nutrients for other plants by being worked into the soil at the end of the season

Cover crops are usually divided into legumes and non-legumes. Legumes, which include beans, peas, and lentils, are able to fix nitrogen, and can provide at least some of the nitrogen requirement for the next crop in rotation. Legumes generally provide more nitrogen, but less total organic matter than non-legumes. The advantage lies in their nutritional value, so they are often used anyway. Non-legumes include wheat, rye, corn, buckwheat, oats, and barley. They are vigorous growers and will provide organic matter to be worked back into the soil.

Within both legume and non-legume groups, there are species specific to either a warm season or a cool season. By using both types of plants, it is possible to improve the overall productivity of the soil. During the growing season, cover crops prevent soil erosion and help control weeds. At the end of the growing season, the cover crop is dug under, without pulling the plants, to improve soil structure, aeration, water holding capacity, and nutrient content. Even with cover crops, it is important to have a plan for rotating different grains. Using the same cover crop year after year will increase plant-specific pathogenic organisms. By switching out to a different cover crop, the gardener will interrupt the life cycle of the organism and discourage it from multiplying.

If you are not using raised beds, you can actually mow cover crops to provide instant organic mulches for the growing plants. Think of a large orchard planted with special grasses; mowing them back helps keep the growth in check and produces good mulch for the orchard.

Planting cover crops is easy if you are using seeds, which is one of the easiest and cheapest ways to plant large areas; you can sow the seeds like you are spreading chicken feed to your fowl. Walk forward through the garden and toss out handfuls of the seed in a circular motion, attempting to cover the area evenly. If you are sowing several different kinds of seeds, you can either mix them into one general seed pile first and then throw them all out together, or you can sow first one and then the other. If you are sowing raised bed gardens, you cannot walk forward so it is best to walk along the side and try to spread the seed evenly throughout the bed.

Now that you have an understanding of how to start companion planting, you will want to decide on what kind of plants to include in your companion garden.

Ways to Choose your Companion Plants

Every gardener has different tastes and different needs and every garden will present growing conditions that offer up a challenge. The growing conditions between your yard and your neighbor's yard can be different, and there can even be differences between your front yard and your backyard. And, as any gardener will tell you, the geographical area of the country in which you live will often dictate the way that your companion plants work together. A distance of only a few hundred miles can present an entirely new set of landscape, temperature, and humidity conditions. Soil may be rockier or sandier or the pH may be higher or lower, affecting conditions enough to change the transplanted gardener's approach to his or her garden.

Every garden contains sun, shade, sheltered spaces, open areas, dry spaces, and places that retain water. These mini-ecosystems must be understood and taken into consideration before designing a garden or choosing the plants to go in it. If space is unlimited for the garden, then crops, herbs, flowers, and shrubs may all be placed where it best suits them. Few gardeners have that freedom in most cases, so space is at a premium.

As with any garden, you need to understand what you have to work with before you create your companion garden. The type of soil, the amount of water available or that you will need, and the amount of sun or shade available should also be considered. Then you have to consider the types of plants that will fit into and flourish in your garden. If you are looking to incorporate a more intensive companion gardening system into your plans, the soil will need to be rich and heavy in nourishment to accommodate the extra plants.

You must select the right plants to accommodate the planting area, rather than the other way around. Let us take a closer look at some of the ways you can select plants for your garden.

Choosing by climate and geographical location

When you purchase plants in a garden shop, they will be tagged with a hardiness zone number.

The hardiness zone is a system the U.S. Department of Agriculture (USDA) developed as a rough guide to the plant's hardiness. The term "rough" applies because hardiness depends on many factors, such as:

- Duration of cold or hot weather in any given year
- Force of wind
- Depth of roots
- How much water is in the soil at the time frost first hits

The USDA has divided the United States and southern Canada into 11 planting zones or USDA Plant Hardiness Zones. The USDA has defined these regions by a 10 degrees F difference in the average annual minimum temperature in the area. The higher the USDA hardiness number, the warmer the temperatures are for gardening in those planting zones. This means that areas within northern Minnesota are in USDA planting zones of 2 and 3, and southern Florida is in the USDA zones 9 through to 11. However, most of the United States falls into the USDA zones of 4 through 8, which cover areas where the average lowest temperatures range from -20 degrees F to 20 degrees F.

Plants and seeds will normally be labeled according to these USDA planting zones, meaning the zone on the label is the zone in which a gardener will be the most successful in the growing that particular plant. The zones can be closely linked, so it is possible that although you live in zone 7, your weather this year (or this season) will act like zone 8. This means that severe winter weather may kill off some plants or an especially hot summer may do the same.

There is an interactive USDA hardiness zone map available through the U.S. National Arboretum Web site at **www.usna.usda.gov/Hardzone/ushzmap.html**. Find your location on the map and understand the zone you are in and what this means for your garden. No matter how much you love a wisteria plant, if you are located in the far north it will not survive. Likewise, if you love ferns but live in Arizona, you probably will not have a lot of success — besides, wilting plants are not attractive in any garden.

Microclimates

A **microclimate** is defined as a mini-climate or a small, specific place found within a larger or macroclimate. This happens as a result of a different type of exposure to the elements. For instance, sunny hidden places in the garden that are sheltered from harsh winds and frosts can contain microclimates.

Consider a south-facing home surrounded by half an acre of land. The front yard receives hours of hot sun and the brick house and the brick wall separating the front from the back will reflect heat, so plants that are closer to these areas may bloom earlier and later into the seasons. They are also more likely to overheat in the summer. Moving to the back or the property, the small deck has a shady part closest to the house, while the outer edge gets more reflected light. The border of the brick wall receives no light at all and is perfect for a shade garden.

Such unique microclimates can be great for experimenting with plants that might otherwise be considered not hardy enough for you geographical location. If you have a plant reported to be for zone 4 and you live in zone 3, you can try growing the plant in a warm sheltered microclimate.

Vegetables are also classified according to frost survival, and these too may be manipulated somewhat if your garden has microclimates. In addition, they can be covered using old cotton sheets or heavy plastic if there is danger of imminent frost. This is a common practice with strawberries if night temperatures drop unseasonably low.

Choosing by light/shade

Another major consideration is the amount of sun the garden and plants will receive in a day. Most gardens will require at least six to eight hours of sunlight a day, even during the spring and fall. Many times when the gardener is unsuccessful with a plant, it is simply because it is not receiving the full amount of sun, even though the gardener feels that the plant was placed in a sunny area.

The number of hours of sun available for your plants is not the only factor to consider; you also have to consider the intensity of the sun. Gardens that are exposed to the east receive cool morning sun and are shaded in the afternoons. Gardens with a western exposure are shaded in the morning and receive very hot sun in the afternoon. If delicate plants are placed there, even if they are considered sun loving, you may notice bleaching and sunburn — browning, dying leaves — especially in warmer climates. The flowers will also fade quickly in the intense heat.

Here is a list of light conditions you might see on the plants at your local nursery:

- **Full-sun plants:** These must go in areas that get a minimum of six hours of direct sunlight every day.

- **Partial sun, also called semi-shade:** These plants thrive underneath a trellis, a tree branch, or a place where the sunlight is filtered. They need some direct sunlight, but it can alternate with periods of shade.

- **Full shade:** These plants require light, but not direct sun. They should be planted under dense trees or in the shadows like on the north side of a house or wall area.

Choosing by nutrient needs

All plants have specific requirements to make them grow and produce in the way they are meant to, but these requirements differ from plant to plant. Some vegetables deplete the soil of particular nutrients. For example, sweet corn is a heavy feeder that takes a lot of nitrogen (and plenty of other nutrients) from the soil. If you plant climbing beans at the base of each growing corn stalk, then the bean's roots can fix the nitrogen from the air into the soil where the corn can make the best use of it. Other legumes, like peas, grow well with other nitrogen-hungry vegetables like cabbages, broccoli, and cauliflower.

Another way of choosing companion plants is by how they grow and where they receive their nutrients. Two different types of vegetables can feed at two different soil levels, which is what happens when you grow carrots and onions together. Onion roots stay just under the surface of the ground whereas carrots push their roots very deep, which is where they feed. By growing the two together, you boost the productivity of your beds.

Choosing by water needs and availability

Water requirements vary from plant to plant and water availability varies from garden to garden. Some dirt is porous and the water will seep away quickly while other garden beds are made with mulch and rich compost that will hold water for longer. If your garden is on a hillside, you need to watch that all the plants' water does not drain down the hillside and away from the plants' roots.

Another consideration is the type of watering system you have available. Are you close to a lake and is there ground water close to the surface? Or do you live in the desert and you need to water a minimum of twice a day? Are you prepared to face an increase in your water bill, or are you looking to have plants that do not need heavy watering? Do you already have enough hoses to cover the size of the garden you are planning? Have you considered using soaker hoses? They work well in many gardens as they can deliver a slow and steady water supply.

Choosing by soil conditions

The soil that is present in the garden must be rich with nutrients to help the plants grow to their full potential. Soils may consist of clay, loam, sand, shale, or rock. You can test what kind of soil is in your garden by taking a shovel, digging a hole in the ground, and pouring a bucket of water into the hole. A very hard soil, like one with a clay base, will never drain; the water may stay there for days. Clay soil will drain, but it may take three hours or even more. A clay/loam mixture will drain somewhere between 30 minutes and two hours. A loam or a sandy loam will drain between ten minutes and an hour. Pure sand will drain so quickly you are unable to keep the hole filled. And of course, if you find rock just below the surface, you will not be able to dig a hole at all. You will need to keep the soil condition in mind when you choose your plants or you will need to improve the soil first.

Soil pH

The acidity of the garden soil is also important and is referred to as its pH level. It is measured on a scale of 1 to 14 with 7 being neutral. A value above 7 means the soil is alkaline, or basic, and if the soil is below 7, it indicates an acidic soil. The acidity reflects the amount of calcium, in the form of chalk or lime, in the soil. This level can change over time and can be affected by rain and the crops growing nearby. Clay soils tend to be alkaline and sandy soils tend toward acidic levels. There are three common terms used to describe the soil pH. Sweet soil has mid-range pH (between 6 and 8) and is ideal for most plants. Sour soil is acidic with a low (below 7) pH, and bitter is used to describe alkaline soil, meaning it has a pH higher than 7.

The pH level is so important because it can affect the release of nutrients and have an impact on worm and micro-organism activity. The pH of a garden soil will affect plant growth. Most vegetables do well in a slightly acidic soil (around 6.5 to 7) as they can more readily access the nutrients in this type of soil. Some plants do not have a preference and some are highly susceptible to pH conditions. You can check with your local nursery to discover what the soil needs are for any plants you wish to plant in your garden. If you are going to test the pH levels in your garden, it is recommended that you take soil samples from two to three different locations in the garden.

None of these garden conditions need to be permanent; it is possible to off-set nearly all of the circumstances listed above. If a drought situation exists, irrigation can be put into place. Windbreaks can be built to keep off the worst of the wind. But it is always the easiest to work with the natural conditions that exist in your area. The goal of the garden, after all, is to be beautiful and productive, whether what is being produced is food or flowers.

Regardless of the soil's existing condition, adding good topsoil will help your garden grow. Adding compost will enrich the soil with nutrients, as will adding well-rotted manure. Some gardeners use fertilizer throughout the blooming season to increase the amount of flowers and increase the yield of the plants. If you prepare the soil well with topsoil, compost, peat moss, and manure, the garden will need minimal to no fertilizing throughout the season.

Where to purchase the ideal soil for your garden

Most major garden centers offer topsoil, either bagged or in bulk, fertilizer, compost, and manure from various sources. If you are uncertain about what you need, speak with a specialist to get advice on the right products. Many of these centers will also offer bulk sales where you can purchase large quantities of dirt. It is better to go to a garden center or a landscaping supply store for this type of material because if you purchase these materials online, you will usually have to order in large quantities, which will make shipping expensive. Your local center will also be able to advise you about problems with the soil in your area.

The compost and fertilizer will add nutrients and improve the texture and workability of the soil; the manure will add nitrogen; and the peat moss will increase the water-retaining capacity.

Choosing by color or appearance

Some gardens appear to have been designed by an artist with the beautiful use of colors, textures, and shapes and appear to meld into a beautiful harmony. Many times, this sort of garden has been carefully laid out with a particular color sequence in mind. Spring might be for the cooler colors — white, yellow, and purple — and in summer the hotter colors come into play — red roses, yellow dahlias, marigolds, and bright asters. Many gardeners love to mix violas and blue delphiniums with the yellow and reds. Other gardens may contain loads of white flowers, sweet alyssum, and climbing roses, mixed with the soft grays of artemisia, lavender, and lamb's ear. The Hosta "Royal Standard" works well in these arrangements too.

If the garden area is very small, using a two- or three-color spectrum can be dramatic. When considering planting for color, consider what appeals to your eye. It may be the cooling whiteness, gray-green foliage, or the extreme hot of ruby red flowers. It may also be the combination of colors that appeals to you, such as lemony-yellow with blue and purple contrast.

Even a garden of all green can be beautiful. In this case, texture and pattern take the place of color. Green is restful, especially in the heat of summer. Consider planting glossy and waxy leaves, hairy or woolly leaves, or toothed and smooth leaves. Together these add interest to the green garden.

Many gardeners like to work with a color wheel to decide the best relationship between their garden's colors. The color wheel is made of six segments containing the three primary colors (red, blue, and yellow) alternated with the secondary colors (green, purple, and orange). Green is between yellow and blue because it is a mixture of these two colors, purple is between red and blue, and so on. The color wheel is helpful because by looking at it, you can determine what effect a certain combination of colors might have. Colors that are close on the wheel, like orange and yellow, are more harmonious; colors that are opposites, such as purple and yellow, will present more of a contrast. This can help you determine whether you would like an exciting, dazzling garden, or one that is more gentle and relaxing.

The strength of the colors used will have an effect on the overall grouping. For example, a soft yellow, such as moonlight coreopsis, will have a soothing effect; a stronger yellow will be much more dramatic. If the garden has been planted and you find the colors are too strong, it is easy to lighten the contrast by adding a lighter shade of the same flowers that already exist. Make sure the softer tones of flowers or their foliage have a definite shape, and that enough of them are used to create the contrast. Otherwise, the lighter-colored plant will be overwhelmed and lost within the stronger colors. If your goal is to develop a scheme that offers richness, consider a garden of golds, reds, and shades of blue/purple. Foliage in this garden should vary from dark green to a purple shade.

White is often omitted from the garden because it tends to look chalky. White draws attention, especially in summer plantings, so it is usually not scattered throughout the garden. However, if used in small doses and mixed among red, yellow, and oranges, whites can accentuate the heat of these colors. If white has been rejected in the past because of its starkness, try a creamier shade instead (like the edges of hosta variety called "Francee"). Pastels and whites are especially enjoyable during twilight hours, particularly if backlit by the sun. Many gardeners select white jasmine, moonflower, and the climbing rose variety rosa x fortuniana just for these purposes.

If planting a first-time garden in a single color, consider using all green. Green is a very restful color and offers many shade varieties, including deep purple-green, true green, blue-green, gray-green, and yellow-green. Blue-green leaves will have a deepening effect, just as blue flowers will. Rustling pale or variegated ornamental grasses planted against deep green hollies or other glossy, strongly shaped leaves offer textural appeal.

A popular garden theme is to use a single color like an all-purple garden. To avoid the color coming across as monotone, use the many different shades like mauves, periwinkle, lavender, violet, and purplish-black. Some good plant choices for the purple garden include:

- Purple smoke bush
- Bronze fennel
- Purple basil
- Eggplant
- Burgundy bush beans
- Ruby perfection cabbage
- California lilac
- Cornflower
- Catmint
- Turquoise blue fruit

If you are gardening for color, consider these tips to have a long season filled with beautiful blooms:

- Determine your color scheme and then stick to it so the garden will not look chaotic.

- For extra interest, include a wide variety of plants: annuals, perennials, flowering shrubs, trees, roses, and bulbs. In the food garden, tuck some of these into the bare spots.

- Consider the seasons. The biggest challenge you will have when developing a new garden is to provide color from early spring through late fall. Do not forget to look for shrubs with bright fruit or trees with a great winter shape or fall foliage color.

- Use one or two bold plants to give focal points to your garden area. Foliage with a strong shape or texture can make everything else stand out. Consider adding cardoon to your garden.

- Plan to work through all the seasons because a garden evolves over time.

- Be willing to take out the plants that are not working and replace them with something else.

Choosing by genetically similar crops

Attempting to garden with natural conditions means much more than gardening by zone, climate, and soil type; it also means selecting plants according to their similarities or differences. When you select plants that are from the same botanical family, you are choosing those that are genetically similar. Grouping the plants together is an easy way to garden because in general their light, moisture, and soil requirements will match. They also often have the same pest problems and similar diseases, so it is possible to end up with trouble if you are not careful. Just be sure to read up on the problems that might exist such as a certain fungus in the tomato family.

When this book talks of families, this refers to these genetically similar groupings. An example of a plant family is the Asteraceae, or aster, family that contains more than 20,000 recognized species. Most of these plants have an astrakhan "flower" (actually a grouping of tiny flowers, called a floret, centered together on a series of petal-like bracts) and they usually live in an open, dry environment. Their leaves can be simple, lobed, alternate, opposite, or whorled. Some of the members of this family include:

- Aster
- Daisy
- Sunflower
- Dandelion
- Lettuce

The cabbage family, called Brassicaceae, is another good example. The cabbage family includes:

- Brussels sprouts
- Cauliflower
- Broccoli
- Kale
- Chinese cabbages

These family members will all grow well together. They also mix well with the aster family mentioned above.

Choosing by the critters that plants attract or repel

Certain plants fall into the "pest control group" of plants and the goal of planting them may be to attract beneficial pests or it may be to repel those that are harmful. Many gardeners also purchase beneficial insects, such as ladybugs and praying mantis, and grow the plants required for the insects to flourish. It is also possible to grow specific plants that will attract these "good" insects to your garden.

Here is a list of some easily attainable plants that attract a wide range of beneficial insects:

- Golden aster
- Goldenrod
- Marguerite
- Bachelor's buttons
- Black-eyed Susan
- African daisies
- Calendula
- Dwarf morning glory
- Cosmos
- Sunflower
- Zinnia
- Buttercups
- Dandelions
- Lamb's quarters
- Wild mustard
- Queen Anne's lace

Just as some plants attract certain insects, others deter them. By combining specific deterrents with the vegetables, herbs, or flowers that bugs normally damage, you can successfully harvest plants without adding harmful chemical pesticides. Note that some of the deterrents are trap crops, which means they act as a decoy, drawing the pest away from the plants they are most fond of. For example, nasturtiums will trap aphids and mustard plants attract harlequin bugs.

Now that you know a little bit more about ways you can choose the plants for your garden, the next chapter deals with attracting the good bugs and repelling the bad bugs in greater detail.

CHAPTER 3

Critters in Your Garden

The garden is a den of activity; it teems with life both seen and unseen. Most of the garden creatures are insects, birds, and mammals and they are all there for a purpose, even if only to feed themselves. The trick is in knowing which of these insects are good, which are bad, and how to define these two terms in regard to your garden.

Even if flowers are not on your plant of choice list, you may wish to add some. Experienced gardeners recommend that you utilize 5 to 10 percent of your garden for flower growing because flowers attract many beneficial insects. For example, the flowers are often used as a place for insect mating and the sugar in the flowers' nectar becomes a fuel for the insects' near-constant movement as they search for prey and lay eggs. Protein and fats are contained in pollen, which support development inside the insect's body, and the nearly microscopic prey that lives inside the flowers are a food source for the young predatory insects.

Understanding Insects in Your Garden

There are many creatures living in your garden on a regular basis, and knowing something about the types of bugs helps determine which you want to keep around and which you want to get rid of. A general classification places insects into one of four categories:

- Insect predators
- Insect parasitoids
- Insect pollinators
- Soil builders

Insect predators

Insect predators are the most familiar and beneficial of all the groups of insects and include some of the most distinctive and visible insects like the lady beetles (ladybugs), dragonflies, lacewings, paper wasps, and praying mantises. These insects are predators, meaning they hunt down their prey. In general, predatory insects are larger than their prey and will often hunt while in the various life cycle stages like the larva stage, as well as in the adult stage. They are hunters for longer than many other bugs, therefore their food requirements are larger while they are growing, making them excellent additions to any garden.

Insect parasitoids

To understand the insect parasitoid, which is part of the parasite family, you have to understand the parasite first. For example, fleas are parasites. The parasitoid lives on the body of its host for a part of the insect's life. They lay eggs on or inside the host, and a host can be an insect, larva, or even an egg.

When the larvae of the parasitoid hatch, it feeds on the host. Examples of this type of insect include braconid wasps and tachinid flies. The wasps' preference is to lay eggs inside the tomato hornworms, which is the caterpillar stage of the five-spotted hawkmoth. Tomato hornworms are common and if you see them with white lumps attached, they already have wasp's pupae attached. When the hornworm is close to death, the pupae develops and emerges as adult wasps.

Insect pollinators

Pollinators are the important insects that help plants flower, reproduce, and bear fruit. The most common pollinators are bees, flies, butterflies, beetles, wasps, and moths. There are more than 4,000 species of bees in North America alone. This group includes bumblebees, mason bees, squash bees, and of course the common honey bee. Regardless of the type of pollinator, they are all necessary to keep your garden blooming and producing all season long.

Soil builders (garbage/trash collectors)

Soil builders are the bugs that break down the soil and other decaying garden matter. They work the compost pile from garbage to nutrient-rich soil for the garden. Included in this group are millipedes, centipedes, earwigs, and brown lacewings. Encourage the presence of beneficial insects by covering any bare dirt spots in the garden with dead leaves, grass clippings, or other mulch. Be sure it is thick enough to actually shade the soil beneath it; this will provide shelter for spiders. Also, provide a water source for these insects just as you would a birdbath for birds. A shallow pan hidden behind a few plants is sufficient, if kept full of fresh water, for the bugs to dine on.

Insects and Bugs You Want to Attract

Our gardens are teeming with life – some we want and some we do not want. This section looks at the insects, birds, and wildlife that help companion gardens and the plants that you can add in to attract these helpers.

A **garden insectary** is a type of garden full of flowering plants designed to attract or harbor beneficial insects. It is one form of companion planting where plants share in their beneficial properties to deter pests, acquire nutrients, and attract natural predators. By planting some of these plants, the garden provides natural housing, shelter, and alternative food sources like pollen and nectar, which is a basic requirement for all insects as part of their diet. You can make a separate garden for an insectary or you can incorporate the concepts and plants into your normal garden.

If you are going to create a garden insectary, know that it does not need to be large; five or six types of plants are enough to attract the right insects. As the garden matures, the insects soon go to work. Think of this type of garden as a long-term project because the results are not instantaneous. For beneficial populations of insects to become established, young plants should mature for one life cycle if not several. With time, your garden will evolve into a naturally balanced space that grows healthy vegetables and flowers.

There are many good insects that you should consider welcoming into your garden. These, for one reason or another, kill other "bad" bugs in the garden. By having these "good" bugs around, you will minimize the bad bugs. Let us take a closer look at various bugs you want to attract.

Ambush bugs

These pale yellow to greenish-yellow bodied insects have especially strong front legs for grabbing up their prey. They are named after their ambush-like behavior of laying in wait in flowers then snatching the prey as it flies near. This bug injects paralyzing saliva into the prey to immobilize it. The ambush bug eats flies, some moths, and other bugs. Some gardeners might consider this bug a pest as it also eats bees. Before trying to attract this bug into your garden, you have to consider the purpose of your garden and what purpose you want your insects to have. The ambush bugs love asters and goldenrod.

Aphid predatory midge

These tiny insects, less than $^1/_{16}$ inch long, feed almost entirely on aphids and are a small, two-winged, mosquito-looking fly. They find aphid colonies by their odor and then lay their eggs alongside the colony. If it is a huge colony, more eggs will be laid. Adult females can lay up to 100 eggs in their life span of six to seven days. It takes a couple of days for the larva to hatch and they feast on the aphids until they mature to adults.

Because the aphidoletes, which are the larva of the tiny fly, require a strong food source and aphids love roses, if you keep roses in the garden, then both insects will show up. Because the aphidoletes are so voracious in their appetites for aphids, commercial rose growers and fruit orchards use aphid predatory midges in the greenhouses and fields.

Assassin bug

These long, oval-bodied bugs have a thin, stretched out-looking head with big eyes and come in many different colors from traditional brown to hot red. They also come in various sizes and shapes. Some like the wheel bug are more than 1 ½ inches long. They love meadows, fields, and gardens of all kinds. They are particularly happy with perennials and ground covers and are common throughout most of North America.

The assassin bugs eat aphids, all types of flying insects, larvae, eggs, and caterpillars, making them another workhorse in the garden. If you are keeping honey bees, you may not want assassin bugs as they will prey on bees as well.

Aphidius

Aphidius are part of the parasitic wasp group and are a common predator of aphids. The adult aphidius are tiny, dark, non-dangerous wasps that grow to approximately ⅛-inch long. The adult females lay eggs inside the aphid, and ten days later the aphid turns into a mummy, which then hatches into a full adult aphidius five days later – and the cycle continues.

The aphidius are excellent hunters and can find aphid colonies even when there are only a few of them around, which makes them invaluable to have in the garden. In order to encourage their presence in your garden, plant sunflowers and/or lupin as they are happy with both.

Beetles

There are countless beetle species around the world and they are actually the largest group of insects, including both predator and pollinator types. Some of the beetles that you are likely to find in your garden include:

- **Fireflies (Lampyridae)** — also called lightning bugs, these common insects can be found under debris and in moist, dark places. Of course, they are easy to spot in the evening as the flash across the lawn. These insects are helpful as larvae as they are predators of slugs, snails, and other insects. They do not feed as adults.

- **Ground beetles (Carabidae)** — these can be found under most stones or grown covers in a garden. They are a shiny black and run very fast when disturbed. It is hard to identify within this species as they are a family of more than 3,000 species. Both the larvae and the adults are active predators of many damaging insects like the diamondback moth, spider mites, tent caterpillars, and the Colorado potato beetle. They are voracious in their appetites, so grow perennials, shrubs, or have wood and rocks for them to hide under and they will keep your garden healthy. They are particularly fond of amaranthus.

- **Rove beetle (Staphylinidae)** — the rove beetle can also be found under rocks, boards, and ground covers because it prefers dark and moist locations. These beetles are effective in both the adult and larvae stage and will consume insect larvae and are particularly fond of fly maggots. These beetles are particularly appreciative of dense ground covers, like alfalfa and clover, which provide them with shelter close to a food source.

- **Soldier beetles (Cantharidae)** — Soldier beetles are happiest on flowers, so keep milkweed, hydrangeas, catnip, and most other flowers in your garden. If you have flowers, perennials, or cover crops in your garden, you will give these beetles a place to reproduce. These beetles, both adults and larvae, feed on many different insects including maggots, eggs, and soft body insects. They are particularly fond of cucumber beetles so keep catnip close to the cucumber patch to bring in the soldier beetles.

- **Tiger beetles (Cicindelidae)** — The tiger beetles are some of the fastest of the beetle species but unlike the others, these are often seen in the sunny, drier areas of the garden. They will stay over the winter in a garden and love most perennials and groundcovers to live in.

Beneficial nematodes (parasitic nematodes and predator nematodes)

These are microscopic-size roundworms that are an incredible addition to any garden. They are predators of many other insects, infesting and killing their prey within 24 to 48 hours. They will continue to live in the area and reproduce as long as there is food, which for them includes white grubs, root maggot, cabbage root maggot, carrot weevils, strawberry root weevils, and fungus gnats. They are known to kill off most turf insects.

These insects do not do well in hot, dry areas and thrive in moist, dark corners of the garden where they can hide in the soil or within woody plants. Some gardeners have luck attracting beneficial nematodes with French marigolds. This is also one of many beneficial insects you can purchase commercially from local nurseries or mail-order seed companies.

Big-eyed bugs

This is a stout, flat bug and as you might expect they have huge eyes that point sideways. They also have clear wings that are dark and silver in color. They are small at only ⅛ to ¼ inch in length. Despite their small size, they are powerhouses at feeding on garden insects and their eggs. Their main diet consists of caterpillars, aphids, blister bees, chinch bugs, spider mites, and all their eggs.

They are usually seen on the surface of the ground, particularly in low-growing ground covers like clover, alfalfa, and they have a fondness for the potato plant.

Butterflies

Butterflies are at their most active during the summer to late summer months and they are great pollinators so it is important to have many nectar-producing plants all summer and fall. It also helps to have food sources for the butterfly larvae and caterpillars. Most butterflies prefer being in full sun and large patches of blooms will help to attract the butterflies. Consider planting a butterfly bush, purple coneflower, Black-eyed Susan, catmint, lavender, phlox, goldenrod, asters, and do not forget the heavy blooming annuals like zinnias, marigolds, cosmos, sweet alyssum, and lantana. The larva will eat leaves off parsley, dill, fennel, hollyhocks, and butterfly weed. There will be a slightly chewed look on the leaves until the caterpillars turn into butterflies, at which time they will head for the nectar in the flowers.

Damsel bugs (Nabidae)

These bugs are quite distinctive with a thin body and curving beaks with strong forearms. You will find them racing around in the groundcovers. If you have fields of alfalfa or other cover crops in the neighborhood, you will find them full of damsel bugs.

They hunt out aphids, caterpillars, leafhoppers, mites, and plant bugs. Keep clover close to your tomato plants to keep the tomatoes free of insects.

Plants that attract damsel bugs include caraway, white sensations cosmos, fennel, alfalfa, spearmint, goldenrod, and lemon gem marigolds.

Dragonflies

Dragonflies are one of the most easily recognized insects in the garden with their long, slender bodies, huge bulging eyes, and four long wings. These insects are strong predators and feed on smaller insects like flies, mosquitoes, gnats, and aphids. There are thousands of different species and they are commonly seen throughout North America.

Dragonflies are wonderfully unique additions to your garden, as they are beautiful to look at. They need a water source to stay in your garden like a pond or half barrel full of water, and close to the water source they need some tall natural grasses. The buttonbush will do well at the edge of a pond and bring in the dragonflies as well. They like a selection of plants so offer grasses, native shrubs, and perennials. Leave them plenty of tall grass or plants for perches and cover as well.

Damselfly (not to be confused with Damsel bug)

The damselfly has forelegs that are built for catching aphids and getting rid of insect larvae. They come in a full range of colors commonly seen as blue or a blue-green shade and they make a great addition to any garden. This insect is often mistaken for the dragonfly, but can eas-ily be told apart by the way the damselfly folds its wings down when the body is at rest.

Damselflies like to be close to water, so if you have a pond, water garden, fountains, or something similar, you will probably see them. They are great for eating water-based insects or insects attracted to water conditions like the mosquitoes. The adult damselfly is a predator of many types of insects and has a particular fondness for aphids. They are attracted to the same water type of conditions and plant selection as the dragonfly.

Hoverflies

These flies are also known as flower flies or syrphid fliers. They are small, approximately ½ inch in length. With their black and yellow/white striped bodies, they are often mistaken for bees. Their movements are quite different in that they hover over flowers unlike bees that land on the flowers.

They are a friend of the garden and are wonderful pollinators that prey on aphids, leafhoppers, small caterpillars, corn earworms, thrips, and mealybugs to name a few. The adults need nectar and pollen and require flowering plants and shrubs, with particular preference to yarrow, wild mustard, and herbs.

Lacewings

This is another group of insects that comprises hundreds of species in North America alone. The most common two varieties you will hear about as being beneficial to your garden are the brown and green lacewings.

- **Brown lacewing** — These lacewings have brown, transparent wings covered with a fine netting pattern. These insects are approximately ¼ inch long and are evening flyers that love woodlands, orchards, fields, and gardens. Both the larvae and adults are heavy feeders and enjoy eating aphids, mealybugs, and most soft bodied insects. Because they are heavy aphid eaters, these insects are always welcome in the garden. The females lay their eggs on the underside of the leaves and the larvae use leaves or organic material on the ground to hide under as they develop. This is how they have earned the nickname of "trash collectors." They need nectar and pollen for the adults to feed on. They love many flowering herbs and plants and have a particular fondness for yarrow.

- **Green lacewing** — This insect is greenish as compared to the brown lacewing and they also have transparent wings with a netting pattern. Adults are slightly larger than the brown lacewing and have a life cycle of between four and six weeks. The females lay eggs on the underside of leaves near aphid colonies and when the larvae emerge, they feast on the nearby food source. Besides aphids, the green lacewing loves to feed on mealybugs, thrips, cabbage worms, cutworms, leafhoppers, potato beetles, and even spider mites. Some of the adults will not prey on pests and will need nectar, pollen, and honeydew close by in order to feed. Green lacewing insects enjoy flowering plants and herbs like dill, cosmos, sunflower, carrots, and dandelions as good sources of pollen and nectar for adults. They do need some water source during the dry season.

Ladybugs (Lady beetles)

Ladybugs, easily recogniz-able red and black insects, are huge predators of the aphid and many other garden vari-ety insects. They love a gar-den with tansy, angelic, and spring flowering bushes and ground covers. They particu-larly love zinnia and yarrow.

Minute pirate bugs

Minute pirate bugs appear as tiny black dots. Even when they are fully grown they do not exceed ¼ inch in length. The nymphs (the insects after hatching) are microscopic in size. The young come in different colors like pink, yellow, and tan with red eyes and these bugs change to black as adults. Both adults and nymphs consume large numbers of insects, preying on aphids, thrips, whiteflies, spider mites, leafhoppers, insect eggs, and when they are found in the corn silk, they are eating the corn earworm eggs.

They are attracted to flowering ground covers. Plants that attract the min-ute pirate bug include alfalfa, angelica, cow parsnip, goldenrod, cinquefoil, yellow coneflower, and Canada anemone. If you plant several of these, you will have blooms all season.

Praying mantis

The praying mantis is another distinctive and easily recognized insect. They have a large 2-inch long green or tan body and are one of the best insects at camouflaging. They are well-known for their body positions, in which their forearms are held up as if they are praying. Unlike many insects, you will not see hordes of these in the garden because they have specific territories. One in your garden (depending on the size) is all you will probably see.

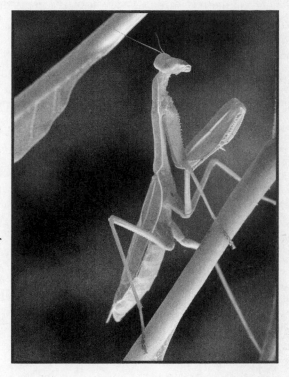

These bugs are expert hunters. They are happy in most gardens where there is an abundant supply of food such as spiders, crickets, grasshoppers, lizards, and even mice. As they are not too particular in their choice of foods, they will consume most prey that they can catch. They can be difficult to attract into a garden and are most often purchased commercially either through your local garden center or mail order.

Spiders

Spiders are not technically insects as they belong to the class arachnida and not class insecta. When it comes to garden predators, the more than 3,000 species of spiders are a pest control army. Spiders are rarely dangerous to people and will try to run away if they can. It is hard to imagine a garden existing without spiders. The more common spider types include:

- **Crab spiders** — these are the small, crab-like spiders that move in all directions and they come in many different colors, usually camouflaged to their surroundings. These insects eat anything they can catch and they can be found in most gardens close to flowering plants like daisies and cosmos, where they wait until their prey comes along.

- **Wolf spiders** — these spiders live mostly in the ground, some in actual burrows. These are night hunters and eat many different kinds of insects including aphids, mites, flies, moths, and beetles. They can be found under the mulch, on the rocks sunning themselves, and in their burrows with egg sacs.

- **Orb weavers** — these spiders create the huge webs that crisscross throughout the garden, eating the remaining web in the morning before moving onto another location for a new web that night. Orb spiders catch their prey in their webs, eating grasshoppers, flies, moths, and any jumping insects that are caught.

Wasps (parasitic)

Wasps belong to the same insect group as bees, sawflies, and even ants. All wasps have two pairs of wings and the females have a stinger. The majority of wasp species are parasitic. Almost every bad insect species has at least one wasp group that preys on it.

- **Aphid wasp** — these tiny black wasps feed heavily on mid-summer and fall aphid populations. The females prey on aphids, killing them before the aphids are able to reproduce, successfully keeping the population down. These wasps can be found close to the aphids with particular success in controlling pear, bean, potato, and cabbage aphids.

- **Spring Tiphia wasp** — this wasp looks similar to the winged black carpenter ant. The female is heavier than the male and is better at digging in the ground to search for beetle grubs. The female is slightly more than ½ inch in size and the male is slightly smaller at approximately ⅜ inch long. They are mainly predators of the Japanese beetle. Plants that this wasp species uses include tulip poplar, choke cherry, Norway maple, American elm, forsythia, firethorn, and pine trees.

- **Chalcid wasp** — this is another tiny black wasp that is only about ¼ inch long and it is quite colorful in metallic blue and green. The females lay eggs inside the skin of the caterpillar. These wasps feed on many different insects including aphids, whiteflies, caterpillars, and whiteflies. They can be found on most garden flowers like sea hollies, foliage like euonymus, and have a particular preference for leaf litter.

Insects You Want to Repel

Just as there are many insects that you want to have in your garden, there are many that you do not want. That is why you bring in the good bugs — to hunt the bad bugs. These bugs are bad because they cause damage to the flowers and vegetables in the garden.

Ants

Ants can be a nuisance in any garden. They can take over any space inside and out. To help keep them in control, use plants that either by smell or by something excreted through the roots repel them from your area, such as pennyroyal, mint, southernwood, and tansy.

Aphids

There are several kinds of aphid including greenfly and whitefly. They can be found in almost all gardens and will eat your plants' roots, leaves, and shoots. Plants that will repel the aphids include rue, anise, garlic, catnip, marigolds, dill, fennel, mint, chives, and the coriander/cilantro plant. Aphids are also a main food of most predatory insects.

Cabbage looper

These light green caterpillars have two white stripes down their sides. They are easily identified by the way they move as they make a loop of their back before stretching forward then pulling their back end forward, creating another loop. They cause a lot of damage to the garden by chewing holes into the leaves of broccoli, Brussels sprouts, cabbage, cauliflower, and sometimes they will eat beets, celery, lettuce, peas, and even spinach. One of the best predators of this insect is parasitic wasps. There are no known plants guaranteed to repel them, although garlic works occasionally, so the best answer is to attract the wasps in.

Colorado potato beetle

This larger beetle has a hard round shell with black and yellow stripes running down the length of the shell. The beetles and larvae can quickly eat the leaves off plants. They feed on cabbage, peppers, tomatoes, petunias, and have a special taste for potato plants. The natural predators of this beetle include spined soldier bugs, stinkbugs, birds, toads, and ground beetles. The tachinid flies and parasitic wasps also help control this beetle population. Research has shown that bush beans deter the Colorado potato beetle so plant bush beans between the potato plants. Another trick is to interplant garlic and keep horseradish close by as they deter the Colorado potato beetle. As toads are a good predator, keep water close by to encourage the presence of toads.

Cutworms

Cutworms are the larvae of several night-flying moths. They get their name because they cut young plants down by feeding on the stems at soil level.

There are also some species that climb up the plant to feed on the foliage and flower buds. They can be up to 2 inches long, brown, tan, pink, green, black, or even gray, and will curl up into a circle when disturbed. The best plant to repel cutworms is tansy and many predatory insects feed on cutworms as well. If you do not have any tansy growing where the cutworms are feeding, squeeze a tansy stem to get the juice on your fingers and then smear it on the stems of the young plants that are in trouble.

Earwigs

These small, beetle-looking insects come out at night and can make a mess of your garden. Many insects prey on them but there is another way to grab control of an infestation. Leave piping, like bamboo or an old busted hose, in pieces in the garden and then check them in the morning because these pipes will probably be filled with earwigs. You can then take the pieces of hose and sink it into water to drown the earwigs or throw the pipe in the garbage.

Eelworms

These bugs are hardly visible to the eye and are also called nematodes. They weaken plants by attacking both the stems and the roots of a plant. Marigolds can be used to repel them.

Flea beetles

These small black beetles have yellow or white stripes. They eat the leaves on plants like eggplant, radishes, potatoes, and most of the cabbage family. However, if you do not have any of these plants in your garden, they are happy to move on to most any crops. Planting trap crops like radishes and Chinese cabbage helps to keep them in control. Catnip will also deter flea beetles. They also do not like moist, dark areas so keeping plants close together and under moist conditions will help deter them. Ground beetles and parasitic wasps feed on these insects.

Flies

The common house fly is a well-known irritant for most gardens and households because it carries serious diseases and lays maggots wherever it can. You can repel this insect by placing pots of basil, tansy, and cologne mint in the garden and around the house. Try placing these plants on your deck or patio to keep them away when you are entertaining outdoors.

Imported cabbage worm

These worms are light green and have one single yellow stripe down the back. They are known to chew holes in the leaves of all cabbage family plants. The best way to get rid of this insect is to attract one of its main predators like the parasitic wasp.

Japanese beetle

These blue-green bugs have bronze wing caps and chew on the leaves and flowers of a wide variety of fruits, vegetables, and flowers. Use trap crops to keep them in one place and then bend the stalks of the plants into a bucket of soapy water to drown them. The best trap crops are the four-o'clocks. During high season, it can be necessary to check your plant stalks every day. The best predator of this beetle is the parasitic nematode.

Mealy bugs

These bugs are white, fluffy insects less than ¼ inch long and look like tiny bits of cotton on a plant. They weaken a plant by sucking the nutrients from the stems. They feed off a wide range of plants including geranium, ivy, chrysanthemum, and fruit trees. Some predators of the mealy bug include the ladybug and hoverflies.

Mexican bean beetle

These are oval-shaped, tan-colored beetles with black spots in three rows down the back and resemble brown lady bugs. They chew on bean leaves and can have such a strong effect that the plant's yield is severely reduced. This bug's natural predators include the spined soldier bugs, assassin bugs, and parasitic wasps. For plant repellants, try interplanting your garden's bush or climbing beans with chamomile, sage, savory, dill, and potatoes. Soybeans are a good trap crop for this beetle because it keeps the bugs away from bush and runner beans. Marigold is known to repel the Mexican bean beetle as well.

Thrips

Thrips are small, skinny insects that have wings with fringes on them. These small insects eat away at fruits, vegetables, and flowers, leaving silvery scars behind. One of the best ways to stop them is to grow pyrethrum. Natural predators of the thrip are the dicyphus insect.

Slugs

These easily recognizable creatures can cause havoc in a garden, eating most plants in their way. However, they cannot navigate over crumbled bark or rough, crumbly surfaces. Toads are a natural predator of the slug. Marigolds and comfrey are a trap crop for slugs so plant the flowers close to lettuce that you are trying to keep healthy. Other plants to deter slugs include garlic, chervil, lavender, wormwood, thyme, sage, stinging nettles, borage, mint, tansy, geraniums, and lemon balm.

Sow bugs

These insects are known by many names such as wood louse, armadillo bug, and slater. These are not, in fact, an insect but are related to the shrimp family and hide under compost, organic debris, logs, and any damp place. They have six pairs of legs and a series of armor plates rippling along their back that allows them to curl up into a small ball as their defense system. They are usually brown and can grow up to ½ inch long. They feed on all types of young plants and young, newly emerged seedlings, as well as decaying matter. The toad is a helpful predator of the sow bug.

Spider mites

Spider mites are known to attack many species of flowers, sucking the sap out of the underside of the leaves. The spider mites look similar to spiders with their eight legs but they are barely visible to the eye and come in many colors, with one of the most common being red. Often the best way to get rid of them is to spray them with a mixture of soap and water or a spray made from onions. Natural predators include beneficial mites, lacewings, pirate bugs, and ladybugs. Pyrethrum, coriander, dill, and rhubarb are said to repel spider mites.

Squash bug

These bugs are oval-shaped, dark gray or black bugs. They suck out the juices from leaves and stems of many vine crops like cucumbers, melons, pumpkins, and squash. This causes the leaves to shrivel and the tips will blacken, making the plant to look sick and diseased. These bugs like heavy mulches so avoid using those. Pick them off the plants when you see them. The natural predators of this bug include tachinid flies. For companion planting, try planting clover, dill, fennel, and yarrow in between the squash and pumpkin plants to keep the squash bugs away from these two plants.

Other Creatures in the Garden

Aside from insects, there are other creatures that you may want to attract to your garden. Again it depends on whether you view these creatures as a great addition to your garden or something that needs to be chased away.

Birds

Birds can be both a pleasure and a pain, depending on the type of garden you are growing. They are a beautiful addition, adding both color and song to your space. Some birds are ferocious hunters of insects, like the swallows who love mosquitoes, but not everyone appreciates a swallow's mud nest under their roof. One of the best reasons to welcome birds to your garden is pollination. Insects can pollinate many flowers, but some plants, like the columbine that is shaped like an inverted bell, require the hummingbird's long tongue to reach down to the nectar.

Some birds can be pests, particularly if you have an orchard or grow berries, but they are very beneficial in the garden as they consume many times their own weight in insects. They consume all kinds of bugs, including aphids, caterpillars, grubs, beetles, and grasshoppers.

Some of the most common birds that you want to have in your garden include:

- **Blackbirds** — these birds will eat berries in your garden when they ripen; however, before then they will scratch through the top layers of the garden looking for insects.

- **Bluebirds** — bluebirds like to feed on insects, especially grasshoppers.

- **Hummingbirds** — these beautiful birds can be found all over North America and are active predators of several small insects like fruit flies, gnats, and aphids. Because hummingbirds require nectar and are great pollinators, your garden will benefit from having bright colored flowers throughout the growing season to attract these birds. Plant bright red flowers to bring the hummingbirds into the garden and they will then go to every flower in your garden. There are many plants that attract these tiny birds including Indian paint brush, trumpet flowers, columbine, larkspur, lantana butterfly bush, globe mallow, honeysuckle, scarlet runner bean, and even foxglove with its purple flowers. Hummingbirds like to feed on the rich nectar from all kinds of flowers.

- **Robins** — there are many species of the robin, which fall into the thrush family, and they have a varied insect diet that includes caterpillars, grubs, and winged insects. They also love earthworms. Because earthworms work the soil, you need as many of these as possible so cover any earthworms you see on the surface of the soil where the robins will get them and move those worms caught on cement and rocks over to the garden.

- **Sparrows** — these are more known for eating seeds but they will hunt and eat insects of all kinds from gardens and shrubs.

- **Wrens** — these are another of the common birds in the backyard. They are prolific insect eaters and because they reproduce frequently, there are always new up and coming hunters.

Gardening for birds

Birds are a wonderful addition to your landscape with their bright colors, antics, and beautiful songs; they are also an asset to flower and vegetable gardens because they feed on insects. To attract birds to your garden and keep them close, you need to offer them shelter, food, and water.

Hedges, thick shrubs, or trees of some kind, will offer the birds nesting sites and protection. A dense hedge gives birds protection from predators and heavy winds. Good choices are viburnum, pyracantha, and cotoneaster, which offer attractive foliage, flowers, berries, and leaf color in autumn and winter. Allow a new hedgerow to become established before inter-planting other plants around it so there is no competition for the nutrients.

Birds need water to drink and to bathe in, plus a spot (preferably more than one) to sit in the sun and dry off. A birdbath is a great addition to your garden as it will offer you and your birds hours of entertainment. Using a fountain not only attracts birds with the trickling water but the fountain part of this birdbath also helps keep the water clean and prevents the buildup of slime. If you have swallows around your garden, they will reduce the pests that will also be attracted to the water such as mosquitoes.

Because the birds are at their most vulnerable when bathing or drinking, make sure you locate the birdbath somewhere that the birds will be safe. Also, keep the birdbath out of reach of the cats, which may take some ingenuity depending on the type of birdbath. Light birdbaths can be hung from tree branches and filled with a hose. For heavier fountain-style birdbaths, find ones that have a dry perch spot in the center where a cat cannot reach without getting wet itself – a deterrent in its own right. Make sure you are able to access the birdbath easily because you will need to clean or hose it out regularly. The birdbath will also require some shade to stop the water from evaporating and overheating. You should also remember to refill the water often or change it out to keep it fresh tasting.

If you have a pond or are considering adding a pond, make sure it is a safe environment for the birds and away from the predators. If you have cats, place a couple of large rocks in the center of the water for the birds to sit on while drinking and preening. Large branches are also good to add to the pond. You want a space big enough for the birds to be comfortable but not large enough for a predator. A pond also provides water at different depths. Some birds only use shallow water versus larger birds that like deeper water.

Ideally, you want plants, shrubs, or large plants to offer shelter and safety for the birds while not providing cover for predators.

When it comes to feeding the various birds, you have to remember that not all birds eat the same foods and some of them eat more than one kind of food. Some eat only seeds and others eat insects, worms, and seeds. Birds like variety in their diet and would appreciate a mix of plants. They like seeds, nuts, fruits, berries, and even flower nectar. To keep birds happy, incorporate a variety of flowers in your garden, but in particular consider planting sunflowers (plant a lot if you want some for yourself), petunias, and marigolds.

The seed eaters include sparrows, towhees, juncos, jays, finches, and quails. Some birds eat off the ground, but others do better with feeders, particularly if you have cats around. Do not forget native grasses like bluegrass and wheat grass for providing seeds for the birds to eat. Keep in mind that some plants like coreopsis, thistles, and cosmos provide seeds for the birds throughout the season and trees such as spruce, fir, birch, and pines are fall and winter food sources for birds. The mountain ash offers large, grape-like clusters of red berries throughout the winter for any birds that live in your climate. You also might consider hanging balls of suet in netting or setting it on a birdfeeder. You can also supplement the birds' diet with commercial bird seed. Sunflower seeds would be the best for attracting the widest variety of birds.

Critters

Not everyone views wildlife in the garden in the same way. Many people are happy to see a deer wander through their garden and take a nibble here and there but there are others who will put up a 7-foot fence to keep them out. The decision behind what wildlife to have in your garden depends on the goal of your garden. If your goal is to grow a year's worth of vegetables, then rabbits are not going to be your best friend as they will consider your garden their grocery store. There are many garden creatures to consider when you are choosing your plants.

Cats

Cats are hardly wildlife but there are domestic and feral varieties in most neighborhoods and both can be a problem if they come in after the birds. However, few people recognize that cats offer great value as well. They are predators of various insects like grasshoppers and spiders, particularly the bigger varieties, and they keep a garden free from mice and rats. Often cats will be drawn to a garden as they need greens, usually grasses, to nibble on. You can provide a nice oat grass for them to chew on and they will appreciate catnip to roll around on (the leaves act as a stimulant).

Dogs

Most dogs are not a problem, but then there are those that willfully dig up every bed in your garden and chase everything that is alive and moving just for fun. If you want to deter a dog from going into your garden, you will need to put up some kind of barrier or use mothballs around the edge of the bed as the smell deters the animals. Do not try the mothball method if you have small children as they might try to eat them. If they are your dogs, you can train them to not enter the garden area, but if they are neighborhood dogs or wild ones, you might need to consider adding a fence.

Rabbits

Rabbits are night gathers and although you may see them in the garden, they will not usually forage until night time. They can be adorable to look at and if you are happy to have them in your garden, plant a few extra vegetables and flowers to compensate for what they will eat. Rabbits will eat mostly growing vegetables, young fruit trees, young flower blossoms, and they have a particular fondness for grapevines.

There are several methods to deter rabbits from invading the garden and the first is to avoid planting the types of plants that they come in for. You can also plant foods they do not eat such as squash, cucumbers, tomatoes, corn, potatoes, or peppers. Try planting clover around the perimeter of the garden because rabbits love clover and if there is a nice supply available to them, they will choose to eat that plant instead of those in your garden. Be aware that clover spreads rapidly, so this system may not be the right one for you.

You can also use onions as a companion to cabbage and lettuce plants because the onion discourages the rabbits. The next best way to keep the rabbits out of the garden is to fence it well. In general, you will need to use a chicken wire fence several feet above the ground that sits either beneath the ground or tight to the ground so that they cannot get under the fence. The holes of the wire need to be very small as baby rabbits have small heads and can get into a hole just bigger than 2 inches.

The other alternative is to put something around the perimeter of the garden that they will not like. For example, you can include strong smelling soap, fox urine, or dried blood, both of which are available at your local garden center. You can also try sprinkling wood ash, ground limestone, and cayenne pepper around the perimeter of your garden. If you do try this method, remember to reapply after a rain.

Squirrels

Another animal that is fun to have around but can be a potential pest is the squirrel. One of the simplest and easiest methods to deal with squirrels is to feed them. There are special squirrel feeders available and cheap seed that you can give to them. Flying squirrels and gray squirrels are found in most wooded suburbs and nuts, seeds, various mushrooms, and insects are all part of their diet. Gray squirrels are active during the day, but flying squirrels are nocturnal. Both love peanut butter spread on a feeding stand.

If you do not want squirrels in your garden, you can try a strong odor repellent that will need to be reapplied after every rain. You can purchase a squirrel repelling product, similar to one used to repel rabbits, at your local gardening center. These repellants come in powdered and liquid form. Another method to try is to dice or mince extremely hot peppers that are still full of natural oil and place them around the garden, preferably on the pathways the squirrels travel, including fence posts and walkways. Also remember that those pesky cats and dogs are a great deterrent for the squirrels.

Mice and rats

If you have cats and dogs, the mice and rat problem will be decreased. Depending on where you live, mice may not be a problem, but most gardeners are not so lucky. Catnip, besides attracting cats, also repels mice quite nicely. You can cut sprigs of this mint and place it throughout the garden or grow it in the four corners of your garden to deter them from entering. This system also works well on outbuildings. Other plants that can repel mice are chamomile, corn, sea onions, and spearmint.

If mice and rats are a problem in the garden — and they will be if your garden is in a rural meadow — try repelling them with mint using either the oil or fresh or dried leaves. Mint generally becomes rampant once it takes hold, so consider including one plant from the mint family just outside the garden area on the back side. If you use it in high traffic areas, the oils are released, filling the air with fragrant mint. Luckily mint is hardy and will tolerate some trampling. Other good choices for mice repellants include sea onion, white lavender, wormwood, and spurge.

Snakes, lizards, and salamanders

Lizards, snakes, and salamanders are critters that are welcomed into any garden. Snakes are very beneficial to gardens as they catch and kill many insects, and, as long as it is not a poisonous snake, it will do very little damage to you. Leave them alone to sun themselves on the rocks. An excellent online resource Herpedia.com, **www.herpedia.com**, provides a guide for reptiles and amphibians in the United States. When starting to work in the garden, brush the plants around noisily and the snakes will move away. Other creatures to consider allowing in your garden are lizards and salamanders as they eat insects in vast numbers. They will stay in cool corners of your garden where large, leafy plants can shelter them.

Frogs and Toads

These garden creatures are a great help as they do little damage and eat problematic insects, feeding for hours on end. One toad is said to eat more than 1,000 earwigs in a summer. They eat a selection of different insects and have a particular fondness for slugs, sow bugs, cutworms, and gypsy moths. These critters can be purchased and placed in your garden if you cannot find any around to entice into your garden. Frogs and toads are happy if there is ample food, water, and shelter. Toads come out at night to hunt and like to hide in cool, dark places during the day. If you are serious about attracting these critters to your garden, consider buying or making a toad shelter. You can create one of these shelters from an old clay pot with an entrance cut into the one side. Turn the pot upside down in a shady part of your garden that is near a water source. You can also create a toad hole, which is a 10-inch by 10-inch hole in the ground with sand on the bottom and flat stones used to create a ceiling. Place a short section of pipe from the bottom of the hole to the surface for the toad to travel into his home and plant a shady bush at the entrance to hide it and provide shade.

Some frogs will stay under water through the winter, requiring a permanent water source (pond, stream, or lake edge) that is at least 6 feet deep. Toads, on the other hand, spend their winter on land and only require shallow and temporary ponds for breeding. They can also make use of the shallow edges of bigger water sources.

Toads and frogs require some native plants or vegetation at the edge of the pond to give them cover. Remember to make the slopes shallow at the entrance to the water so they can easily move in and out. It also helps to leave sticks or logs at the pond edge for them to use as well.

Bats

Bats can eat up to 3,000 insects in one night alone, and one of their favorite insects is the mosquito. Bats are attracted to ponds and will roost in bat houses in the garden. Bats can be seen in many backyard habitats, especially those near a pond or stream. Most are gentle, harmless, and eat many destructive insects like leafhoppers, ants, cicadas, stink bugs, and flies. They may sleep in trees or seek out an abandoned building for roosting. Some gardeners enjoy providing them artificial roosting boxes.

Now that the insects and animals have been covered, the next section deals with the best way to feed your garden to keep it healthy and happy.

CASE STUDY: JOSH KIRSCHENBAUM

Territorial Seed Company
Product Development Director
PO Box 158, Cottage Grove, OR 87424
www.territorialseed.com

Josh Kirschenbaum, a plant biology graduate from Ohio University, has worked at Territorial Seed Company for over a decade where one of his major responsibilities is to coordinate and evaluate the yearly trials.

"Territorial has a 44-acre, certified organic trial ground where we test vegetable, flower, and herb varieties. Not all 44 acres are used each year for trials but rather we rotate the fields. So, if one area was planted last year for trials, we will not use it for trials this coming year. Instead, we plant a cover crop in the fall and leave it in over the winter. Depending on the type of cover crop that we use, we may till it under in the spring or summer and plant another type of cover crop that is suitable for growing in the summer. By doing this, we replenish some of the nutrients that were used previously and incorporate as much organic material into the soil as possible.

Compost is an integral part of our gardening/farming system. The company grows its own trials and seed crop production (we grow plants, harvest the seed, clean it, and then package it), and consequently have a large amount of vegetative material that can be composted at the end of the season. The main way that we compost this is by vermicomposting — using worms to break down the plant material and turn it into rich compost. The compost is then used in our fields and in our soil mixes that we use for our mail order plants.

We mainly sell seeds and one of the most common problems that I see is with starting seeds indoors. If someone lives in an area with quite a good amount of sunlight in the early spring, then seedlings can be put in a south-facing, sunny window. Most of us, however, need to use some sort of supplemental light to get our seedlings off to a good start and avoid them becoming leggy and weak. This doesn't mean that you have to go and spend lots of money on an expensive grow light system — a simple fluorescent shop light can work just fine. The important thing to remember if using a standard fluorescent light to grow your seedlings is that the bulbs are typically not very powerful so you want to have the plants as close to the light as possible without actually having them touch the bulb. As the plants continue to grow, move the light fixture accordingly.

Another common problem is putting plants or seeds in the ground too early. Several vegetables are frost sensitive and plants will die if temperatures dip below freezing. Even if a frost does not occur, if a particular plant thrives in warm temperatures, it might become stressed by cold temps or just not grow. If planting from seed directly into the garden, it is very important to plant when the soil temperature is ideal for the particular type of seed. If the soil is too cold or wet, the seed could potentially rot before having a chance to germinate. Remember that soil temperature is quite different than air temperature and I highly recommend purchasing a soil thermometer to know for certain.

In regards to common problems people have with their insects, I recommend to:

- Make sure that you let us know when you would like to receive them. Most of the insects can be purchased year-round for those folks who have greenhouses. If a customer plans on putting the insects outside, they should wait to order them when it is warm enough.

- Try to introduce the beneficial insects when the pest population is present but low. If a ladybug doesn't have any aphids to eat, it won't just wait around for them!"

There is a good chance that the garden that you are planting will need soil enhancement at some point in time. If you are going to follow some of the companion planting concepts, you will need to nourish your garden throughout the year. There are only so many nutrients naturally in the soil and it will not take long before you will need more to feed your plants.

Ways to Feed Your Garden

There are many options available to feed your garden. Some require commercial fertilizers, but the best are ones that you can use without adding chemicals to the soil. These include:

- Monoculture
- Rotation
- Mulches
- Compost
- Garden teas
- Fertilizers

Monoculture

Monoculturing is the process of planting just one type of plant. In companion planting, this practice is used to enrich the soil through the benefits one plant can give. This monoculture plant is then turned back into the soil to increase the nutrient level of the soil. One example of this is to grow alfalfa or another grass crop and turn it back under before it goes to seed to let it decompose further before planting that area of your garden. By doing this, the soil has a chance to rest and replenish itself.

Rotation

Crop rotation is a great way to control insects, weeds, and diseases, and it also enhances soil fertility. Vegetables in the same botanical family will require similar nutrients in similar amounts. Some will be considered heavy feeders like broccoli, sweet corn, and tomatoes, and will utilize more of the soil's nutrients, whereas others are considered light feeders, like carrots, onions, peppers, and potatoes, and will use fewer nutrients. To go along with these plant types, there are plants that add nutrients and improve the soil, like peas and beans. If you practice crop rotation by alternating these three types of crops in one bed, the soil can be enhanced.

Mulches

Mulch is a protective layer placed over the soil. There are many benefits to using mulch including:

- **Minimizes weeds** — the mulch will suffocate weeds and stop light from reaching the seeds, which stops new weeds from germinating.

- **Improves the garden plants** — the mulch covers the plant's roots that are on the surface, saving them from damage caused by cultivation and drying out.

- **Retains moisture** — mulch reduces the amount of evaporation, which keeps the soil moist, and allows for a more even growth.

- **Minimizes temperature differences** — the mulch minimizes the temperature extremes at the soil level so it stays warmer at night and cooler in the day.

- **Improves the soil** — if you are using organic mulch, it will add nutrients to the soil as it decomposes, encouraging microbial growth. It also encourages earthworms to burrow in the soil, which aerates and drains the soil. The mulch also prevents the soil from packing down.

- **Creates a more even-looking garden** — mulch stops the dirt from splashing up onto the plants during rain or watering and from washing the soil away from the plants during too heavy rain or watering.

- **Gives the garden a finished look** — the garden looks professional with a nice mulch covering it. A uniform layer of good looking mulch throughout the garden gives the area a uniform, "finished" look.

The following are some forms of mulch you may want to consider.

Organic mulch

There are many types of organic mulch to choose from. There are some you may have readily available and others you may need to buy. Most will be available through your local garden center.

The best organic mulches include:

- **Bark or small wood chips** — these come as small or large chips (or chip your own if you have a wood chipper) and work well under trees and shrubs. You can purchase finely shredded cedar mulch in various colors that can add an interesting designer component.

- **Leaves** — fall leaves are great for mulching large open areas, particularly around squash, pumpkin patches, or other sprawling areas. If you are short on another type of mulch, like compost or newspaper, leaves make a great second layer. Not only does it cover up something unsightly, but it also helps with decomposition.

- **Eucalyptus** — this mulch has to be purchased from your local garden center and comes shredded or as fiber mulch. The advantage of this type of mulch is that the oil in the eucalyptus repels termites, fleas, ticks, and insects. The disadvantage is that it can be hard to obtain and it can be twice as expensive as other types of mulch.

- **Grass clippings** — when they are fresh, they are smelly and will stain your hands but are high in moisture and nitrogen, making them good for the garden. Avoid using clippings that are full of grass seeds because these seeds are likely to sprout in your garden. This mulch is easy to work with and can be placed throughout the garden where the seedlings are more delicate or closely planted, such as around lettuce, spinach, and carrots.

- **Straw** — if you have access to straw, it offers excellent winter protection for your garden. The only problem with using straw is the potential for some of the seeds to germinate. Straw should be seed free but because it is often confused with hay, which still has seeds, it is possible to end up with seeds in your bales. Another disadvantage is that it is not very attractive and looks worse as time goes on.

- **Pine needles** — this is a long-lasting mulch that can slightly acidify the soil under it. This makes it good for potatoes and strawberries, which benefit from the more acidic soil. It is also an easy mulch to put into small or hard-to-reach places. Pine cones can also be used and make an attractive addition to any woodland garden.

- **Pine bark** — this is a mulch that decomposes slower than other varieties and will last a year or more. It comes in different sizes, ranging from fine to 2-inch chunks. The disadvantage of this mulch is that it can lower the pH slightly. You can still use it around the same plants that prefer a more acidic environment like strawberries.

Non-organic mulch

There are several non-organic mulches available on the market. These types of mulches keep the weeds down and do not need replacing like organic mulches. Some of these mulches include:

- **Plastic sheeting** — these are large sheets of dark plastic. They are great to use in the spring to warm up beds and are also great for suppressing weeds. If you use a heavy grade plastic, which will last many years, you can lay it down between rows of plants where you want more heat, like between tomatoes, or on paths where you want to suppress weeds. You can use the sheeting to help improve the soil by stuffing the underside of the black plastic with organic matter to compost underneath the sheet. Some gardeners even lay the plastic down and cut holes into it to transplant seedlings. The plastic can stay on throughout the whole season as a weed suppressor. The problem with doing this is that it will not let water through it.

- **Landscape fabric** — this is a loosely woven fabric that helps retain moisture and slows or even prevents weed growth. The disadvantage of this type of mulch is it is usually one of two layers with a top layer covering the fabric to make the garden bed look better. Also consider that some landscape cloths are nonporous and will not let moisture through. If you purchase the nonporous type, the plant roots can suffocate and rot.

- **Rubber** — this product is made from recycled tires and will not decompose, making it permanent mulch. It can be purchased as mats, tiles, and nuggets and is available in various colors. It will not blow away or wash away under a heavy watering. It also comes in many attractive colors, giving it a strong design element. In practical terms, insects avoid the rubber and it does not sink into the ground like gravel and rocks. However, the product can give off a strong odor and can be both expensive and hard to find.

- **Stone (pebbles and gravel)** — stones can be as small as pea gravel or as large as small boulders. The small gravel will stop the weeds better, but when topped with an assortment of boulders, together they create a nice contrast for the garden. Stones are another permanent cover as they do not break down over time but offer great color and texture to a garden. The disadvantage is that some of the smaller rocks will disappear into the soil over time and working with this type of mulch is physically demanding.

When to mulch

Lay the mulch down in the garden after the soil has warmed up in the late spring or the early summer. Placing an even, shallow layer of mulch approximately 2 to 4 inches deep will be effective against wind, sun, weeds, and pests. Be careful of the plants and avoid putting the mulch close to the crown of the perennials and the stems or trunks of shrubs and trees as you do not want to damage new growth and you need to leave plants space to obtain water.

If you live in a winter climate, one of the best times to mulch is in winter. Depending on where you live, the freezing and thawing process causes the soil to expand and contract. This can break new roots and even force your plants out of the ground in a process called frost heaves. If you cover the garden with something loose and full of air, like straw, when the ground first freezes, you can help keep the ground frozen until winter ends. Once spring arrives, you can remove the mulch.

Another benefit of winter mulching is protecting all types of plants, including perennials and ground covers, from **winter burn**, which can happen when the winter temperatures damage the plants. When the ground freezes and there is a strong wind, the moisture is pulled from the plant.

Compost

Compost can be the best natural fertilizer for your garden, regardless of the type of plants you are growing. It is a mixture of decomposed plant and animal material (manure) and many other organic materials that then go through decomposition in the presence of oxygen, called **aerobic decomposition**, to create a rich black soil. This soil is excellent for your garden as a soil conditioner and fertilizer.

The best compost materials include fruit and vegetable material, garden trimmings (not weeds gone to seed), and animal manure from horses, goats, sheep, and chicken. Other materials to consider adding if you have them available include leaves, coffee grounds, paper, cardboard, seafood shells, tree bark, eggshells, and even "humanure" (human waste).

How to make compost

Choose a spot close enough to be easily accessible but out of sight. You can choose to purchase a compost bin or alternatively build a system to work in the space you have available. You can make a heap in one corner of the garden and use the area to make your compost pile; you can use a single bin and place all the organic material into it; or you can create a three-bin system (made from wood). If you leave the bins open on one side, you can easily add to the pile, and to turn it over occasionally. Only cover the tops of the compost bins if your area receives a lot of rain. The three-bin system allows you to turn the compost from one bin to the other so that the compost in the final bin is ready to use while the pile in the second bin is in the middle stage and the first bin is just starting to decompose. However, you will need to manually move the compost from one bin to the other.

When starting a new compost pile, making a pile with two parts of brown materials to one part green will help the materials break down faster. The **green garden materials** are grass clipping or old annual plants pulled from the garden, and the **brown garden materials** are dry leaves and twigs. The green material is high in nitrogen and the brown material is high in carbon and both are required to make your compost work successfully. If you add in too much green, the compost will have a foul odor.

Pile or layer the green and browns into a heap until you have a compost heap that is about 3 feet by 3 feet by 3 feet. You want the pile close to this size because it will heat up quickly and will therefore break down faster. Once a week, check the moisture content of the pile. To decompose properly, your pile will need water, but if there is too much moisture, the pile will not be able to maintain the required heat level. Your compost should feel damp like a wrung out sponge; any more water content than this and the pile will start to smell worse than normal. If your pile is too wet, you can add more leaves; if it is too dry, you can water it gently with a garden hose.

Once a week, the pile needs to be turned over, meaning you turn the outside material into the center – where there is internal compost heat. Oxygen is required for the decomposition process, which is why you turn the pile. Turning the pile also stops it from becoming hard and compacted. Some people keep a perforated PVC pipe standing upright in the center of the compost pile to let oxygen reach the center of the pile.

If you turn your pile over once a week, you could have finished compost in eight to ten weeks. The compost pile that is not turned over will not be as active and will take longer to decompose with the good compost sitting at the bottom of the pile. During the decomposition process, the temperature of the pile will reach between 110 and 160 degrees F. You can monitor the temperature with a long probe thermometer pushed into the center of the pile. Turn the pile when the temperature drops below the 110 degrees F mark to speed up the compost process. If you decide not to monitor the temperature, you can turn the pile every month.

The compost from the bin system is ready when the temperature lowers until it is barely warm and the original materials in the pile are no longer recognizable. It is possible you will have a few pieces that are not quite "finished," which is fine; throw them into the first bin to start the next pile of compost. The compost should also be a rich black-brown color, moist, and have an earthy smell.

How to use compost

Now that you have this great rich soil, it is time to add it to your garden. If you do not want any bits left in your compost, you can run it through a compost sifter, which is wire mesh in a frame, that will leave you with only soil. The bits and pieces that do not go through the sifter can go back into the compost pile. You can do several things with this nutrient rich-soil but treat it as you would any rich fertilizer or potting soil. There are several ways you can use your compost:

- **As a mulch to hold water** — you can spread it about 3 inches thick on the base of plants, trees, shrubs, or perennials in the garden. If there are some unfinished pieces in your compost, they are fine to use here as they will continue to break down over time.

- **To fertilize the garden** — you would want to dig the compost into the existing garden, going down several inches or more to work the compost in.

- **To make a compost tea** — some compost tea is natural byproduct of compost. If there is no liquid in your compost, you can steep a shovel full of compost in a bucket of water for a few days. After a few days have passed, remove the compost material, put it back in the compost pile, and simply water the plants with the compost tea. If you want, you can put the compost into something like an old towel, cheese-cloth, or burlap bag before putting it into the bucket of water.

- **As a topping for your lawn** — often called a **lawn dressing**, you can add a 1- to 3-inch layer of compost on top of the existing grass. The compost works its way into the ground as the grass grows through it. Because it is a great way to fertilize the grass, adding compost in the spring or fall may eliminate the need to fertilize throughout the rest of the season.

Many people add the compost into their gardens in fall or spring, whenever it is ready, digging it in as they turn their beds over. Whichever way you choose, your plants will benefit from adding compost.

Garden teas

Garden teas are similar to compost tea except there are several variations to consider making, depending on the type of materials you have available. Making teas for your garden will give them an extra boost of nutrients to help them fight off disease and grow strong. The teas are good for any garden, especially companion planting gardens. Here are some suggestions to consider, depending on what materials you have available:

- Alfalfa tea
- Comfrey tea
- Manure tea
- Scrap tea
- Seaweed tea
- Swiss chard tea
- Weed tea

Alfalfa tea

To make this kind of tea, you will need a 5-gallon bucket and a sack of some kind like an old pillow case or rice bag. You want something that will allow water to soak through the material. Fill one quarter of the sack with alfalfa meal/hay. Fill the bucket with water, place the sack in the bucket, and let sit. The tea will need at least a week to ten days to steep. When the tea base is ready, remove the pillow case and dump its watery contents in the garden. Take 1 cup of the tea and put it in another bucket or gallon-size jug and fill it with water, diluting it down. This is the finished tea. Water the crops once a week with this high-phosphorus content tea.

Comfrey tea

You can make an instant comfrey leaf tea that is high in calcium, potassium, phosphorus, and other various minerals. For this tea, take several cups of comfrey leaves, place them in the blender, add enough water to make it blend, and liquefy the leaves. Take the pulpy liquid and put it into a 5-gallon container. Fill the container almost to the top with water with a strong pressure so that your mixture gets a frothy appearance. After your tea has mixed, it is ready to go onto the garden. Tomatoes and potatoes love comfrey tea as do most vegetables.

Manure tea

To make manure tea, take an old pillowcase or cloth sack and fill it about one quarter full of manure (cow, horse, chicken, or a mix) and place the sack in a 5-gallon bucket. Fill the bucket almost to the top with water and let the mixture sit for a couple of days. Stir it a couple of times while it is steeping. When it is done, remove the manure sack and dump the contents in the corner of the garden where it can finish decomposing. Then take the brown liquid and dilute it down to a pale amber and water the garden once a week. Manure is high in nitrogen, making this a great additive to the garden. When you are working with manure, it is better to use gloves and wash your hands to avoid transmitting bacteria.

Scrap tea

Fill a cloth sack with kitchen food scraps like potato peelings, apple cores, and broccoli stems. Make sure the scraps are not animal-based but do remember to include tea bags and coffee grinds. Place the sack in a 5-gallon bucket and fill with water. Let the mixture sit for three to six days. When enough time has passed, remove the sack and dump its contents into the garden. Dilute the remaining liquid down to an amber-colored liquid and water the garden with this tea once a week. The tea can be left in the bucket outside until the next watering session.

Seaweed tea

For those who live in coastal areas, seaweed products and concentrate are available at many garden centers. If you live near the beach and are able to find your own seaweed, take a large bucket and fill it three quarters full of rinsed seaweed collected from the beach. Fill the bucket with water and let it sit for several weeks or months. (The liquid gets stronger the longer you leave it.) Once the liquid is done steeping, pull out the seaweed, add the plant to your compost, and use the liquid to fertilize your garden.

Swiss chard tea

This tea is made the same way as the comfrey leaf tea. It is just as rich a mixture as the comfrey tea and is rich in calcium, phosphorus, potassium, and trace minerals.

Weed tea

This tea is made of the nuisance weeds you are trying to get rid of from the garden. Fill a cloth bag with harvested weeds and put that sack into a large bucket of water, making sure the bag is completely submerged to kill off the weeds. Some weeds may not be dead even after two weeks submerged in the water, particularly running weeds like sorrel that will regrow from just a small piece left in the garden. After a month to six weeks, check to ensure there is brown sludge in the bucket and the weeds are completely dead. Take out the bag and let all the liquid drain. Put the contents from the bag into the compost pile, not the garden. The remaining liquid is weed tea and it can be poured straight onto the compost heap to accelerate the compost process or it can be added to the garden as a liquid fertilizer. To add to the garden, dilute the weed tea at a rate of one part weed tea to ten parts of water.

Fertilizers

Fertilizers are additives that help your garden grow. There are natural fertilizers and of course commercial fertilizers. There are many different commercial fertilizers that contain mixes of chicken manure, blood, bone, seaweed, sheep manure, and cow manure. For information on what commercial fertilizers are available for purchase in your area, check your local garden center.

There are other additives that you can mix into your garden that will fertilize the area. Consider adding the following items, which are all readily available at your local garden center, to your garden to increase its health and well-being:

- Blood and bone meal
- Mushroom compost
- Lime and dolomite
- Seaweed
- Wood ash

Blood and bone meal

Blood and bone meal fertilizer is a mixture of ground-up animal bones and dried up blood that is rich in phosphorus and nitrogen and have been used for centuries as a fertilizer. All plants will benefit from this fertilizer. It is usually mixed with potash, a potassium compound, for a total plant fertilizer. Check with your local nursery center to see what they have available.

Lime and dolomite

Lime is calcium carbonate and dolomite is calcium carbonate with magnesium carbonate added. They are made from pulverized limestone or chalk. These elements will raise the pH, reducing the acidity level in your soil, and will provide calcium and trace minerals for the garden. It is best to add this to the garden in the fall and let it work into the ground over the winter.

Mushroom compost

Mushroom compost is more than 75 percent straw, wood shavings, and manure, and the rest is a mixture of gypsum and limestone. Mushroom compost is a byproduct of the mushroom growing industry and is rich in organic matter and nutrients. You can buy it in bulk if you have a producer close by or you can buy it in bags. Check your local garden center to see if it is available.

Wood ash

Wood ash in small amounts is great for any garden as it is a good source of potash, potassium, and also contains phosphorus and micronutrients. If your soil is very acidic and has a pH lower than 5.5, the wood ash will raise the soil's pH. However, if your soil is neutral or alkaline, it might interfere with the plant's ability to absorb the available nutrients. Do not put it around acid-loving plants like rhododendrons and blueberries for that reason.

Now that you have an idea of the plants to put in your garden, the insects that you want to attract, those you want to repel, and the ways to nourish your garden, the next chapter takes a look at the type of maintenance is required for your garden and when to do these tasks.

· CHAPTER 5 ·

Garden Maintenance

S ome people are in their gardens on a daily basis, taking joy in simple garden maintenance tasks. Others want to spend minimal time working in the garden so they can sit and enjoy the garden. Regardless of the type of gardener you are or the type of companion planting you are looking to practice, there are some simple tasks that will need to be done.

Maintenance Tasks

In the spring, it is time to pull weeds, remove mulch that was put on in the fall, and turn the beds over. Spring happens at different times around the world so understand the growing season for your area so you know when to get started. There are a couple of Web sites that will show you the last expected frost dates in your location if you are in the United States. The first one is through the Farmer's Almanac at **www.almanac.com/content/frost-chart-united-states**. Another Web site called Dave's Garden lets you put in your ZIP code and it will tell you the expected frost dates for both spring and fall for your area **http://davesgarden.com/guides/freeze-frost-dates**.

Early spring – pre-planting season

When it is too early to plant because the ground is still too wet or the danger of frost is still present, you can start weeding if you already have a garden bed to work on. This is a good time, provided the frost is out of the ground, to pull weeds that will cause problems later on as the ground is soft and the softer the ground, the easier the weeds will be to pull. When you can, trim the perennials that survived the winter. Some take longer to show growth than others so do not immediately throw away a plant that has not started to sprout new growth. Pull up the old leaves and plant debris, and if you left the seeds in place for the birds, cut the branches back now.

As the garden dries up, add in compost if you have it and start to dig your beds over. If you do not have a garden already, this is the stage you should be laying out your design, building raised beds if that is your choice, and starting to work the area into a garden. You can start seedlings indoors if you can offer them enough light, and you can plant early crops outdoors if you have the ability to keep them safe from frost. Otherwise, hold off a few more weeks until the weather warms.

Another thing to do is to sort out your watering system and lay down hoses that you are going to use. You may want to have timers regulate your hoses to cover all your garden areas. You can have them go off each evening after the sun has gone down so the plants have the benefit of the water overnight during the cooler hours. If you water during the day, most of the water evaporates, robbing the plants of the necessary moisture.

You should be sorting through the plants you are interested in having in your garden and considering which plants should go where. Consider if you are going to have separate gardens for vegetables, herbs, and flowers or if you will interplant for maximum space usage. Will you need to put up trellises for plants to climb, or use another plant like corn stalks for beans and nasturtiums to climb up instead? If you know your garden will have insect problems based on your experiences from past years, consider which companion plants will help to solve these problems this year.

Once the ground has warmed up enough, it is time to plant.

Late spring – planting season

This is the busiest season next to harvest time for your garden. This is the time to make sure your garden has been dug over, enriched, raked, and is ready to put down seeds and plants. At this point, you can plant most plants with the exception of the tender ones like peppers, basil, and eggplant. Certain plants may need a cover to keep them warm for a few more weeks, like tomatoes.

You can put down the seeds, buy seedlings, or plant the seeds you started in the house. You can also buy annuals for window boxes and containers. If you are doing garden bed rotation and planting a cover crop in one bed, now is the time to get those seeds in the ground. This is also the time to keep weeding so the weeds do not have a chance to get established. If you notice certain bugs creeping into the garden area, such as slugs, it is time to remove them and start attracting the predators you want to have in your garden. Set up toad houses, create rock piles as hiding places, and have bird baths and bird houses as well as tall perches for the birds to sit on.

Digging the garden over

To dig the garden over effectively, the ground should be dry and crumbly. If you can squeeze it and form it into a flat cake of mud, chances are it is too wet. You can still dig it; however, it will take extra effort and it will not be as effective. The purpose of this stage is to break the crust that has formed over winter, kill the growing weeds, and open up the grubs and seeds to the birds.

To dig the garden over, put your shovel into the ground, lift up a hunk of soil, turn it over, and put it back down on the same place, breaking it up slightly before moving over to the next piece. You can use a piece of equipment called a rototiller to do this same job if your garden is too big to dig by hand. Work the garden over about one to two weeks ahead of planting. Any longer than this and the ground can harden again; any shorter than this and the birds will not have had a chance to pick up the grubs that you have moved to the surface. When you are ready to plant, you may need to break the dirt up slightly again. This is particularly helpful when growing plants with long roots like carrots. The ground needs to be well dug and preferably sandy to grow the long carrots. If the ground is dense and full of clay, the carrots will be stumpy and short. This is also a good time to work any organic matter like peat moss or compost into the garden to improve the soil. It is also a good time to add fertilizer as you work the ground. As companion planting often means making the most out of the space available, the soil needs to be rich in nutrients to sustain the plants throughout the long growing season.

Seeding

Seeding is the process of sowing the seeds of the plants you want to see in the summer and fall. Generally, this refers to vegetable seeds but this is also the way many wildflower and annuals are started. Water the ground well before putting out the seeds.

If you are sowing in a row, gently create a trench using your fingers or a hoe and lay the seeds evenly spaced in the dirt as per the directions on the package of the seeds you are planting. Cover with a light layer of dirt. If you are scattering the seed in a general area, try to sow them evenly throughout the area. Once the seed is covered, label the garden row or bed and note the date planted. When planting is done for the day, water the area with a gentle mist so as to not disturb the seeds. Water daily until the seed is sprouted.

Transplanting

Transplanting the seedlings that you have bought or grown in the house is simple but requires a gentle hand because these young plants are easily damaged. Start by letting your seedlings acclimatize by setting them outside during the day and then bringing them in again at nighttime. This is a process called **hardening off** and will help the plants adapt to the outdoor cooler weather. It is best to transplant on a cooler, preferably cloudy day, as the transplants will transplant easier when they are not in the hot sunshine.

If you are planning to use newspaper or black plastic/landscape cloth to keep the weeds down, then cut holes in the center and dig big enough holes for the seedlings to settle into easily. You do not want to force them into the ground as the young roots may break off. Water the seedling well, remove it gently from its current home, open up any matted roots slightly, and place it in the new home. Form a slight hill of dirt around the base of the plant and press the dirt down firmly.

Thinning seedlings

When you sow seeds, it is easy to sow too many in one spot. In fact, it is almost impossible to not sow them too thick. That is where thinning comes in. Once the seeds have sprouted and have tops that are several inches high, then the process of **thinning** starts. This is the process of pulling out the plants that are too growing too closely together. The seed packet will tell you how far apart the plants need to be for optimum growth and you will have to pull any plants that are closer than this recommended distance. The idea is to have a couple of inches minimum between two healthy seedlings. You should look for the healthier of the seedlings and pull all plants out of that healthy plant's space. By doing this, you avoid overcrowding. If you do not thin the seedlings, the plants become so overcrowded that they will not grow properly and will eventually die. This is particularly important if you are going to add other plants to maximize your space in your garden.

Divide mature plants

After several growing seasons, some plants need to be divided. You will know they need to be divided because they have reached the point where they begin to die off in the center and leave a brown ring. It is better if you catch the plant before it gets to this point. You can start when the plant has grown several times its size over a couple of years. Division is done by dividing the plants into several smaller versions of the original to keep the plants vigorous and happy for a long time.

Any time these plant have outgrown their location, they can be divided and moved. The best times to divide plants are in the spring and fall. The reason for dividing the plants in the spring is because the roots have not started actively growing yet and will be able to recuperate from the disturbance faster. In the fall, the growing season is over and the plants can be moved to a new location where they will have the winter to put down roots.

Before dividing the plant, soak it well because disturbing the roots will affect the plant's ability to take in water and nutrients for a short time. If the plant you are dividing has a lot of foliage on top, you may need to cut the leaves back by a third because this makes it easier for the plant to recover. Make sure you have the new location picked out, dug out, and well watered to receive the new plant because the plant will respond better if it is not left out of the ground for any length of time. Make sure to give the new plant sufficient space. Treat the new plant piece like a seedling and give it extra care until it is established.

The actual division process can take several different forms. The right way to do this usually involves digging out the entire plant and slicing around and through the roots to separate off a healthy chunk. Some plants like daylilies have twisted roots that can be gently pried apart with two pitch-forks. Some people will take a sharp spade and make a clean cut through plants (especially grasses) while they are still in place. Regardless of the method, after cutting the plant, lift it out of the ground, keeping as much roots and dirt attached as possible, and place it into the new location so the roots of the main plant have only a minimal disturbance. When you are done, hill the dirt around the new plant and the main plant's exposed roots and water them thoroughly.

Keep in mind that large plants can be divided several times and spread throughout the garden to create more plants. Also realize that some plants are so overgrown and root bound, like large ornamental grasses, that they will require an axe to help split the plant into two.

Taking cuttings

Another way to divide or create new plants is to take cuttings from a healthy plant and planting them in a pot full of potting soil. There are different types of cuttings that can be done. The most common methods include:

- **Stem cutting** — a piece of stem that needs to include one leaf node is planted in the soil and will produce new roots

- **Root cutting** — this is a section of root that when separated and planted elsewhere will produce new shoots

- **Leaf cutting** — a leaf is placed on moist soil and will need to produce both new roots and new stems

Some species, such as blackberries and geraniums, will produce new plants easily, while others will require more care. For more information on how to work with cuttings, see the Hortus USA Web site (**www.rooting-hormones.com**).

Summer – heavy growing season

In the summer, your garden will be an explosion of color and produce. The more you harvest, the more your plants will produce. They will need ample sun and nutrients, but if you have prepared your beds properly, they will grow beautifully.

Watering

During the summer months, it is important to keep up a regular watering routine. Keep an eye on your garden and try to avoid overwatering. Also remember that with companion planting, the nutrient and water requirements are heavier when you plant a lot of plants in a smaller space as they have to share the resources among themselves. It is also easier to revive a dried-out plant than to dry out and save a waterlogged plant.

You should water your plants when the soil is dry several inches below the surface. To see if you have watered your vegetable and flowers sufficiently, use your fingers to check that the ground is damp at least 4 to 5 inches below the surface. In some regions of the country where fungus is a problem, morning watering will minimize the fungal growth. The normal rule of avoiding watering during the daytime should be ignored if your plants are wilting and stressed due to the heat. If your schedule does not allow you to water early in the morning or in the evening after the sun has gone down (which is the preferred time to water your plants), watering the plants during the day is still better than not watering them at all. Some plants will need more water than others and tomatoes are definitely one of them. These fruit are full of juice and you cannot have big, plump tomatoes without regular, preferably drip-type, watering. The problem is when you forget to water then attempt to make up for it with an extra heavy watering the next time, particularly if the plants are not mulched, they will take up a lot of water faster, causing the inside of the fruit to grow faster than the skin and the tomatoes will split. You can tell if your plants are not getting enough water because the foliage will wilt and the stems will hang limp.

Staying ahead of the pests

Always keep an eye out to monitor your garden's pest population. If you are companion gardening and have done so for a while, there should not be any major problems. If you have just started companion planting, it will take a bit of time for the balance of prey and predator to establish itself. It is important to keep an eye on the situation. Walk up and down the rows and inspect the plants by checking the undersides of the leaves, the tops of the leaves, the growing tips, and at the base of the stem for insects.

You may also find signs of disease, but this does not have to be a major problem. If you find a plant that is heavily diseased, pull it out of the garden and throw it away. Do not put it into the compost pile as the disease could spread. If there is just a leaf that shows signs of disease, pluck it off and throw it away.

Pinching off/deadheading

The process of snapping of dead blooms and in some cases growing tips is called **pinching off** or deadheading. The reason for pinching off the dead blooms is to encourage more flowering. Some plants, like coleus, are grown for their foliage and not their flowers so when the plant shows signs of flowering, you pinch off the starting blooms to encourage the plants to become bushier and thicker. The decision of whether to promote more flowering needs to be determined by whether you have enough flowers in the garden now to attract in the pollinators like birds and bees. If you are cutting flowers for vases, make sure you leave enough for the pollinators as well.

Some plants bloom and leave only beautiful dry pods full of seed that are often left in place. An example of this is the astilbe, which only blooms once a season. Pinching off the finished bloom will not bring on more flowers. Deadheading is normal with annuals like petunias, pansies, and even roses will benefit from having the dead blooms removed to promote new growth.

Cutting back

Some early-blooming plants start to get tired and scrawny looking in the summer and the older leaves start drooping and looking worn and damaged. The hardy geranium is a prime example. In the spring, it is a thick, beautiful clump but by the time the heat of the summer sets in, it is no longer as attractive. This is a great time to cut the plant back and have it regrow.

Some of these early bloomers will have new growth coming out of the center of the plant, which is a sign that the plant is ready to start again. You can cut the old foliage back to where the branches look livelier or you can cut it all the way back to the new growth, which is basal growth. Many plants will bloom a second time after you cut them back and coreopsis is another example. Wait until the plant has finished blooming then shear the plant down and wait for it to bloom again. All plants are different and require a little care to make them look gorgeous all summer long.

Another reason to cut back is because sometimes plants become tall and spindly and when they are ready to bloom, their stalks are not strong enough to support the flowers. To encourage the plants to grow stockier and stronger, you cut the plant back to about a third of its height once it has reached 8 to 10 inches tall. Let it grow again and then cut it once more. When the plant grows for the third time, it should be strong enough to support big, healthy flowers. The flowers may bloom a bit later than if you had not cut the stalks but there will be more flowers than ever. By doing this, you also allow the plants around to spread out and maximize their growth.

Fertilizing throughout the growing season

If you are growing a garden heavy with vegetables, you may want to fertilize mid-way through the growing season. When you fertilize mid-season it is called side dressing. The garden will need this second boost of nutrients to keep some long-producing plants like tomatoes growing and producing strong throughout the season. To apply a commercial product, you can make a trench along the row of vegetables that you want to fertilize. You should never put fertilizer directly on the plants because it can burn the plants. Apply the fertilizer and then cover the trench. Because companion gardening makes heavy use of the available nutrients in the soil, it is important to replenish these nutrients on a regular basis.

If you are fertilizing with garden teas, they can be poured around the plants every week throughout the growing season and your plants will appreciate it. You can also add compost that is ready for the garden any time. This soil can be place around plants or up and down the rows.

Late summer – harvesting

Harvesting is the fun part of gardening and every plant has a different time to harvest. Here are some basic tips to keep in mind when you harvest:

- Pick only the items that are ripe – like tomatoes. Leave the others on the plant to ripen a little later.

- Pick the produce every few days. Plants like beans, peas, okra, and cucumbers will produce more if you pick often.

- Avoid picking vegetables in the rain or when the plants are wet to avoid spreading disease.

- Avoid damaging the plants when harvesting.

- If the plants are wilted, water and wait until they recuperate before harvesting.

- Once harvested, put the fruit and vegetables into a cool place. Enjoy the harvested fruits and vegetables as soon as possible.

- Disturb the plants as little as possible. If you are reaching under the potato plant to steal the new potatoes, make sure to avoid disturbing the roots. You can pull the whole plant if you want, but if you leave the potatoes you missed in place, the smaller ones will continue to grow. If you want potatoes for storage, you need to leave them in the ground until they have a firm skin. The potatoes will often continue to grow under the ground even after the plant above the ground has died.

- Some plants need to stay in place until after a frost before you harvest because a light frost will convert the starch in some vegetables like parsnips to sugar, improving their taste. Brussels sprouts will keep better after a frost as will the flavor of kale and collards. Pumpkins are not generally picked until a light frost kills the plant so the pumpkins can reach their maximum growth.

- Harvest for your taste. Some people like zucchinis only a few inches long and others prefer them when they have grown bigger than a foot.

- It is also okay to let some of the plants go to seed; the insects and birds will thank you for it.

Fall – cleaning up/preparing for next year

The fall is the best time for garden cleanup. This is also the time to cover the soil for winter and set up havens for the insects and wildlife.

Some plants will have an extended season – at least until a hard frost occurs. Many flowers will still be blooming throughout September like the asters, mums, stonecrop, pansies, and some of the clematis varieties. Plants like carrots, spinach, and Swiss chard can survive several frosts so do not be in a hurry to pull those plants. In fact, if you cover these plants with a thick layer of straw, cover the straw with a waterproof tarp to stop the straw from getting wet, and place heavy rocks on the tarp to stop the tarp from blowing away, you will be able to harvest these vegetables throughout the winter.

Sheltering insects

Many of the insects that have helped you throughout the summer are going to stay in your garden over winter. If you plan on using cover crops and mulch, they will burrow into these during the winter. Leave water dishes out in the garden until the water has frozen. If you have boards around the garden, leave them in place. You can clean them up in spring and the insects will move into the garden then as well.

Planting fall plants

If you have new perennials, trees, or shrubs, this is a good time to plant them. It is also a good time to transplant and divide plants to set them out in new locations if you did not do it in the spring or if you find you have to do it again. Remember to deadhead the flowers of the perennials and keep in mind this is the right time to plant spring-flowering bulbs like tulips.

Taking care of perennials

In the fall, trim or prune back your perennials. You can either cut off any seed heads left on the stalks or you can leave them on for the birds.

Cleaning up the garden

This is the time of year that the plants look old and worn out; some are crumpled to the ground and the others sag because of the effort of producing all summer long. Clean out all the old and dead plants in the garden and put them into the compost pile.

When you are going through the garden beds, check for plants that have suffered from insects or diseases. If you find one, pull the entire plant including the roots to make sure the problem is not there next year. Remove all the plant material of the cabbage and squash family plants as well, as they are prone to disease and can cause problems in the garden next year. If you have potatoes or tomatoes in the garden, be sure to harvest the plants completely and if you are planning on composting the plants, make sure you have an active compost going. Some diseases can survive winter in the compost heap as well so you want to make sure the compost is actively breaking down the plant materials.

Putting the garden to bed

Once the garden has been stripped and the perennials have been taken care of, it is time to lay down compost and fertilizer and either till the soil or dig it under. This will add nutrients to the garden that will decompose in time for spring planting.

If you are still in the mood for gardening at this point, you can prepare the beds for spring, plant a simple cover crop to add nutrients to dig over in the spring, or just let it all sit for the winter as it. This is time to relax and enjoy the silence of the winter. Spring will be here soon enough and the process will start all over again.

Now that you know the basics to establish a garden and are familiar with maintenance and garden critters, the book will now describe the various plants to consider for your garden. This next chapter starts the discussion on herbs.

CASE STUDY: MARY (MOOSEY) RUSTON

Moosey's Country Garden
www.mooseyscountrygarden.com

*Mary Ruston is a New Zealand gardener whose country garden is crammed full of foliage plants, roses, phormiums, and cordylines. She hosts a gardening forum for gardeners from all over the world at **http://forums.mooseyscountrygarden.com***

"No real gardener can be a perfectionist, can they? Imagine a garden in which no shrub grows too big too quickly; no expensive little treasure gets monstered by its neighbor; and no unwelcome bug dines out on gourmet foliage plants. But real gardeners will happily spend a lifetime trying to get everything in their garden just right. Here are six tricky little tips to make your garden appear closer to perfection than it actually is. This isn't really cheating — think of it as gently nudging the truth.

1. If your garden looks too messy, there is a simple solution: Sweep and/or rake all the paths, and make sure the path edges are well defined. Mow any lawns and cut the grass edges sharply. Introduce edging material into your garden — stones, bricks, logs — whatever suits your style.

2. If some piece is annoying you — an ugly trellis, an abandoned bathtub, a concrete slab — don't be a gardening wimp and camouflage it, celebrate it! Make the eyesore a quirky feature. Put plants or pots around it, decorate it, or place a seat nearby. Have it say 'Look at me. I'm meant to be here.'

3. Let the weeds lurk in the interior of your garden borders, but keep visible areas close to paths well weeded. Install colorful buckets where you can pop offenders as you wander past. And don't feel guilty that you're a cosmetic weeder. Enjoy your garden; don't become a slave to it.

4. Let differences be your guide when 'designing' a planting scheme. Contrasts make life interesting, and it's the same for gardens. Think fat and thin for leaves, blobby and spiky for shapes. Put a refined cane garden chair next to a wizened tree trunk. Grow a feathery perennial next to a rough and tough evergreen.

5. No garden should be totally predictable and controlled. Allow yourself as many random gardening events as you cope with. Encourage flowers that self-seed. Buy that interesting new plant; if it embarrasses your planting design, you can always stuff it into a flashy pot. By all means, make serious garden plans, but embrace the unexpected.

6. Gardeners often get terribly serious about their timing. When should they shift a rhododendron? Or put compost underneath the roses? The answer is simple: If it's free, then the time is right. A free load of rotted manure? Take it and spread it. A free rhododendron? Take it and water it. However, if 'it' costs you money, then do your 'When is the right time?' research and follow the instructions. "

· CHAPTER 6 ·

Companion Herbs

This chapter is an alphabetical listing of the most common herbs to use in companion planting. Each section discusses the basic growing conditions, the benefits of the plants, best companion plants, and the worst companion plants, if any, to plant with.

Aloe Vera (Aloe barbadensis)

This green or gray-blue-green succulent plant has thick, fleshy leaves coming out from the base and is one of the most useful plants to have around because the plant's juice has long been used as an emergency burn remedy. This herb is easy to grow in  warm, frost-free, sunny environments, preferably in shallow containers that can be brought indoors for winter. It is one of the few plants that is free of disease and pests.

If you cut of a tip off one of the leaves, you can squeeze the aloe gel onto plant limbs that have been cut from tree trimming, rose pruning, and you can even use it on yourself if you cut yourself when working in the garden. Aloe grows well with asters and chrysanthemums because their water requirements are the same. There are no known bad companions for aloe vera.

Anise (Pimpinella anisum)

Anise is related to the caraway and dill plants. It has white flowers atop of lacy leaves and can grow up to 2 feet high. Anise likes a well-drained soil with a sunny exposure. The plants should be approximately 6 inches apart and the rows should be 2 or 3 feet apart. The plant prefers drier conditions so water when necessary but avoid over watering as the plants do not like to sit in water. Many people mix up anise and fennel *(Foeniculum vulgar)*, but they are two different plants even though they share a similar flavor and are from the same family. Then there is star anise *(Illicum verum)* which is known by its eight-pointed star seed pod shape.

Anise has a strong licorice flavor and is good to plant near the brassicas family of cabbage, broccoli, and cauliflower because the anise odor camouflages its companions' smell so the pests cannot find them. The plant makes a good host for predatory wasps that love to feed on aphids. It is also supposed to repel aphids and to increase the vigor of any plants growing beside it. Anise is a good companion plant to coriander. Ointments made with anise protect against stings and bites.

Basil (Ocimum basilicum)

Basic is a leafy, green, bushy plant that usually grows 1 foot high. It produces fragrant purplish flower on single spikes. There are both spicy and sweet varieties that offer hints of anise, lemon, and cinnamon. Basil should be sowed outdoors after all

danger of frost has past. It grows very well in pots. Choose a sunny location where it is protected from strong and cold winds. Basil likes a fertile, well-aerated soil. Pinch off the flowers as they arrive to send the growing energy into the leaves, which is the reason most people grow the herb.

Plant basil with your tomato plants to improve the growth and flavor of the fruit. Basil also grows well paired with peppers, oregano, asparagus, and petunias. It can be helpful in repelling thrips, flies, and mosquitoes. Avoid planting basil beside rue and sage. Rue is bitter and basil is sweet and they do not work together in this case. To keep fruit flies off picked tomatoes, place a sprig of basil on top of the fruit.

Bay Leaves (Laurus nobilis)

Bay leaves are the harvested leaves of the bay Laurel bush, which if left unpruned can grow 30 feet. Consider growing them in containers as that will limit their growth naturally. The leaves are used when they are fresh picked or dried. When eaten whole,

they have a slightly bitter taste and are better known for their fragrance that is similar slightly to oregano and thyme. This is one plant that is easier to grow from nursery stock than from seed. Bay laurel needs a mild, warm climate and a location protected from strong winds. If the climate is hot, plant the tree where it will receive partial-shade; in most other climates, the plant is happy in a sunny location. Trim the plant to several inches above ground during winter and it will sprout again next year. This plant likes to dry out between waterings.

The bay leaf plant will deter weevils and moths so plant in various corners of the garden to deter pests. If you dry the leaves, crush them then spread them around the garden to deter insects. A good combination of dried herbs for an insecticide dust includes the bay leaves, cayenne pepper, tansy, and peppermint. Bay leaves grow well with most herbs and there are no known bad companions.

Bee Balm (Monarda didyma)

This pretty perennial, also known as wild bergamon, horsemint, and bergamont, can be purchased from a garden center or grown from seed with some difficulty. Plant in a partial-shade to a full-sun location and set the plants at least 10 inches apart for optimum growth. Keep the soil moist but do not overwater. The entire plant above ground is edible and is used as a flavoring in cooking. The edible flowers are often used in salads.

Bee balm is a good companion for tomatoes as it helps them improve their growth and flavor. It is a popular plant that attracts beneficial insects and pollinators like butterflies and bees. It is a good companion plant to Black-eyed Susans, coneflower, daylily, false sunflower, gayfeather, goat's beard, rose mallow, Shasta daisy, speedwell, and yarrow.

Borage (Borage officinalis)

Borage is also known as star-flower. It will grow up to 3 feet tall and has hairy stems and leaves. It produces five-point blue flowers. Borage grows best in a full-sun location, but it can do well in partial-sun. It needs fertile, well-drained soil but needs a  mulch to keep it moist. It will benefit from strong nutrient-based mulch like compost. Borage flowers are edible.

Borage makes a great companion plant for tomatoes, squash, and strawberries. It makes a good neighbor for most plants by increasing resistance to pests and disease. It is said to deter tomato hornworms and cabbage worms and is also one of the best plants for attracting bees and wasps. The leaves are rich in vitamin C, calcium, potassium, and trace minerals. This annual will self seed if you let it. There are no known bad companions for borage.

Caraway (Carum carvi)

Caraway looks like carrots in the first year when it will grow close to 8 inches tall. By the second year, the stalks have developed, and they are then topped with pink or white flowers. The flower seeds are the spice used in cooking. Caraway is a bit of a wild card to grow. Some gardeners say it does well in moist, heavy dirt and other say it grows well in sandy soil with good drainage. If it is planted in fall, it can be ready for sprouting in the following spring.

If you choose to plant in the spring, realize that this is a biennial plant and you may need to sow new seeds two years in a row. Once the plant is established, it will self-seed and you could be overrun. Thin the seedlings to 10 inches apart and make sure the rows are 10 inches apart as well. When the plant flowers, the plant's life cycle is over and you should harvest the dry flower pods on a hot, sunny day so the pods are dry.

The plant has long roots, making it a good plant to work the subsoil. This also makes it a good plant to locate close to shallow-rooted crops such as lettuce as they will search for and use nutrients at different levels. It does not do well close to fennel or dill but it does well close to strawberries. The flowers are great for attracting many insects, in particular parasitic wasps.

Catnip (Nepeta cataria)

Catnip is also called catmint and is a member of the mint family. This strong-smelling herb grows several feet high and wide, producing leaves with a minty, aromatic scent. The plant produces purplish-colored flowers. It is relatively easy to grow and is happy in full sun or partial shade. Space the plants 3 to 4 feet away from each other and be prepared for them to self-seed. They like a soil with good drainage. Prune catnip to keep the plant size in control. This plant is one that is well-loved by all felines. They will rub against it and even lie in the middle of the plant. You can dry the leaves, flowers, and branches and then use them in your cat's toys.

Catnip has insect-repelling oil. If you steep the catnip like a tea and sprinkle it around the plants, it will deter fleas, aphids, Japanese beetles, squash bugs, and weevils. Grow catnip in areas where you want to deter mice and cut fresh sprigs to place in areas where you want to deter ants. Catnip has a strong, pleasant aroma and is very safe for humans and animals. Catnip makes a good companion for cucumber plants, chamomile, mint, radishes, bee balm, hollyhock, pincushion flower, Shasta daisy, yarrow, and roses.

Chamomile (Matricaria chamomilla)

There are two common types of chamomile – German and Roman (Anthemis nobilis)— and both are happy in full sun or partial shade. The flower heads are used for teas and ointments. German chamomile is the taller plant, growing up to 3 feet high, and produces small daisy-looking flowers with white petals surrounding a raised center. Roman chamomile is low to the ground, grows under any condition, and can be considered a weed by many. The German chamomile, also called wild chamomile, has a strong aromatic odor and is an excellent companion plant for cabbages, cucumbers, and onions as it can improve both their vigor and flavor. Also, the flowers can be soaked in cold water for a couple of days and the liquid can then be used as a spray against plant diseases and to combat **dampening off**, which is when young seedlings die suddenly seemingly from rot. Another benefit is that the plant is host to hoverflies and wasps.

One of these plants in your garden is enough unless you are planting acres. The plant will re-seed itself if the flowers are left unpicked. It is also said to increase the oil production of other plants when grown with herbs like peppermint. It is known to deter the Colorado beetle and carrot flies. It makes a good companion to beans, peas, cucumbers, dill, tomato, pumpkin, and squash.

Chervil (Anthriscus cerefolium)

Chervil is a lacy, fern-like leafed plant that is related to parsley. The herb is used to season various dishes and offers a faint licorice taste. Chervil is happiest in a shady spot in the garden and will **bolt** (go to seed quickly) in the heat. The seeds will germinate faster if you soak them overnight because the seedlings need a lot of moisture. Thin the seedlings when they are a couple of inches tall. As the plant grows, you can trim the branches and use the herb for your own use – the plant will continue to grow. This plant does not like to be transplanted so if it is not shady enough, plant a taller plant beside it.

It is a good companion plant for radishes, lettuce, and broccoli and improves their growth and flavor. Some gardeners have luck with chervil keeping aphids off lettuce, others with repelling slugs.

Chives (Allium shoenoprasum)

Chives are an easy plant to grow. They have tiny, tubular leaves that can be eaten in place of onions. The plants will grow around 1 foot tall. They prefer full sun but do fine in partial shade and once established, they can be divided into several plants over and over again. If the ball-shaped flowers appear, cut the plant down to an inch or two off the ground and it will spring up again quickly with fresh herbs. When the flowers start growing, the herb becomes less flavorful and tough. The onion chives have purple flowers and the garlic chives produce white flowers.

Chives are a good companion to carrots, brassicas, and tomatoes, improving both growth and flavor. If you have apple trees, chives will help prevent apples scab and when planted with roses they can prevent black spot fungus, which are small black spots on the leaves. However, expect it to take at least three years before these diseases can be prevented.

Chives are said to keep aphids off tomatoes, mums, and sunflowers. They have had some success in driving away Japanese beetles and carrot rust fly. You can make chive tea to spray for apple scab and to prevent powdery mildew on cucumbers and gooseberries. Chives are bad companions for beans and peas.

Cilantro/Coriander (Coriandrum sativum)

Cilantro is the plant and coriander is the seed of this plant. It is an annual herb that grows in warmer climates. It will grow to 3 feet tall and will produce leaves that resemble parsley in the first year. In the second year, the seeds are produced. The leaves are used fresh or cooked and the seeds are dried and used in cooking. It loves damp, cooler springs and long, hot summer days. It is happiest in full-sun and prefers a well-drained soil. Coriander has a **taproot**, meaning one long single root, that once established, does not transplant well. Thin the seedlings to 4 inches apart and if you want a steady supply of the leaves, sow new seeds every couple of weeks. The seeds will ripen in late fall. The plant is full of carotene, calcium, protein, minerals, riboflavin, and several B vitamins, in particular B6, B12, and niacin (B3).

Coriander is good for repelling aphids, spider mites, and the potato beetle. Coriander tea is an effective spray for spider mites. It is a good companion for anise as it helps it germinate. It is a bad companion for fennel because it hinders seed formation.

Comfrey (Symphytum officinale)

Comfrey is a perennial herb with a soft hairy leaf, black root, and small pastel-colored flowers. It is part of the borage family. Comfrey leaves have long been used as a medicinal herb because it was believed to have strong bone healing properties, hence its other name: knitbone. It is high in calcium, potassium, phosphorus, and is full of vitamin A and C. This plant is never taken internally; instead, the leaves are used in topical treatments.

It is an easy to grow plant. Russian comfrey has a high calcium/nitrogen blend, making it ideal for the compost.

It is happiest in a wetter spot in the garden, and likes full-sun and partial-shade conditions. Plant these herbs 3 feet apart and do not plant close to other small herbs. When you want to harvest the leaves, cut them at the base. This will also stop the plant from flowering and extend its growing season.

It is a trap crop for slugs, and is beneficial to avocado and most fruit trees. There are no known bad companions for comfrey.

Dill (Anethum graveolens)

Dill is easy to grow from seed and can reach 2 feet in height. The plant has slim stems and thread-like divided leaves. Dill flowers are white to yellow. Plant the seeds in early spring about ½ inch deep and about 4 inches apart. Once the plants are a couple of inches tall, thin them to 9 inches apart. The leaves can be harvested in five to six weeks. The dill will continue to grow throughout the season. Once the plant flowers, the leaf growth stops and the plant will begin to produce flower heads and the much sought after seeds. Harvest the seeds when they have turned brown. If you are growing the plant for the leaves, then cut the down to the base of the plant as soon as the flower heads start to develop. The fresh and dried leaves are used in cooking and pickling. Dill seed is a spice with a hint of caraway flavoring.

Dill is a good companion to cabbage and lettuce, improving the plants' health and growth, and does well beside onions, sweet corn, and cucumbers. It is a bad companion to carrots and can greatly reduce the yield of caraway and tomatoes as it is known to attract tomato horn worm. Dill also attracts hoverflies, swallowtail butterflies, bees, and predatory wasps. It can repel aphids and spider mites and sometimes squash bugs.

Fennel (Foeniculum vulgare)

Fennel is classed as a herb but is a common vegetable as well. The bulb base and stalk are eaten raw or cooked similar to celery. The leaves and seeds have a taste reminiscent of anise. The plant has bright green fern-like leaves, grows 3 to 4 feet high, and will produce strong scented yellow flowers. Plant fennel in late fall. It does not transplant well so make sure you start the plants where you want them to grow. They like a sunny exposure and well-drained soil. Plant three seeds 6 inches apart and in a hole 6 inches deep. Fill the hole in and water well. Cover the spots with a thick mulch to help insulate them against winter and stave off the insects. Once the danger of frost is over in the spring, begin watering every couple of days. The plant needs three months to mature.

Fennel is one of the few plants that has mostly bad companions as it inhibits the growth of any nearby plant. It has a particularly strong inhibiting effect on kohlrabi, bush beans, eggplant, caraway, and tomatoes. When planted close to coriander, fennel will not produce seed and it also does not do well with wormwood. Find a location away from most plants to let it grow. It will produce copious quantities of foliage that attract birds and the leaves, and its seeds and bulbs are all commonly used.

Garlic (Allium sativum)

Garlic will reach 2 to 3 feet in height while producing long, flat leaves with white flowers. The bulb is the most commonly eaten part of the plant, which is used cooked or raw to season dishes. Garlic bulbs split into individual cloves and it is the largest and the healthiest of these cloves that are planted in the fall at least six weeks before the ground freezes. If you live in the South or have mild winters, you can plant the cloves at the end of January. Garlic likes full sun and well-drained soil. Dig a hole 10 to 12 inches deep and fill the hole with about 8 inches of compost. Plant the cloves, pointed end up, 2 inches deep and 5 inches apart. Cover the bulbs with a thick layer of compost and mulch to protect them over winter. Remove the mulch in the spring so the sun can warm the ground and then mulch again when the garlic breaks ground. Garlic will not grow well if it surrounded by weeds because they will take over, so keep weeding until it is well established. Cut off the flowers as they start to appear to promote large bulbs. When the foliage turns yellow or falls over, you know the bulbs are almost mature. There are several opinions of when to harvest, but a simple rule to follow is that when the plant is one-half to three-quarters brown and one-quarter green, the bulbs are probably ready to harvest.

Garlic repels aphids, so plant it near the roses, apple trees, pear trees, cucumbers, lettuce, and celery. Garlic is also known to accumulate sulfur, which is a naturally occurring fungicide that helps prevent disease. It is effective against diseases that damage stone fruit, cucumbers, spinach, and nuts. You can plant garlic with tomatoes to prevent red spider mites. Garlic is a bad companion to beans, peas, and strawberries as it can inhibit their growth.

Horehound (Marrubium vulgare)

White horehound or Common Horehound is a flowering plant that can reach 1½ feet tall. The leaves have a crinkled surface and are covered in downy hairs. The flowers are white, and the leaves and young shoots are invaluable as a flavoring for candy and cough drops. Horehound is a member of the mint family. Sow horehound seeds ⅛ inch deep when the ground has warmed up nicely. Thin the seedlings until the plants are 15 inches apart. In the first year, the plant will stay small but will eventually reach 3 feet tall. It thrives in many places that other plants will not and it can withstand harsh winters but it does not like sitting in excess moisture and is an extremely drought-tolerant plant so water rarely.

Horehound is a good companion to tomatoes and peppers, improving their quality, increasing their yield, and helping them fertilize and grow fruit better. The plant blooms from early summer to fall. Like many other mint plants, the tiny flowers attract braconid and icheumonid wasps, tachnid and syrid flies, as well as many other insects. Grasshoppers and other insects do not like the taste of horehound.

Hyssop (Hyssopus officinalis)

Hyssop is a tall flowering herb that can grow up to 2 feet in height. The plant has narrow long leaves and branched stems that are covered in tiny hairs at the tip. The plant produces blue flowers at the ends of the branches. The leaves have a mint flavor and can be added to soups and salads. You can start hyssop by seed, although you might find a young plant in a garden center. Plant the seeds ½ to ¼ inch deep, 1 foot apart, in a sunny location. It can tolerate a shady location. In colder temperatures, hyssop is considered an annual but in warmer climates it is considered a perennial. Hyssop is a great plant for a container, but requires a pot at least 10 inches deep due to its large root system. The plant will deteriorate with time and should be replaced every five years.

This is a good companion plant to cabbage and grapes, deterring cabbage moths and flea beetles. If planted close to grapevines, their yield will increase. It is safe to interplant with most plants, but it is not a companion plant to radishes as they grow poorly beside them.

Lavender (Lavandula vera)

Lavender is an easy to grow plant with few known pests of its own. It is a small shrub with gray leaves and violet flowers that is known for its pleasant, sweet scent. The fresh and dried flowers are used in for various things including scent pouches. The  flowers can be candied and used in baking, and its leaves and flowers are used in home remedies and aromatherapy. You can start cuttings in the fall indoors or purchase plants from garden centers and plant in the spring. It is harder to grow this plant from seed. Lavender prefers alkaline soil and a sunny location. The plant also does not like a lot of water so it will not do well close to sprinklers, low ground, or beside plants that require a lot of water. It is a long lived perennial that lives an average of ten years. You should space these plants several feet apart.

The constant flowering aspect of the lavender attracts and nourishes many insects. It protects other plants from whitefly and when planted close to fruit trees, it will deter codling moths. It is considered deer resistant and rabbit resistant but will attract butterflies. It is a good companion to dianthus, yucca, daylily, coreopsis, and yarrow, and there are no known bad companions.

Lemon Balm (Melissa officinalis)

Lemon balm can easily grow 3 to 4 feet, producing leaves containing a gentle lemon scent. The plant produces white flowers toward the end of summer. Lemon balm is used in herbal teas and desserts, as well as many medicinal uses. The lemon balm herb requires moist soil and a full-sun or partial-sun location. You can plant seeds or propagate by cutting off a large piece of root from an existing plant. The seedlings should be no closer than 2 feet and you should make the rows 2 feet apart as well. The plants will grow quickly.

The plant is easily recognizable by its lemon-scented foliage and has similar compounds to the citronella plant, which helps this plant keep the mosquitoes away. Rub the leaves and the mosquitoes will avoid you. It also repels squash bugs, which makes it a good companion plant for squash and pumpkin plants. There are no known bad companions for this plant.

Lovage (Levisticum officinale)

Lovage is a large perennial plant, reaching 6 feet in height, so plan to give it space in the garden. It has ribbed stalks and hollow stems with dark green leaves and yellow flowers. Lovage tastes similar to celery and parsley whereas the roots have a nutty flavor. It prefers shady, slightly moist conditions. It can be planted in spring or sown in late summer and early fall for sprouting the following spring. Lovage will die down every winter and spring up again the following year.

Lovage improves the flavor and vigor of most plants and offers a good habitat for ground beetles. Lovage is a good companion plant for cucumbers, asparagus, beans, beets, the brassica family, onion, leeks, peas, potatoes, lettuce, squash, zucchini, corn, and tomatoes. It is not considered a good companion for celery.

Marjoram (Origanum majorana)

Marjoram is an evergreen with reddish-brown stems that produce gray-green leaves and tiny flowers throughout the summer in white or pink. There are several types of marjoram. Some will act like a perennial in warm climates and others will act as an annual in colder climates. This plant requires a full-sun location that is protected from the wind. You can buy young plants or sow the seeds after the danger of frost has passed. Plant or thin the seedlings 6 inches apart and do not overwater because they are happier in a drier location.

Marjoram is a friend to all plants and helps improve growth and flavor. It is a good companion to asparagus, beets, the brassica family, cucumbers, lettuce, onion, peas, potatoes, radishes, squash, corn, tomato, sage, peppers, and zucchini. There are no known bad companions for this herb.

Oregano (Origanum vulgare)

Oregano is related to marjoram, especially sweet marjoram. It is hardy herb that is an easy addition to any garden. You can sow seeds or plant nursery plants but you will need to plant them 2 feet apart as they will grow to 2 feet wide.

Oregano is a companion to most plants but is a good companion to cabbage and grapes. Plant near broccoli, cabbage, and cauliflower as it is repels the cabbage butterfly, and plant close to cucumber plants to repel the cucumber beetle.

Parsley (Petroselinum crispum)

Parsley is an easy to grow herb that likes a full-sun or partial-shade location in well-drained soil. The plant will grow approximately 1 foot high and can have a curly leaf *(P. crispum)* or a flat leave as in Italian parsley *(P. neapolitanum)*. It makes a good container plant. Seeds can be planted several times a year in either spring, summer, or fall. Lay the seeds on top of the ground and keep moist until it germinates; after that, thin until they are 3 inches apart. Once germinated, do not let the dirt dry out between watering. A layer of mulch will help keep it moist.

Parsley is a good companion to asparagus, carrot, chives, onions, roses, and tomato. Parsley also attracts hoverflies and when the plant goes to seed it will attract the tiny parasitic wasps. Parsley is said to increase the fragrance of roses when it is planted close by. Parsley is a bad companion to mint as neither plant does well when planted close together.

Peppermint (Mentha x piperita)

Peppermint will easily reach 3 to 4 feet in height producing smooth stems and strongly scented dark green leaves with different colored veins and purple flowers. Peppermint likes a partially-sunny or partially-shady location. Sow the seeds anytime in the spring or summer. The ground should be moist but not wet. When the seedlings are almost 2 inches high, thin or transplant the seedlings until they are 12 inches apart from each other.

Peppermint contains menthol that repels white cabbage moths, aphids, flea beetles, and bees. Peppermint can repel red ants from shrubs. If it is grown close to chamomile, the peppermint will produce less oil but the chamomile grows better. To increase the oil in the peppermint, grow it close to stinging nettles. There are no known bad companions for this herb.

Rosemary (Rosmarinus officinalis)

Rosemary is a hardy perennial that produces aromatic leaves and blue flowers. The leaves are used in cooking and aromatherapy. Rosemary seeds take a long time to germinate so it is better to buy young plants from the nursery. They like full-sun or light shade and require well-drained soil. The plants need at least 2 feet between them. Rosemary can **overwinter**, or survive the winter temperature, in warmer climates and can be taken inside for the winter in colder climates.

Rosemary is a companion plant to cabbage, beans, carrots, and sage and repels cabbage moths, bean beetles, and carrot flies. There are no known bad companions for rosemary.

Rue (Ruta graveolens)

Rue is a evergreen shrub that grows 1 to 1½ feet tall. It has green to blue-green leaves with yellow flowers. It is very bitter plant and is used medicinally instead of for cooking. Rue is an herb for warmer climates. It likes a sunny location and well-worked soil that offers good drainage. It is easier to grow rue from nursery stock than from seed as it germinates slowly. Plant the seedlings 18 inches apart.

Rue is a companion plant to figs, strawberries, raspberries, lavender, or roses it as it repels the Japanese beetles. It is also known to deter aphids, onion maggots, slugs, snails, fish moths, and fleas. Rue is a bad companion to basil, mint, and sage with all plants suffering if they are together. It also slows the growth of cucumbers, cabbage, basil, and sage.

Sage (Salvia officinalis)

Sage is a hardy perennial with pale green leaves and produces purple flowers in summer. Sage has a slightly peppery flavor. It likes a sunny location and well-drained soil. It needs some space as it grows to 2 feet high and there should be 2 feet between plants. Sage can be grown indoors or outside.

Sage is a good companion plant to broccoli, cauliflower, rosemary, cabbage, and carrots because it repels cabbage moths, beetles, black flea beetles, and carrot flies. It is a bad companion plant to cucumbers, onions, or rue. If you allow the herb to flower, it will attract many other beneficial insects and the flowers are visually appealing.

Spearmint (Mentha spicata)

There are thousands of varieties of mint, and spearmint is just one of those. It is a gently scented perennial with green leaves and white, pink, or lavender flowers. Mint is one of those hardy perennials that is hard to kill and will take over your garden once it is established. It needs space in your garden and likes partial shade and a moist rich soil, but it often does well anywhere. You can plant early in the spring, but they are hard to grow from seeds so it is better to purchase a young plant.

Mint is a good companion to cabbage and tomatoes, improving their vigor and flavor. Mint is strengthened when close to stinging nettle. Mint deters the white cabbage worm, ants, rodents, flea beetles, fleas, and aphids. It attracts hoverflies and predatory wasps. Mint is a bad companion to parsley so keep these plants apart.

Summer Savory (Satureja hortensis)

Summer savory will grow up to 2 feet high with slim bronze green leaves and lavender flowers in the summer. It is a sweeter flavor than winter savory and is used extensively, often in place of sage. Summer savory likes a full-sun location well away from most of the garden and it will re-seed itself. The seeds should be planted ½ inch deep and 3 inches apart with rows 3 feet apart. The soil needs to be well-drained and the stalks can need support over the summer as the plant grows.

Savory is a good companion to beans and onion, improving their vigor and flavor. It also discourages and repels cabbage moths, Mexican bean beetles, and black aphids. It attracts the honey bee. There are no known bad companions for summer savory.

Tarragon (Artemisia dracunculus)

Tarragon will grow up to 4 feet tall, with slender stems producing long, skinny glossy green leaves. The flowers are greenish-yellow. Tarragon is used extensively in cooking, soft drinks, and baking and offers a similar flavoring to anise, only milder. Tarragon

makes a great garden or house herb. The seeds require a full-sun location, dry soil, and shelter from the wind. Thin the plants to 12 to 14 inches apart if you plant them in the garden. You can plant them in pots and easily bring them inside over winter.

Most pests do not like tarragon, so you can plant it all over the garden. It is recommended to improve the growth and flavor of all vegetables.

Thyme (Thymus vulgaris)

Thyme will grow about 1 foot high, can have solid or variegated leaves, and produces either white or purple flowers. The leaves are used either fresh or dried in cooking. Thyme is an easy to grow, hard to kill perennial. Its seeds take a long time to germinate and you are better off buying young plants. They like a full-sun, well-drained spot in a drier location. Put the plants at least 6 inches apart. Plants can be divided after several years and you can cut them back whenever they outgrow their spot.

Thyme is an excellent groundcover and also comes in an upright form. It is known to deter cabbage worm so plant near your cabbage, broccoli, and kale to ward off any potential problem. It is a good companion for eggplant, potatoes, and tomatoes.

Wormwood (Artemisia absinthium)

This herb is also known as absinthium and artemisius. Wormwood will grow up to 5 feet tall with silvery-green branches and greenish gray leaves with white undersides. The flowers are yellow. Wormwood is used medicinally and rarely in culinary dishes. Its strong odor however makes it invaluable in the garden. Sow the seeds in early spring after the danger of frost has passed. Put the seeds in a separate corner of the garden and thin the seedlings to 18 inches. The chemical absinthin can be toxic to other plants so once they are planted, keep that location for wormwood year after year;

you can also choose to grow it in a container. It likes partial shade and needs to be watered regularly in the heat.

Planting wormwood as a border on the outside edge of the garden is an excellent way to deter many insects like moths, flea beetles, and the cabbage worm butterfly. Wormwood is a good companion plant for asters, purple coneflower, geranium, lamb's ear, Black-eyed Susan, and yarrow. A garden tea made from this herb will repel cabbage moths, slugs, snails, black flea beetles, and fleas. One variety, the Powis Castle, attracts ladybugs that breed directly on the plant. It is a bad companion for peas, beans, anise, caraway, fennel, and sage.

The next chapter deals with the companion planting issues as they relate to specific vegetables.

· CHAPTER 7 ·

Description of Vegetables

T his chapter offers you an in-depth look at how to plant the various vegetables and the best and worst companion plants to go with them. Remember that most vegetables like a nutrient-rich soil full of well-rotted compost and mulches. Even if the individual plant instructions do not mention this fact, make sure your garden bed is richly prepared before beginning. There are a few vegetables that do well in sandy beds, like carrots, but most do better in well dug over dirt that has been enriched with nutrients in preparation for the long growing season. All beds will also benefit from additional nutrients throughout the growing season.

The following are guidelines you can follow, but take the time to make this fun. Mix up the planting and interplant carrots with beets and radishes or try planting kohlrabi with both to take advantage of the nutrients at the surface level versus deeper root levels. Vegetable gardening can be a fun and rewarding experience.

Asparagus

Asparagus prefers to grow in the same spot year after year, so pick a full-sun location for best results or partial shade in a spot where it will not need to be disturbed. You will need to purchase asparagus crowns from your local garden center or nursery catalog. The

crown will have a strong root system but the top growth will be dormant. Plant the crowns in early spring for most locations; if you live in a warmer climate, you can plant in late winter. The asparagus will need to be planted deep so make a trench approximately 6 to 7 inches deep. Spread the bottom of the trench with wood ashes or bone meal and compost if you have it. There will be instructions on the asparagus when you purchase it, so make sure you read and follow them.

In general, soaking the roots first, preferably in a compost tea, is a good start. Then lay them on their side in the trench approximately 1 foot apart. Make sure the rows are 3 to 4 feet apart. You will the fill in the trench slowly as the sprouts appear but only cover the stalks and be sure to leave the foliage uncovered. With time, the trench will fill in and the asparagus foliage will now be above ground level. It is important to be diligent with the weeding and you should aim to lay down mulch once the trench is filled in.

Asparagus has many companion plants, including the family of aster flowers, dill, coriander, basil, comfrey, and marigolds, which will deter beetles. Parsley appears to increase the growth of both plants when they are grown together. Tomatoes and asparagus help each other; tomatoes protect against asparagus beetles and a chemical in the asparagus juice deters nematodes from tomato plants. There are no known bad companions for asparagus; however these plants do better when they are not close to onion, garlic, or potatoes.

Beans

There are different types of beans available, like snap, dry, and bush. Some will have different companions, both good and bad. There are some basics that apply to all types of beans. Plant in a full-sun location or partial shade if you live in hot climates.  Sow seeds only after danger of frost has past. For scarlet runner beans, which are climbers, supply support of some kind. Thin the seedlings to 5 or 6 inches apart, but leave slightly more space for pole beans.

All beans have the ability to enrich the soil with nitrogen. They all do well when planted with carrots, cauliflower, peas, radishes, potatoes, strawberries, the brassica family, chard, and corn, and they are of great benefit to cucumbers and cabbage. Summer savory is another good companion to beans as it improves the beans' growth and flavor and deters the bean beetles. Marigolds, rosemary, and nasturtiums also deter bean beetles.

Bad companions for beans include garlic, onion, and shallots as they appear to stunt the plants' growth. They are not happy planted close to gladiolas. Beans are prone to diseases, but crop rotation will prevent most of them. There are also companions specific to individual types of beans.

Bush beans

Bush beans, a shrub variety of the snap bean, do well with celery if planted at the ratio of one celery plant to six bush beans. Bush beans do well close to celery and leeks but only if there are only one or two bean plants there. If more than this are planted, then none of them do well. Bush beans will give and receive benefits when planted with strawberries and cucumbers. Bush beans are a bad companion to fennel and onions.

Pole beans

Pole beans, a climbing variety of bean like scarlet runner beans, do particularly well with corn, summer savory, and radish. They do not particularly like beets. They make bad companions with onion, beets, cabbage, eggplant, kohlrabi, and sunflowers.

Broad beans

Broad beans, also called fava beans or horse beans, produce large, flat pods with large beans inside. They are excellent companions for corn, potato, cucumbers, strawberry, celery, and summer savory. They are bad companions with onions.

Beets

Beets are an easy-to-grow crop that prefers a full-sun location and well-tilled soil with good drainage. They germinate well and will need to be thinned to 4 inches apart with rows at least 2 feet apart. Beets are great for the garden as they add in minerals to the soil.

Beets are good companions for lettuce, onions, kohlrabi, and the brassica family. Mint, garlic (which improves the beet's flavor), and catnip help beets grow. If you do not want to plant mints around the beets, you can use mint foliage as mulch. Beets are bad companions to pole beans and gives mixed results next to bush beans.

Broccoli

Broccoli grows best in full sun or partial shade in a well-drained soil. In terms of minimizing disease, plant broccoli where no other brassicas (including cabbage, Brussels sprouts, kohlrabi, and cauliflower) have been planted in the previous two years as per

crop rotation rules. Broccoli is a large plant and can reach 3 feet in height so the seeds or nursery seedlings should be planted 18 inches apart after danger of frost has passed. If they do not form heads (broccoli florets) properly, they are deficient in lime, phosphorus, or potash. You can purchase these nutrients at your garden center and add them to your broccoli plants.

Broccoli, like all the brassicas, does well with aromatic plants including dill, which improves the plant's growth and health. Broccoli is a good companion to beets, celery, chard, cucumber, lettuce, onion, potato, and spinach. Flea beetles like broccoli so plant Chinese Daikon and Snow Belle radishes to attract flea beetles away from the broccoli.

Do not plant close to tomatoes, strawberries, pole beans, peppers, or mustards as they are bad companions.

Cabbage

Cabbage needs to spend at least half the time in the shade. You can grow from seed or purchase the plant from a nursery to get a jump on the season. Insects like young cabbages so consider covering the plants with a lightweight cloth when they are first growing. They love compost, fertilizer, and water. If the cabbage's florets do not form properly, the plant is deficient in lime, phosphorus, or potash and you should purchase some from your local garden supply store to add to your beds.

Cabbage, like all the brassica family, does well with aromatic plants including dill, while sage, peppermint, and rosemary help repel cabbage flies. Celery and dill improve cabbage's health and growth. Clover will reduce native cabbage aphids and cabbage worm. Other good companions include onions, potatoes, hyssop, thyme, and southernwood. Wormwood repels white cabbage butterfly. Tansy deters cabbage worm and cutworm, and thyme deters cabbage worm. Nasturtium deters bugs, beetles, and aphids from cabbage.

Bad companions for cabbage are strawberries, tomatoes, peppers, lettuce, eggplants, rue, grapes, and pole beans.

Carrots

Carrots prefer full sun and need a very loose, preferably sandy soil for the roots to grow easily downward. If your soil is high in lime, humus, and potash, you will have sweeter tasting carrots. Low nitrogen levels in soil will decrease the flavor of your carrots. Sow seeds directly into the garden several weeks ahead of the last frost (in warm climates you can sow in fall, winter, and spring). Sow seeds around ½ inch deep and thin to 3 to 4 inches apart. Thin early before the roots entwine and be careful to not damage the remaining plants.

Plant onions, leeks, rosemary, and sage to deter the carrot fly. Other good companions include lettuce, onions, chives, beans (which are a good source of nitrogen and can help increase your carrots' flavor), peas, peppers, radish, and tomatoes. Tomatoes can stunt the carrot's growth but they will have a great flavor. Bad companions for the carrot are dill and parsnip. If you want to use carrots to attract insects, they need to be able to flower, so plant a few carrots with the intention of leaving them in the ground instead of harvesting them for eating.

Cauliflower

Cauliflower likes a full-sun location in a well-drained soil. Purchase nursery stock to get a jump on the season or sow outdoors after danger of frost has past. Sow in small clusters of several seeds but once they have sprouted, keep only the strongest cauliflower plants. Keep the plants moist when they are young.

For growing instructions and companions, see cabbage as most members of the brassica family have similar growing requirements.

Celery

Celery needs to have a lot of sunshine but can have partial sun for half of the day. Celery requires a rich, moist soil. It is easiest to work with plants from the nursery that you can transplant into the garden when there is no danger of a frost. Plant 8 to 10 inches apart and be generous with compost and water over the growing season.

Good companion plants for celery include beans, leeks, onions, spinach, tomato, and the brassica family. Garlic and chives help keep aphids away from celery. If bush beans and celery grow together, they will strengthen each other. Friends to celery include cosmos, daisies, and snapdragons. Bad companions for celery are corn, lettuce, and aster flowers.

Chard

Chard is an easy-to-grow vegetable. It prefers full sunlight
unless you live in a hot climate where they prefer partial
shade. Well-drained soil with
compost helps chard produce
well. For most climates, sow
the seeds in the spring and
thin to 8 inches apart when

the seedlings are about 6 inches high. You can either eat these seedlings or
transport them to another spot in the garden.

Good companions for chard include beans, brassica family members, and
onions. There are no known bad companions.

Corn

Corn likes full sun and a rich, well-draining soil covered in mulch. Sow
several seeds in a hill approximately 1 inch deep and 6 inches apart. When
seedlings are close to 4 inches tall, thin them to 1 foot apart. Corn needs a
steady supply of water and mulch.

Corn helps beans when grown together (as in the Three Sisters example)
and sunflowers, legumes, peanuts, squash, cucumbers, melons, amaranth,
white geranium, lamb's quarters, morning glory, parsley, and potatoes all
help corn. Marigolds help to deter the Japanese beetle away from corn.
Planting radishes around corn and letting them go to seed deters an insect
called a corn borer, which is known to be a pest for several agricultural
crops. Bad companions for corn are tomato and celery. Pigweed is said to
raise nutrients from the deeper earth level to a place where the corn can
reach them.

Cucumber

Cucumbers like full sun and can also do well with afternoon shade. Seeds are sown several inches deep a couple of weeks after danger of frost has passed and once the soil has warmed slightly. Plant the bush varieties approximately 1½ feet apart and the vine varieties 2 to 3 feet apart.

Cucumbers have many good companions including corn, beans, sunflowers, peas, beets, and carrots. Radishes can deter cucumber beetles. Keeping dill close to cucumbers attracts beneficial predators and cucumbers attract ground beetles. Nasturtiums improve the cucumbers' growth and flavor. Bad companions for cucumbers include tomatoes and sage.

Eggplant

Eggplant loves heat, so plant it where it can have full sun. It is easiest to purchase started plants then transplant them when there is no longer any danger of frost. It is preferable to wait a week or two after frost has passed to allow the soil to warm up. There are dwarf and standard varieties of eggplant. Plant the standard versions approximately 1½ to 2 feet apart and the dwarf varieties can be 1 to 1½ feet apart. Tie the taller varieties to stakes to keep the fruit from touching the ground.

Good companions for the eggplant include amaranth, peas, spinach, and marigolds, which deter nematodes. Eggplant helps beans and peppers. They are good to plant with corn as they deter raccoons from eating the corn and the corn protects the eggplant from a virus that causes wilt. Bad companions for eggplants are pole beans, fennel, and potatoes. There are mixed results when planted with aromatic herbs.

Horseradish

This is an easy plant to grow and will take over your garden in no time. Find a corner away from most of the plants and consider planting horseradish in containers. It is easiest to purchase a small plant from the nursery and it will grow in most conditions. Plant 1 foot apart and bury the top of the root 4 inches below the surface. Make sure you water this plant well.

If you grow this plant in a container, you can move the containers around. Keep 1 plant in the potato patch to deter the blister beetle and help deter Colorado potato beetle. Horseradish also improves the potatoes' resistance to disease. If you are going to plant it in the potato patch, be sure to dig it up and remove it in the fall to prevent the plant from spreading.

Kohlrabi

Kohlrabi is a cooler weather vegetable that can be planted for both spring and fall crops. Plant in full sun and in well-drained soil. Sow seeds outside four weeks before the last frost. Plant the seeds ½ inch deep and 3 inches apart but thin them to 6 inches when the seedlings  are several inches high, which will not take very long as these plants are very fast growing.

Kohlrabi is a good companion with cucumbers, beets, onions, and chives and appears to help protect members of the mustard family. It is a bad companion to strawberries, tomatoes, peppers, and pole beans.

Leeks

Leeks like a full-sun location that offers well-drained soil. It is easiest to buy leek plants to transplant into the garden around the time of the last frost. Place the seedlings approximately 6 inches apart. Set the plants closer together if you are planting long,

thin-stemmed varieties or set them wider apart for thick-stemmed varieties. (Always check the package for specific planting instructions.) Make a hole and set the seedling down so that only an inch of the top of the plant is exposed. Fill it in loosely with soil.

Leeks will improve the growth for celery, onions, and apple trees. Carrots help leeks by repelling carrot flies. Bad companions for leeks are legumes including beans and peas.

Lettuce

Lettuce does best with a mixture of sun and shade. It does not like extreme heat and will need shade during the hottest months or else it will go to seed. Sow the seeds outdoors once the ground has thoroughly thawed and can be worked. If you purchased plants, set them approximately 1 foot apart (this may vary based on the variety so read the label) and sow several times for a lettuce supply all summer.

Lettuce does well when close to radish, onions, kohlrabi, beans (both bush and pole), cucumbers, carrots, strawberries, beets, and sunflowers. Chives and garlic are great deterrents of aphids so plant them close to lettuce. Mints like hyssop and sage repel slugs so plant these plants close to your lettuce if slugs are a problem in your area. Lettuce is a bad companion to celery, cabbage, and parsley.

Onions

Onions are another plant where it helps to purchase plants at a nursery instead of starting the plant from seeds. You can transplant onions into your garden up to two months before the last frost is expected. Any earlier than this and it could be too cold for them. They like a partial to sunny spot and appreciate compost. Make sure the soil is dug over well to allow for good bulb development and weed constantly in the early growth stage as the weeds can crowd out the young onion plants. As the bulbs grow, make sure to keep them covered if they start to push out of the ground.

Good companions for the onion include all the brassicas, beets, lettuce, tomatoes, summer savory, leeks, kohlrabi, dill, lettuce, and tomatoes. Plant onions in the strawberry patch to help the strawberries stay healthy and fight off disease. Pigweed has the ability to raise the nutrients from subsoil and makes them available to the onions. Bad companions for onions are peas, beans, and parsley.

Peas

Several types of peas are available for today's gardener including garden peas, snow peas, and snap peas. They all like a sunny exposure and a rich soil. Sow the seeds in the garden a month before the last frost and make sure there is support, like a trellis, fence,

or netting of some kind, ready for them. Plant the seeds 1 inch deep and approximately 3 inches apart in rows and keep 3 feet between rows. Peas germinate quickly and you will need to start the vines twining up the support very quickly. Plant peas several times to keep a fresh supply of peas all years long.

Peas are good companions to carrots, turnips, radishes, cucumbers, corn, beans, celery, chicory, eggplant, parsley, and potatoes. Bad companions for peas include garlic and onions as they stunt the growth of the peas.

Peppers, Bell

Peppers are sensitive to cold so it helps to get a jump on the season by purchasing started plants at the nursery then transplanting them outdoors several weeks after the danger of frost has passed. Set them 1 foot apart in the garden and add in stakes for the varieties that will grow more than 1 foot high. They like full sun and a well-drained soil. You can sprinkle Epsom salts around the plants to supply the magnesium they need for good development.

Good companions for bell peppers are basil, okra, marjoram, parsley, lovage, and carrots. They also do well if planted closely with other peppers and tomatoes as long as the crowded leaves offer the peppers shelter from direct sunlight. The presence of geraniums and petunias also helps peppers. Bad companions include fennel and kohlrabi.

Peppers, Hot

There are many varieties of chili peppers to choose from and most transplant well and fruit heavily. You can sow seeds or purchase started plants from the nursery. Sow seeds in a full-sun location after danger of frost has passed. Peppers need a lot of water but do not let them sit in water. They are fast growing plants and the fruit only takes a week or so to ripen on the vine. The more you pick the plant, the more peppers will grow.

Hot peppers are good companions for chard, cucumbers, eggplant, escarole, tomato, okra, and squash. Companion plants that are good for hot peppers include basil, parsley, oregano, and rosemary. The root of the hot chili plant excretes a substance that prevents root rot and other Fusarium diseases that are responsible for wilt in cantaloupe and muskmelon.

Potato

Potatoes like full sun and a well-drained soil high in phosphorus but low in nitrogen. Nitrogen prevents the potatoes from fully growing their foliage. The ground needs to be well dug 1 foot deep for them to form properly. Plant potatoes a couple  of weeks before the last frost has passed. You can plant the seed potatoes whole or cut larger ones into smaller pieces, making sure each piece has several eyes. The simplest way to plant potatoes is to plant them 7 to 8 inches deep and about 1 foot apart from each other (cut side down). The stems will grow up to the surface. For easier harvesting, plant potatoes in a trench and cover with several inches of soil. When the stems are 6 to 8 inches tall, hill mulch around the plant, leaving just the foliage showing. As the plant grows, hill more mulch around it. The potatoes will form inside the mulch.

Horseradish is a plant that will help potatoes. Good companions for potatoes are bush beans, brassicas, carrots, celery, corn, marigold peas, onions, and peas. Flowers that complement potatoes are petunia and marigold, which deters beetles. Bad companions for potatoes include sunflowers, cucumbers, kohlrabi, pumpkin, eggplant, the squash family, turnip, and fennel. Both tomatoes and potatoes are prone to the same blight so keep them apart to avoid contaminating each other.

Pumpkins

Pumpkin requires a long growing season to allow the fruit to produce and ripen, so it helps to shorten this time by purchasing the plants from the nursery or start the seeds indoors. Plant outdoors three to four weeks before the last expected frost. Pumpkin likes full sun and a light, well-drained soil. Give the plants at least 5 feet of space in every direction as they like to sprawl out. As the vines spread out, you can place the vines in the direction you want them to spread throughout the garden. Once the fruits appear, pinch the vines back so the energy goes into the fruit. Do not harvest the pumpkins until after vines have died but make sure you harvest them before freezing temperatures hit.

Good companions for pumpkins include corn, melon, and squash. Buckwheat, catnip, tansy, and radishes all help pumpkins and they attract spiders and ground beetles, keeping these insects away from the pumpkin. Radishes will keep the flea beetles away; marigolds will deter beetles; and nasturtium will deter beetles and various bugs.

Radish

There are literally hundreds of radish varieties you can plant in your garden. They are all quite simple, easy to cultivate, and can be sown a month before the last frost. Plant seeds in spring or winter (check seed packet for instructions) but plant the seeds ½ inch deep and try to thin to 6 inches apart. You can try spreading the seed thinly then covering it with a mulch. You can plant new sowings every week up until the hot summer months. They prefer cooler weather and intense heat will turn them bitter.

Radishes are a good companion to have in the garden as they deter against cucumber beetles and rust flies. Good companions for radishes include beets, bush beans, pole beans, carrots, chervil, cucumber, lettuce, melons, peas, and spinach. Radish will attract an insect called leaf miners away from spinach yet the leaf miners, although they will eat the radish leaves, do not harm the root from growing. Radishes will deter spider mites when planted close to tomatoes. Radish is thought to protect all members of the squash family from the squash borers. If you plant leaf lettuce close by in summer, it will help the radishes become more tender.

Chervil and nasturtium are known to improve the growth and flavor of radishes with the added value of letting them go to seed to repel squash borers. Bad companions for radishes include cabbage, cauliflower, kohl-rabi, broccoli, turnips, and Brussels sprouts as well as the hyssop plant.

Rhubarb

Rhubarb is available in most nursery centers as a crown. It can be planted in early spring as soon as the ground can be worked. Find a location off to one side in full sun so it can grow undisturbed year after year. Plant at least 1 foot deep with at least 3 feet between the plants. Set deep enough in the ground that the new buds are covered by 1 to 2 inches of dirt. When the shoots emerge, place mulch around them. Rhubarb appreciates mulch and compost when available throughout the season. Snap off the seed heads to have the plant continue producing stalks.

Rhubarb is a good companion for the brassica family. You can add any of the family to your rhubarb patch and watch them do well. Rhubarb is a good companion to columbines as it helps deter red spider mites. Rhubarb also helps protect beans against black fly. There are no known bad companions for rhubarb.

Shallots

Shallots belong in the same family as garlic and onions and like garlic. The shallot bulb will grow other bulbs around it. Like onions, you want the soil well dug over and loose for the bulb to form properly. Plant the bulbs roots down with the tops even to the surface and around 8 inches apart from each other.

Good companions for the shallot are the same as for garlic and onions as they grow well with most garden vegetables. Bad companions for the shallot are peas and beans.

Spinach

Spinach is a great cool weather crop so sow for spring and summer harvest or sow in late summer for fall harvest. It will go to seed quickly in intense summer heat. Plant in full sun for cool weather and shadier areas for late summer planting. Sow into the ground as soon as it can be easily  dug over and two months ahead of the last expected frost. Sow seeds ½ inch deep and 2 inches apart in rows. This plant can be sown several weeks in a row. Thin seedlings to 6 inches apart with the leaves about 4 inches tall. You do not want spinach to be crowded as that can cause them to run to seed early.

Peas and beans are good companions to spinach as they can take advantage of the shade of the vines' height. Spinach is compatible with cabbage, cauliflower, celery, eggplant, onion, and strawberries. There are no known bad companions for spinach.

Soybeans

Plant soybeans after the last frost for your area in a full-sun location. Plant seeds 2 inches apart in rows that are 2 feet apart. Soybeans tolerate drought well but they will produce more if they are kept moist throughout the growing season.

Soybeans attract rabbits so only plant them if you are willing to share or if you have a secure, rabbit-proof garden. They are good companions to corn as they add nitrogen to the soil. There is some question as to whether they attract or dispel beetles.

Squash

Squash is one of the easiest vegetables to grow, and with so many colors and varieties available, they offer a lot of interest to any garden. You can start seeds indoors or purchase started plants from the nursery. Read the labels on the seed package for insect-resistant strains that are now available. (You can look on the package to tell whether your squash variety is insect resistant.) Plant in a full-sun location with a well-drained soil several weeks after the last expected frost. Plant two plants together in a hill to the same depth as the pot they are leaving. Plant the hills 3 to 4 feet apart.

You can include a good companion for squash by sowing radish seeds in the hill with the young plants and letting the radishes go to seed instead of harvesting them. Like with cucumbers, radishes will prevent insects on the squash plants. Other companion plants include cucumbers, corn, melon, and pumpkin. Borage will help to deter worms and improve the squash's growth and flavor. Marigolds help deter beetles and nasturtium helps deter squash bugs and beetles. Oregano provides general pest protection. Squash, like pumpkin, is helped by buckwheat, catnip, and tansy, all of which attract spiders and ground beetles, keeping them away from the squash plants.

Tomatoes

Tomatoes are technically a fruit but as everyone considers them a vegetable, they will be included here. Buy tomato plants from the nursery (or start indoors or in a greenhouse) and plant outdoors after all danger of frost has passed. Tomatoes like heat so give them a full-sun location out of the wind. Like most garden vegetables, they prefer mulch and compost. Dig a large hole (1 foot across) and place compost inside. Set the plants 1 to 1½ feet apart (read the label for more specific instructions). Plant them deep, leaving the top four branches exposed to encourage root development. You can cover young plants with floating covers, which are plastic sheets or tunnels made of special polyester with pores big enough to let in water and air but small enough to keep out insects. These covers help protect plants from wind and cooler temperatures. You can also cut a 6 inch-wide collar or disk with the plant in the center to deter cutworms. Tomatoes require a lot of water so water often and they appreciate compost tea every week for optimum fruiting. Do not water tomatoes from the top – they do better if watered at ground level.

Tomato plants are good companions to roses (protecting them from black spot), peppers, and asparagus (protecting the asparagus from the asparagus beetle). There are many good companions for tomatoes including beans, celery, cucumbers, head lettuce, onion, parsley, and peppers. Garlic between the tomatoes will deter spider mites. Flowers to companion plant with tomatoes include nasturtium, marigolds (as they deter nematodes), and pot marigold (as it deters tomato worm and many general garden pests). Basil will repel flies and mosquitoes along with improving the growth and flavor of the tomatoes.

If stinging nettles are planted close, they will improve the tomatoes' ability to keep longer after being picked. Borage will deter tomato worms and improve the tomato's flavor and growth. Dill is only a companion plant to tomatoes until it matures. While dill is young, it improves growth and health of tomatoes, but after it matures, it will retard the tomato plant's growth. Bad companions include kohlrabi, which stunts the tomato's growth, and all members of the brassica family. Keep tomato and potatoes apart as they can suffer from similar strains of a fungal disease and can contaminate each other. Tomatoes do well with carrots but the carrot's growth may be stunted. However, the carrots will have a sweet flavor when planted with tomatoes. You can plant a few close to the tomatoes then plant rows of carrots elsewhere for harvesting. Other bad companions for the tomato include eggplant and peppers (as they share similar blight issues) and fennel, which can inhibit the tomato plant's growth. Also do not plant tomatoes close to corn as the tomato fruitworm is very similar to the corn earworm and you may end up with both pest problems.

Turnips

Turnips are easy to grow and are easy to store over winter, like potatoes. There are several varieties to choose from, most with similar growing conditions. Turnips like a full sun and well dug, loose soil for the bulbs to develop. Plant the seeds approximately  ½ inch deep and 6 inches apart. Plant rows 1 foot apart. Keep the turnips free of weeds, especially when they are young.

Good companions for turnips are peas and vetch, which deter the aphids that tend to plague turnip tops. Bad companions include hedge mustard and knotweed. To minimize pest and disease problems, do not rotate the turnip bed location with the cabbage family.

CASE STUDY: COLLEEN VANDERLINDEN

Garden writer and blogger
www.inthegardenonline.com

Colleen Vanderlinden is the organic gardening expert for the Web site About.com and the author of Edible Gardening for the Midwest. She also blogs about gardening at her personal garden blog, In the Garden Online.

"I can't imagine not growing vegetables. The fact that $2 spent on seeds results in hundreds of pounds of food for my family still amazes me. I find myself devoting more of my yard to edibles, sticking containers anywhere I can find a bright spot of sun. As far as addictions go, vegetable gardening is a pretty harmless one!

I primarily use interplanting in my garden, mainly because I garden on a small urban lot and space is at a premium. Being able to use one area of the garden for two (and sometimes more) crops just makes sense for my situation. I also do some companion planting to help with pest control, particularly for thwarting tomato hornworm, which can be a big problem for those of us who are always trying to 'push' the season and get our tomatoes planted extra-early.

Tomatoes with borage is probably my favorite companion planting combination. If you plant borage near your tomatoes, you won't have a hornworm problem. And borage is a beautiful, useful plant in its own right. If you plant nasturtiums near your potatoes, they help deter Colorado potato beetles. I made the mistake of planting nasturtiums, for the edible flowers, near my Brussels sprouts one year. The only problem is that nasturtiums attract aphids like crazy, and soon I was dealing with aphids on my Brussels sprouts as well.

I also like to sow lettuce seed near newly-transplanted tomato, pepper, and eggplant seedlings. You can harvest baby lettuce leaves for several weeks before the tomatoes get large enough to completely take over the area. Finally, you can't go wrong with a traditional Three Sisters garden of corn, squash, and beans. They just work so well together, and it really does cut down on work for you as the gardener. I have tried interplanting (or intercropping) as well as pairing vegetables with herbs or flowers that will improve the growth and flavor of the vegetable, or, in some cases, confuse insect pests, keeping them away from the vegetables.

My advice to gardeners is to start small. It's so easy to keep buying seeds and trying new varieties, but things can become very overwhelming. Plant those foods you know your family will eat. Spend time daily with your plants. That will help you recognize little problems, such as pest or disease issues, before they become big problems. Be willing to try new things and experiment. Just because a book or magazine article says something will work (or won't work) doesn't always mean it is true. You just don't know what will work in your garden until you try."

• CHAPTER 8 •

Annuals for Your Garden

Annuals are plants that germinate, grow to produce flowers, and then die all in the same season. In horticulture, most people refer to an annual as a plant that grows for just one season. However, that classification can include perennials and biennials grown as annuals. For example, carrots and celery are biennials that are often grown as annual crops. Tomatoes and peppers would also be considered perennials that are grown as annuals. Ornamental perennials that are often grown as annuals include impatiens, begonia, petunias, and even snapdragons. Then there are the biannual hollyhock and pansy that are often grown as annuals. Marigolds and zinnia are examples of true annuals. Gardeners tend to define plants by the most common classification and not by their true classifications.

The annual cycle can be very quick – from less than one month to seeding or it can go for the duration of the growing season for several month-long cycles. There are also winter annuals that have an annual life cycle but will germinate in the fall or winter and bloom in late fall, winter, or early spring. These plants tend to be low to the ground where they are sheltered somewhat from the winter temperature extremes. Examples of these types of winter annuals include chickweed and winter cress.

This chapter looks at the well-loved annuals that create a beautiful splash of color in any garden. Annuals come in all different sizes, types of foliage, and flower colors. Companion planting with annuals refers to the birds, insects, and butterflies that they attract for the benefit of all plants in the garden. All known good companion plants have been noted; however, there is little information available on poor companions for flowers and shrubs. Those that are known have been listed.

Alyssum (Lobularia maritima)

This annual, also known as sweet alyssum, will feature bright white, pink, yellow, or purple flowers from summer to fall. There are several popular varieties with some growing as small as 4 inches and others growing up to 3 feet tall. They like full-sun locations and a well-drained soil. Sow seeds outdoors after the last frost or purchase some of the readily available plants at a nursery centers in early spring. The plant is great as a ground cover anywhere in the garden and will hang down over rocks and edgings for a cascade of color.

Sweet alyssum is a great plant for the garden as it attracts and shelters ground beetles and spiders. It also attracts bees. The variety Basket of Gold is a perennial that is a good companion to other annuals like creeping phlox, stonecrop, false rock cress, and hens and chicks.

Amaranth (Amaranthaceae)

The name amaranth is confusing in that it represents a family of more than 60 different plants. Some people would recognize the name as a grain or cereal, others as a leaf vegetable, many would consider it a noxious weed commonly known as pigweed, but it probably most commonly known in North America as a hardy annual ornamental plant such as the love-lies-bleeding. If these plants were lined up they would hardly be recognizable as being from the same family because they are so diverse in looks and color. Globe amaranths offer puffball flowers in pink, reds, and cream colors and they make great dried flowers. The love-lies-bleeding plant is a stunning display of foliage and color growing from 3 to 8 feet tall in a full-sun location.

The leaves and the seeds are edible, as is the large tassel flower available in bright red to various purple shades. It makes a great shade plant and trellis plant for vines or those plants that need cover. It helps corn grow better and is known to be a host for predatory ground beets.

Bachelor's Buttons (Centaurea cyanus)

This popular annual is known by several names including cornflower, mountain bluet, and Boutonniere flower. The flower's name comes from the fact the small, 1-inch flowers fit perfectly in the buttonholes of suits. This is another excellent flowering plant as it blooms from late spring to summer with fluffy flowers ranging in color from pink to deep purple with the most common color being blue. They are grown from seed early indoors or directly into the garden in early spring. Do not transplant the started plants into the garden until after the last frost. Bachelor's buttons are known to like full sun but they will also do well in other location and will tolerate dry and average soil. Do not let the plants sit in water. They will flower through light frosts in the fall. Some people consider this plant a wildflower.

They are a welcome addition to the garden as they are one of the first flowers to bloom, offering early nectar for many beneficial insects in the garden. Good companions include coreopsis, gayfeather, lady's mantle, Shasta daisy, and yarrow.

Blue-eyed African Daisy (Osteospermum fruticosum)

Unlike most of the daisy family, which are perennials, this flower is an annual. All daisy varieties are easy to grow. You can plant the seeds outside after frost has passed or indoors during the winter and set the plants out after the frost danger has passed. This plant offers beautiful daisy-like flowers in a wide variety of colors. It will grow 2 to 3 feet tall.

This annual is a great companion plant for any of the cabbage family and tomato family. It offers nectar that attracts and keeps a large selection of beneficial insects.

Calendula (Calendula officinalis)

These are also called pot marigolds and come in orange, yellow, and pale lemon colored blooms on long stems and resemble marigolds. They grow up to 2 feet tall. The plants are prolific with blooms extending from early summer throughout the fall until frost hits. These plants will flower, seed, and then reseed the following spring so they need to be in a location where they can stay for years. Space these plants about 15 inches apart.

They are known to attract a wide range of beneficial insects so plant them anywhere and everywhere throughout the garden.

Calliopsis (Coreopsis tinctoria)

There are both annuals and perennials within this family and this flower is the most common of the annuals. The plant blooms from midsummer to fall with loads of vibrant yellow, daisy-like flowers that have a red band on the petals. They grow 2 to 3 feet high. Sow this plant thickly outdoors in early spring with a second crop in midsummer for fall flowers.

This annual is a great companion for tomatoes and peppers as they attract hoverflies, spined soldier bugs, and tachinid flies and keep them away from the vegetables.

Candytuft (Iberis)

This early-blooming annual, which has some perennials in the family, offers profuse clusters of flowers in white, pink, purple, and red shades. It grows naturally in a mound approximately 10 inches high and wide. Sow the seeds indoors to get a jump on the blooms or sow them outdoors after frost has past. The mounds create an interesting edging along any section of the garden.

This annual is known to attract hoverflies and protect ground beetles. Good companion plants for candytuft include basket-of-gold, gloxinia, peony, creeping phlox, and cushion spurge.

Cosmos (Cosmos)

This tall, fast-growing annual is a gem for any garden and is easy to grow. It offers white, pink, and red blooms with yellow centers all on top of feathery leaves. Sow seeds outdoors after danger of frost has passed. These plants will easily reseed so be prepared  for new flowers to pop up everywhere. Thin these plants to approximately

18 inches apart. They prefer full sun to partial shade and will do well in average and poor soil. They are also tolerant of dry soil, making them excellent for the beginning gardener.

The white sensation variety is very good for attracting beneficial insects such as parasitic wasps, hoverflies, tachinid flies, and bees.

Cypress Vine (Ipomoea quamoclit)

The cypress vine is also known as hummingbird flower and star glory. This flowering vine is a fast growing member of the morning glory family. It is an easy to grow annual that will reach 10 to 15 feet in a single season. All summer, the plant will produce hundreds of small, star-shaped flowers that can be red, pink, or white. If you pick off dead flowers, the plant will produce even more. The plant does need structural support of some kinds like a trellis or fence. These vines are grown from seeds sowed directly into the garden after danger of frost is over. Choose a full-sun location in rich, well-drained soil. The seeds will sprout within a week and should be thinned to 1 foot apart. They will re-seed if you allow the pods to open and drop their seeds.

The plant is well-named as the hummingbirds love these bright flowers. The plant is also known to attract butterflies.

Dwarf Morning Glory (Convolvulus tricolor)

This annual comes as a vine or a bushy plant that blooms from midsummer through the fall. It produces blue and white funnel-shaped flowers with some producing rose and pink flowers. The bush plant grows to 1 to 2 feet tall whereas the vine will easily

reach 10 feet within a few months. All varieties are easy to grow from seed and can be sown outdoors a couple of weeks before the last frost. The seeds germinate faster if they are soaked overnight before going in the ground. They make a great looking border plant.

Be warned that the flower is poisonous. It is known to attract hoverflies and ladybugs.

Gazania (Gazania rigens)

This plant is considered an annual in the North but a short-lived perennial in the southern United States (zones 9 through 10). Gazania blooms in late spring to summer and has yellow, orange, and red daisy-like flowers with dark centers. They grow from 6 to 16 inches high. The plants are easy to grow as they are drought tolerant and do well in poor soil. They make a great ground cover. An odd characteristic of the plant is that the flowers close in low sunlight and open up in strong light.

They are a great companion plant as they offer a long blooming season and are popular with ladybugs and spined soldier beetles.

Geraniums (Pelargonium)

Geraniums are another easy to grow annual and are wonderful for both your garden and in containers with their bright red, white, and pink blooms. There are many different varieties, including trailing and scented. They can be sown from seed, rooted from cuttings *(see Chapter 4 for more information on cuttings),* or bought in spring from nursery centers. They are happiest in full sun and partial shade and do well in most soil conditions. They will flower from early summer until a killing frost. When the weather gets cold, lift the plants and replant them into containers to bring indoors where they will happily bloom throughout the winter.

Geraniums are good companions to roses, grapes, corn, tomatoes, cabbage, and peppers. They are known to repel cabbage worms and Japanese beetles (white geraniums especially) and will deter beet leafhopper.

Larkspur (Consolida orientalis)

Larkspur, often called by its sister's name of delphinium, is a popular flower with its tall spikes of pink, blue, red, or white flowers. It is an early bloomer and blooms several weeks before other flowers. There are many varieties of larkspur and the plants can range from 1 foot high to 7 feet high. They like full sun to partial shade and do well in average soils. Sow the seeds after all danger of frost has passed and thin seedlings to 1 foot apart. Once mature, the plants can be divided by the roots

and the new plant moved to a new location. *For more information, look under delphinium in Chapter 9 on perennials.*

Larkspur is poisonous to humans and cattle so do not plant where livestock can eat them. They are known to attract Japanese beetles. The beetles feed on the foliage, which poisons them. They are also poisonous to most insects including aphids and thrips.

Marigolds (Tagetes)

Marigolds make a great addition to any garden for their long-lasting bloom-ing period. The plants come in single or double flowers in colors including yellow, orange, red, and even rust. There are varieties that reach 5 inches to giant varieties that

can grow up to 4 feet tall. They can be sown indoors early in the planting season or outdoors in early spring. Transplant to the garden after all danger of frost has passed. Young plants are readily available in springtime from nursery centers. Marigolds are very tolerant of average to poor soil but will do better in a rich soil environment.

Most insects do not like marigolds and will avoid being in the area where the plant grows, making them a great companion plant. The Lemon Gem variety is especially attractive to beneficial insects, bringing in hoverflies and parasitic wasps.

The following are types of marigolds you may want to consider adding into your companion garden.

- **French Marigold *(Tagetes patula)*** is one variety that has roots that exude a chemical substance that kills nematodes. If you need nem-atode control, plant many marigolds close together. This chemical stays in the soil for longer than one year so the benefit is long lasting. These marigolds are also known to deter whiteflies when planted around tomatoes. Do not plant this variety next to bean plants – they are not good companions.

- **Mexican marigold** *(Tagetes minuta)* is reputed to be the most powerful at repelling insects and is known to inhibit weed growth – even affecting bind weed, a noxious weed that is almost impossible to get rid of. This marigold is supposed to repel the Mexican bean beetle and even rabbits as the smell is so strong. It is not a good companion to beans and cabbage because it has an inhibiting effect on their growth.

Mexican Sunflower (Tithonia rotundifolia)

This annual blooms all summer long with bright red-orange, daisy-like flowers that are 2 to 3 inches across. The plant grows from 3 to 5 feet high so plant them at the back of the garden. They might need support if you live in a windy area. They grow well from seed either indoors or outdoors after the last frost has passed and the soil has warmed. Keep soil moist until properly sprouted. They do not like the cold so grow them in full sun and they will tolerate most soil conditions as long  as the soil is well-drained. They are drought tolerant. *See sunflowers in this chapter for more information.*

These flowers make great companion plants with tomatoes, peppers, and eggplants. They attract beneficial wasps, flies, and the spined soldier bug, as well as provide shelter for spiders. There is an added benefit to this annual – butterflies love them.

Nasturtiums (Tropaeolum majus)

This easy growing annual offers multitudes of blooms and prefers to be ignored. There are bushy plants, trailing plants, and climbers to add lots of variety to your garden. It likes a full-sun location but will do fine in partial- shade. It needs to have a dry location and will prosper in poor soil. Sow seeds approximately 1 foot apart after the last frost. Nasturtium leaves and flowers are edible, having a slight peppery taste, but you should pick them while they are young. The seedpods can also be used as a substitute for capers.

Nasturtiums make an excellent companion plant for cucumbers, tomatoes, cabbage, and at the base of fruit trees as insects are attracted to them and therefore stay away from the crops. It is known to deter whiteflies, wooly aphids, squash bug, cucumber beetles, and other pests. It is also a trap cop for black aphids. Fruit growers are known to plant nasturtiums close to the root zone of fruit trees, which allows the roots to pick up the pungent odor of the plant to repel bugs without affecting the fruit.

Petunias (Petunia)

Petunias are annuals in North American but are perennials in South America. They grow approximately 1 foot high and produce bright flowers in an amazing array of colors. They are common in gardens and containers as they are easy to grow. They are often grown from seed indoors early or sown directly into the ground early in the season. They are also readily available from most garden centers. Petunias like full-sun exposure and love a rich and loose soil with good drainage although they will tolerate poorer soil.

Petunias are known to repel the asparagus beetle, leafhoppers, tomato worms, Mexican bean beetles, aphids, and many general garden pests. As such, plant them everywhere in the garden. The leaves have additional useful properties as they can be made into an insect spray.

Sunflower (Helianthus annuus)

There are many varieties of sunflowers and some will grow as high as 20 feet tall with blooms as big across as 2 feet. Giant sunflowers are any variety that grows taller than 10 feet or that has enormous flower heads. Sow the seeds outdoors in the garden approximately 3 feet apart. Keep the rows 3 feet apart as well. They like a sunny location where the tall stalks can be protected from the wind. They grow well in average soil but need to be able to spread their roots for stability so sandy soil is not recommended.

Sunflowers make a great companion plant for corn as it is supposed to increase the yield. They also have an interesting relationship with ants and aphids as the ants will herd the aphids onto the stalks where they can do little damage because the stalks are so tough. Plant sunflowers wherever aphids are a problem and you will find the problem disappear. The sunflower also attracts hoverflies, lacewings, parasitic wasps, tachinid flies, and bees. Sunflowers also attract many birds including hummingbirds.

Swan River Daisy (Brachycome iberidifolia)

This beautiful plant resembles the aster plant with its pink, blue, violet, or white blooms and can grow 10 to 18 inches tall. Sow the seeds directly outdoors in early spring after the last frost, sow early indoors and transplant after last frost, or purchase young plants from your local garden center. They like a full-sun location and a rich, well-drained soil.

This annual is a good companion plant for fall lettuces, spinach, and onions. It is known to attract tachinid flies.

Sweet Peas (Lathyrus)

There are both annual and perennial varieties of sweet peas available. The annual variety can be started from seeds six weeks before the last frost and then moved out to the garden. They all like a sunny location with well-drained soil. The plants will need a support structure of some kind for the plants to climb. There are several dwarf bush types available if that is more suitable for the space in your garden. They are grown for their colorful flower display that shines from spring into the fall. The flowers come in a wide array of colors including red, blue, lavender, pink, and white. They are also available in solid or streaked and mixed colors. They will tolerate a light frost toward the end of the season.

The perennial sweet pea is deer resistant, helping to keep deer out of the garden and minimize damage to the landscape of the garden. Both the annual and perennial varieties are fantastic for attracting butterflies. The perennial is called perennial sweet pea, perennial pea vine, and perennial pea. The perennial sweet pea is an easy to grow vine that grows to 6 feet in height and produces pink and white flowers. Unlike the annual varieties, the perennial sweet pea flowers have no scent. It produces suckers that will need to be cut off to keep the plant in control.

Zinnia (Zinnia)

Zinnias are wonderful plants that come in amazing colors with large blooms that last from midsummer until a hard frost hits. The flowers range in color from white, yellow, orange, red, rose pink, and even blooms that are multi-colored. They are another easy annual to grow. Sow indoors early for transplanting outdoors after frost danger has past or sow directly into the garden early in the season. Space the plants 6 inches apart. There are some giant varieties available and these need to be spaced at least 1 foot apart. These plants are tolerant of most soils but prefer a rich, well-drained location in full-sun.

Zinnias are great companions to beans and can be interplanted nicely with broccoli. Their profuse blooms are great for attracting birds like the hummingbird. They also attract ladybugs, parasitic wasps, parasitic flies, and bees. The pastel-colored bloom varieties make great trap crops for the Japanese beetles. All zinnia varieties attract insect pollinators.

CASE STUDY: DIANE LINSLEY

Diane's Flower Seeds
www.dianeseeds.com

CLASSIFIED CASE STUDIES
™
directly from the experts

Diane Linsley is the owner of Diane's Flower Seeds, an Internet business based in Ogden, Utah. She grows heirloom flowers and vegetables, especially rare perennials and unusual tomatoes.

"You can save seeds from most flowers, except for hybrids, which do not come from saved seed. When going out to harvest seeds, I stuff my pockets with small plastic bags that are perfect for small amounts of seed, or take stainless-steel mixing bowls for larger quantities. I use pruning shears and thorn-proof gloves to harvest the seeds off thorny plants.

The best time to collect seeds is when they are fully ripe. Seeds are produced in either pods or seedheads. Pods have seeds enclosed in a shell and are ready to harvest when they become dry and brittle, just before they split open and spill their contents. Other plants produce seedheads, which are open, instead of being inside a pod, with the seeds exposed. After the seeds are ripe, the seedhead shatters. The trick is to harvest the seeds before this happens. You can feel to see if the seedhead is loose as it will be brown, crunchy, and dry. Some seedheads turn from green to brown before they shatter.

Seeds should be dried in a well-ventilated room (70 to 95 degrees if possible), or they can be dried in a garage out of direct sunlight. Small quantities can be dried in plastic cups, on small plates, or in plastic bags propped open with toothpicks to provide air circulation. A thin layer of seeds will dry more evenly. Turn or stir them every few days. Most seeds require two to six weeks to dry completely, depending on the seed size, temperature, and humidity of the room.

Seeds can be cleaned after they have started drying. The chaff or coating is easier to remove when it is dry, but the seeds will need further drying after cleaning. Cleaning equipment includes different sizes of stainless-steel mixing bowls, a fan, and a kitchen strainer with a metal screen. Small seeds are shaken through the strainer to remove the chaff, which is the dried protective coating on the seeds. They are then passed from one mixing bowl to another in front of a gently blowing fan to remove the dust. Be careful not to blow away the seeds. Larger seeds from seedheads are rubbed between gloved hands to loosen them before being passed in front of a stronger breeze to remove the chaff.

Dry seeds should be stored in a cool, dry, dark place. Well-prepared seeds will remain viable in storage for several years."

A perennial plant is one that lives for more than two years, while a biennial plant is one that has a life cycle lasting only two years. The term perennial generally applies to winter hardy herbaceous plants. However, woody plants like shrubs and trees are considered, on a scientific basis, perennials as well.

Herbaceous perennials are the small, flowering plants that grow and flower in the spring and/or summer then die back in the fall and winter before sprouting again in the spring from the roots. However, there are some plants that although they would be a perennial in warmer climates, they are annuals in colder climates where the severe winter kills the plant off.

Perennials can live for a couple of years or they can live for centuries like trees. There are no defining height requirements for perennials nor are there any restrictions on the type of flowers produced. Perennials include many plant groups including grasses, ferns, shrubs, and trees. They provide great interest and variety, making them an excellent addition to any garden.

Aster (Aster)

Asters are an easy to grow perennial that offer blooms in many colors ranging from blues, pinks, and purples with a yellow center. There are annual and perennial varieties, the most common being the perennial. There are shorter asters at under 1

foot tall, and some that soar 3 and 4 feet tall. Asters can be grown from seed or by dividing mature plants. They are commonly found in nursery centers – in some areas aster is considered a wild plant. For seeds, sow in early spring and cover lightly with soil or mulch. They will germinate quickly and flower by midsummer and continue throughout summer and early fall. The plants will grow well for several years and can be propagated by dividing the main plant and replanting the cut piece into a new location.

Asters are companionable to most vegetables, especially asparagus, as they are known to repel nematodes, beet leaf hopper, and other insects. Avoid planting close to corn as these flowers can transmit disease. The plants themselves are not known for any disease or insect problems. They make great companion plants for Black-eyed Susan, butterfly bush, purple coneflower, sedum, and the silver lace vine.

Astilbe (Astilbe)

This plant is known by many names including false spirea and feather flower. This perennial offers fern-looking flowers throughout the summer. There are many varieties that offer different sizes, foliage color, flowering times, and flowering color. The blooms will last longer if they are planted in a shady location. They do well in most locations and soil conditions although they prefer a well-drained, loamy soil.

The astilbe attracts butterflies into the garden. It makes a great companion plant for bleeding heart, hosta, spiderwort, and rhododendrons.

Balloon Flower (Platycodon grandiflorus)

The balloon flower is another easy to grow perennial. This plant produces balloon-shaped flowers, and if the dead flowers are picked off, it will continue to flower throughout the summer. The plant prefers a well-drained soil but will grow in slightly moist soil. It needs a full-sun to partial-sun location. It is very tolerant of being ignored and does well in rock gardens or as a ground cover.

Good companions for the balloon flower include baby's breath, bellflower, tall phlox, and the Shasta daisy.

Blanket Flower (Gaillardia)

This hardy, drought-tolerant perennial is also known as gaillardia. The blanket flower is easily grown from seed. Sow seeds in a full-sun location in well-drained soil. If the plant does not receive sufficient sunlight, the stalks will tend to droop. The plant typically reaches between 1 and 2 feet in height and the daisy-like blooms come in a variety of colors.

The blanket flower offers great cut flowers for a vase. It is deer resistant and is known to attract many kinds of butterflies. Good companions include daylily, gayfeather, balloon flower, tall bearded iris, yarrow, tickseed, and Black eyed-Susan.

Bleeding Heart (Dicentra)

This plant is also known as dicentra. This perennial is well known for its long stalks of pink, heart-shaped flowers and fine foliage. This plant likes a rich, loose soil that is well-drained with good access to moisture. It likes a full-sun to a partial-shade location. It does not do well in windy locations. Some bushes will reach several feet in height.

Good companion plants for the dicentra include astilbe, forget-me-nots, hosta, lamium, and spiderwort.

Carnation (Dianthus caryophyllus)

Carnations are known under many names like pinks, dianthus, Sweet William, and cheddar pinks. This colorful perennial grows well in well-drained soil in full sun or partial shade. It needs regular watering if there are prolonged dry summers in your area. The blooms come in several colors and many have strong fragrances. They make a great border plant for mass planting.

Carnations are known to attract butterflies and are deer resistant. Good companion plants include campanula, gaillardia, harder geranium, hens and chicks, and coral bells.

Chrysanthemums (Chrysanthemum)

This hardy perennial will likely to be the last bloomer in your garden come fall. It is possible to grow them from seed or from cuttings but they are readily available in nursery centers in both spring and fall. They do well in containers or in the garden in well-drained soil with a full-sun or partial-sun location but can tolerate most locations.

These flowers are popular with a wide variety of insects. The painted daisy variety is known to kill root nematodes. It does well beside broccoli or red cabbage. The flowers have been used as a botanical pesticide. The white chrysanthemum will repel Japanese beetles. Costmary is an herb member of this family and it is known to help repel moths.

See also daisy in this chapter for more information on sister plants.

Creeping Phlox (Phlox subulata)

Many consider the creeping flox a wonderful ground cover by many, and it is covered with small pink flowers in the spring. It is also known as flowering moss, moss phlox, ground pink, and moss pinks. This plant likes a sunny location with well-drained soil and makes a great border plant.

Good companions for the creeping phlox include heartleaf bergenia, dwarf iris, lamb's ear, and even snow-in-the summer. It grows well with spring bulbs like tulips and summer snowflake. It makes a good companion plant for rock cress, Black-eyed Susans, star of Bethlehem, and alyssum.

Daisy (Bellis perennis)

Daisies are a hardy, easy to grow perennial, and there are many varieties to choose from. In most cases, they like rich, well-drained soil in a full-sun location. They also tolerate poorer conditions and less shade. You can sow seeds in early spring one year for blooms the following year or purchase young plants that will flower that year. Divide the plants every few years to allow the plant to grow large flower heads.

Daisies do well with most other plants and particularly well with dianthus, Iberis, and coreposis. Bees love the daisy flower nectar. The flowers also attract butterflies.

Delphinium (Delphinium)

There are both annual and perennial members of the Delphiniums family *(see larkspur in Chapter 8 on annuals for more information)*. All delphiniums are poisonous so consider carefully if you have children or animals around. This plant is easy to grow from seed and can be sown directly in the garden after all danger of frost has passed. Thin the seedlings to 1½ feet apart. They do like full-sun but will do well in partial-shade. They grow fast and will reach several feet in height. The perennial members will need to be divided after several years to stop them from becoming too compact.

Delphiniums are another plant that attracts the Japanese beetle and then kills them as the foliage is poisonous.

Foxglove (Digitalis purpurea)

This is another old-fashioned plant that blooms in early summer in shades of pink, rose, cream, and white with contrasting polka dots. They like a full-sun to partial-shade location and will easily reach a height of 2 to 5 feet depending on the variety. They do well in average soils and cool weather. Sow seeds in the garden after the last frost, and thin the garden plants to 2 feet apart. Be warned the leaves are poisonous.

Foxglove is known to stimulate the growth of tomatoes, potatoes, and even apples and will also help protect them from fungus. It is known for giving strength and longer life for all the plants growing close to it. These properties carry over to the cut flowers as well in that if you place a stalk of foxglove in a vase with other flowers, it will help keep them healthier for longer.

Golden Asters (Chrysopsis)

This perennial is another easy to grow plant as it tolerates neglect and grows well in dry to sandy soil. It will bloom all summer long, offering many yellow, aster-like flowers approximately 1½ inch across. Depending on the variety, the plants reach from 1 to 5 feet in height.

They are good companions to coneflowers, other asters, and goldenrods, offering long-lasting blooms. They attract a wide range of beneficial insects into the garden.

Golden Marguerite (Anthemis tinctoria)

This hardy, long-season bloomer makes a great border plant as it does better in poorer soil and tolerates drought conditions. The plant grows 1 foot tall and offers beautiful golden-yellow daisy-like flowers from May through July. The flowers are  small but as there are always many of them. The plant likes to be in a full-sun or a partial-shade location.

This plant is great for attracting ladybugs and parasitic wasps.

Hosta (Hosta)

The hosta plant is also known as plantain lily. This plant is one of the best for growing in the shade. They are very tolerant of neglect and will continue to grow and multiply year after year. The plants come in various colors of green, yellow variegated with  green, blue, gray, and many with stripes. There are also several different leaf patterns to choose from including round, oval, and even heart shaped. Hostas like moist and preferably well-drained soil.

Good companion plants for hostas include bleeding heart, astilbe, and hardy geranium. Hostas also grow well with spiderwort.

Lamium (Lamium)

Lamium is also known as Spotted Dead Nettle and is another easy to grow perennial for warmer climates or an annual in colder climate. They do well in a partial-shade location with the leaves turning brown if they are under hot sun. The plants need to be 1 foot apart as they will spread outward, making an incredible ground cover under trees and shrubs. They cover the area under weeping trees nicely and fill the space with deep purple blooms. They also come in pink and white flowers. They are ideal ground covers for around hostas, under roses, and between ferns. There are a few species that are considered weeds, but these are generally non-flowering varieties.

Lamium is known to repel the potato bugs. Hellebores is a recommended companion.

Painted Daisy (Tanacetum)

The painted daisy is also known as Pyrethrum. The Tanacetum coccineum varieties are a wonderful splash of color in the garden. With a height of 2 to 3 feet when mature, they make great border plants. They produce daisy-like flowers in reds, purples, pink, or white. The leaves resemble fern leaves. They will bloom in the middle of spring through to summer. Cut them back after flowering to encourage a second blooming period.

The painted daisy has natural insecticidal properties, making it an ideal companion plant to keep insects away. They do well with most plants, in particular strawberries. The painted daisy is known to kill root nematodes and attract tachinid flies, parasitic wasps, and many other beneficial insects. They are believed to repel aphids, leafhoppers, spider mites, harlequin bugs, ticks, and imported cabbage worms among other bugs.

Peony (Paeonia)

There are both tree peonies and regular peonies. The tree peonies have a woody stem and the branches do not die to the ground as the garden peonies do. They all prefer a well-drained soil in a sunny or partially-sunny location where they will not be moved often. It can take a year to establish the peonies but they will live for years. Peonies are offered in many unique colors and there are some with fragrant perfume.

Good companion plants for the peony includes hardy geranium, iris, lady's mantle, and the pincushion flower.

Periwinkle (Vinca)

There are several varieties of periwinkle available. This plant makes a great ground cover as the stems often root where they touch ground. The plant will spread very quickly. There are both evergreen and deciduous species.

The plants produce simple, five-petal flowers usually in violet, blue, and white. The vine is very fast growing and can overwhelm other plants. Many of the periwinkle plants grow well in shade to semi-shaded areas and will also do well in full-sun if watered regularly.

The plant makes a great ground cover to choke out weeds and cover unsightly areas. It is also recommended as a fire retardant ground cover. It is thick and strong enough to be used for erosion control on hillsides as well. It is a great companion plant to most bulbs including crocus, iris, paperwhites, snowdrops, and striped squill. It is a good companion as well to coral bells, ferns, hosta, and Solomon's seal.

Pincushion Flower (Scabiosa)

These attractive perennials offer blue, white, and light purple blooms all summer long. The plants are easy to find at your local nursery. They like a full-sun location in well-drained soil. Set the plants 1 foot apart. These plants, with their 2 to 3 inch blooms, make a great permanent edge on a raised bed.

They are good companions to strawberries, bellflower, daylily, hardy geranium, peonies, and lady's mantle. The pincushion plant is known to attract hoverflies and tachinid flies, and offer the added benefit that butterflies love them.

Purple Coneflower (Echinacea purpurea)

These typical prairie plants are easy to grow. Although most people consider them to have a purple flower, they do come in red, gold, mauve, and white. These plants are grown directly from seed and work great in fields as wildflowers. The mature plants can be divided to create new plants but do so in the spring. Plant in full sun in a well-drained location and space the plants 1 foot apart. Depending on the variety, the plants will reach from 2 to 4 feet in height and will bloom until frost. They are dependable flowering plant and do well in clusters.

These flowers are particularly attractive for birds and butterflies. They will attract beneficial wasp and flies as well as spiders and praying mantis.

Rock Cress (Arabis)

This profuse blooming perennial can be found across all the United States. They flower in the spring and are great for rock gardens and places where it is difficult to grow other plants. You can sow seeds or purchase young plants and when mature, divide them to create new ones. Set plants or thin seeds to 1½ feet apart or closer if you looking for rock cress as a ground cover. They will flower in the second year. Plant in full sun but they are tolerant of partial-shade. They do well in most well-drained soils and they like dry conditions.

Butterflies are attracted to the flowers. As well, rock cress attracts bees and offers shelter to ground beetles and spiders. Good companions include creeping phlox, stonecrop, false rock cress, basket of gold alyssum, bugle-weed, and hens and chicks.

Sea Hollies (Eryngium)

This unique-looking plant has stiff spikes or spiny foliage in a soft, blue-gray color. The flowers are blue domes with silver bracts. The plant can be started from seed but will not flower until the second year. You can also purchase started plants but they may not be readily avail-  able at local nursery centers. However, they are available in mail order cata-logues. The plant grows to 1½ feet high and needs a well-drained soil. It does not like being transplanted so set in a long-term location the first time. The plant with its striking looks is a great front for perennial clusters and taller plants. It is known to attract tiny parasitic wasps like chalcid wasps.

Shasta Daisy (Leucanthemum x superbum)

The Shasta daisy will grow 2 to 3 feet high and give a profusion of white daisy flowers in summer. The plant grows well in dry to moist soil and most soil conditions. This cheerful variety is often thought of as a wildflower but has become a common sight in many gardens. The flowers are great to cut and include in your vases and as they start in late spring throughout most of the summer, they provide a constant supply of flowers.

The Shasta daisy is well known for attracting butterflies. The Shasta daisy is a good companion to the balloon flower and bachelor's buttons. It looks great beside coreopsis, dianthus, Iris, phlox, and daylilies.

Solomon's Seal (Polygonatum)

Solomon's seal is unique with its long fronds and small, white flowers blooming beneath them. They can easily reach 4 to 5 feet tall and make a stunning display even when not flowering. There are solid and variegated varieties available. They like a rich, moist soil in a partial to heavily shaded area.

Solomon's seal is known to attract hummingbirds. Good companion plants include coral bells, hostas, hardy geranium, and ferns.

Spiderwort (Tradescantia)

This perennial has a unique spider web-like leaf pattern with buds that last one day. However, the plant flowers almost continuously for the summer. The plant can grow to 4 feet high so find the best location for this large plant. It is quite adaptable to various soil conditions and almost all sunlight ranges; however, it will need more water if planted in full sun. It makes a great border plant or for mass planting.

Spiderwort is known to attract butterflies. Good companion plants include astilbe, campanula, daylily, hosta, dicentra, and Siberian iris.

Tansy (Tanacetum vulgare)

Tansy is another easy plant that requires little maintenance and should not be confused with tansy ragwort (senecio jacobeae), which is a highly toxic plant, especially to children, pets, and livestock. Tansy is a plant that has begun to grow so rapidly in some parts of

North America that it is considered to be invasive. Common tansy is an herbaceous perennial herb that has flowers that are arranged in flat golden clusters that bloom in July and August. They sit atop feathery, fragrant leaves as tall as 3 feet high. This flower is a member of the thistle family and blooms throughout the summer. The plant can be grown from seed during the spring (after danger of frost has passed) in a full-sun location with average or poor soil. Thin the seedlings to 6 inches apart.

Tansy contains volatile oils, making it a great insect repellant as most of them hate the bitter taste and strong odor. The same oils can cause a rash on your skin too. Tansy makes a good companion to cabbages, roses, cucumbers, squash, raspberries, and grapes, but will help most garden crops. Tansy helps concentrate potassium in the soil, benefiting nearby plants. Tansy is known to repel cutworms, cabbage worms, squash bugs, striped cucumber beetles, Japanese beetles, ants, flies, mosquitoes, and fruit moths. Peach trees benefit from tansy around its trunk in particular. It also helps most fruit trees, roses, raspberries, and blackberries, but be aware it has a tendency to take over an area. It wards off flying insects and keeps borers away. If you chop up some plants and toss them into your compost, it will activate the decomposition process. It works well if tied up and hung on a porch as a fly repellent.

CASE STUDY: BETH TRISSEL

www.bethtrissel.com

Beth Trissel is a successful romance author and gardening specialist with an enthusiasm for all heirloom plants and old-fashioned cottage garden plants. She's been successfully practicing companion planting for decades and focuses on creating wildlife sanctuary gardens that bring in the butterflies, hummingbirds, songbirds, and honeybees.

"We rotate our garden vegetables as well as practice companion planting. There are time-honored combinations we've tried as well as making some of our own discoveries. Some that have worked well include:

- Nasturtiums and radishes planted closely around the cucurbit family (also commonly referred to as the cucumber, gourd, melon, or pumpkin family) help to deter the squash vine borer and cucumber beetles, which are deadly to the plants. This family is our most trouble prone, so it gets the greatest attention when it comes to companion planting.

- Radishes are also a good companion for lettuce, spinach, and carrots.

- Interplanting garlic with roses has beneficial effects in warding off some of the pests and diseases that attack them.

- We've observed that old-fashioned sunflowers with multiple heads (planted by birds from the birdseed variety) grow the best. Sunflowers attract masses of goldfinches, a favorite songbird, and when planted in and around corn, reduce armyworms in the ears.

- Marigolds are an excellent companion plant for vegetables and flowers to help ward off Japanese beetles.

- Borage enriches the soil, attracts honeybees, and is another good friend for squash.

- Onions planted near carrots help repel the carrot fly.

- Tomatoes love basil and grow more robustly when planted near that herb. Sweet peppers also like basil.

- Sweet marjoram is beneficial to interplant with vegetables and flowers.

- Mint helps deter cabbageworms.

- Pumpkins and squash survive better when rotated from their usual spots. This year we tucked a pumpkin in among the massive, native clematis vine growing along the backyard fence that we refer to as 'the beast.' The borers didn't find it, plus 'the beast' cradled the orange globes.

My main recommendation for a healthy garden is to use a lot of compost and natural mulch, like well rotted hay or straw or even leaves as healthy plants better resist insects and disease. Some other tips include:

- Earthworms are a gardener's best friend and thrive in natural mulch, humus-enriched soil. Avoid chemical fertilizers and pesticides or you'll kill the worms and other beneficial insects.

- We clear the vegetable plot in the fall and if possible, till it. If not then, we wait and till in the spring. We've tried the heavy mulch/ no till method, but accumulated an unbelievable number of slugs. Some of them were the size of small bananas and even had nests of babies. Now, we add a lot of compost to the soil in the spring and mulch with organic matter but let it break down over the summer and don't leave it in place for the winter."

In today's gardens, it is hard to determine a wildflower or weed from any of the other plants people have growing in their garden. In truth, a wildflower is one that grows naturally in the wild. When people think about wildflowers, they tend to think of those growing happily in deserted lots, in the ditches along the road, or along the hillside out of town. Many of the cultivated wildflowers started in these lowly beginnings and many can be still found there. However, there is a growing interest in many of them for gardens. After all, they are easy to grow, require little to no attention, and require only the water nature provides. As an added advantage, they will often grow in difficult growing areas, allowing gardeners to brighten and beautify "ugly" corners of their yard.

Wildflower packets are generally a wide variety of seeds mixed up for throwing out in fields and yards for a naturalized look. This type of planting will produce continuous blooms over the spring, summer, and well into the fall. This theme has grown in popularity due to its low-maintenance benefits.

More of these wildflowers have made their way into cultivated gardens and are available in both seed form and from nursery stock.

Black-eyed Susan (Rudbeckia hirta)

Black-eyed Susan, also known as Rudbeckia, is an annual or in some locations a short-lived perennial herb. The plant reaches several feet in height and offers prolific flowering of bright, 3-inch, yellow flower heads that have dark centers all throughout the summer. It appreciates a full-sun location but will adapt to partial-shade. If there is too much shade, the plant will produce fewer flowers. This plant is great for sowing small gardens or for tossing seeds across a large field as wildflowers. As it is great for attracting all kinds of pollinators, spreading this seed in an orchard works well. The plants can be mowed back in the fall after the plants have set seed in late July to mid-August.

It attracts green lacewings, butterflies, honey bees, and bumble bees among other beneficial insects. It is also a good companion plant for coneflower, pennisetum, stonecrop, Russian sage, and garden phlox.

Bushy Aster (Aster dumosus)

This plant is yet a member of the aster family and can usually be found dotting the countryside. It is a perennial that grows to approximately 3-feet tall and has many small flower buds. The flowers are white or a soft mauve with a yellow center and are usually about ½ inch across. Like most other family members, the bushy aster flowers from August to October. Technically this plant could have gone into the bulb section as it spreads under the ground but it is better known as a wildflower.

The seeds of this plant are eaten by the American Goldfinch, sparrows, and chipmunks. The leaves are food for rabbits, deer, the Painted Lady butterfly, as well as many others. The flower attracts pollinators like bees, butterflies, and flies. The plant also attracts insect predators like praying mantis and spiders. Bushy asters are known to provide shelter for small ground animals and American Goldfinches have been known to build their nests in them.

Chicory (Cichorium intybus)

Chicory is another common wildflower. It is a perennial that produces blue flowers and dandelion-looking leaves. The bush can grow up to 4-feet and is often seen across meadows and roadsides. The flowers resemble the daisy with a bluish center moving to purple at the edges. The flowers reach about 1½ inch wide, blooming from June to October.

Chicory flowers attract many insects for the nectar and pollen including bees, butterflies, and flies. It also attracts predatory insects like yellow jackets and lacewings. The seeds are eaten by mice while rabbits and deer eat the leaves and stems.

Dandelions (Taraxacum officinale)

Dandelions are maligned in much of the world for being a persistent weed, but they have much to offer in other ways. They are an easy to grow perennial that blooms with yellow flowers on a hollow stalk. They require no care and pop up in gardens, all over lawns, and in crevasses and cracks of cement in ways that defy logic.

For the compost pile, pull the dandelions and add them to the pile before they go to seed as their deep taproots bring up nutrients from deep in the soil to add to the compost. They are known as an early source of nectar for ladybugs and will bring in pollinators like bees, flies, and butterflies, making them great to plant around fruit trees. Dear and rabbits eat dandelion leaves, and birds eat the seeds.

Goldenrod (Solidago)

Goldenrod is a common wildflower found throughout North American with more than 50 known varieties. They are all late summer to fall bloomers, most of them producing long stalks full of bright yellow flower clusters. They can found in full sun,

partial shade, rich soil, and poor soil. They are often considered a weed but with so much natural interaction between insects, birds, and animals, the plant is an essential part of nature.

This plant attracts bees, wasps, butterflies, moths, flies, and other insects with its nectar and pollen. It also attracts wasps, spiders, praying mantis, lacewings, ambush bugs, assassin bugs, and beetles. Birds are attracted to the flowers and the insects. Deer and rabbits will feed on this plant. It is known to shelter many critters like goldenrod spiders, moles, mice, and birds.

Lamb's Quarters (Chenopodium album)

Lamb's quarters is also known as pigweed. Like most wildflowers, lamb's quarters, which offers edible leaves, is easy to grow. It thrives in rich or poor soils and can be sown in the garden or you can toss the seeds by the handfuls out on a fields. The plants bloom in the summer through to the fall, offering tiny green flowers on the 1- to 3-foot tall plants. The flowers change to tiny fruits with even tinier black seeds. They self-sow freely so to control the spread, snip the flower heads before they go to seed.

Lamb's quarters is a great companion plant for corn. They are also a good worker in the compost pile but pull them before they go to seed. Lamb's quarters is also known to attract parasitic wasps. The seeds attract chipmunks, squirrels, and birds. Deer will eat the entire plant.

Oxeye Daisy (Leucanthemum vulgare)

This rapid-spreading perennial can be found through many parts of the United States and is often confused with the Shasta daisy, which is a larger, more robust plant with larger flower heads. The oxeye daisy is a rampant weed in some area and in southern

British Columbia, it is considered a noxious weed, meaning it is troublesome and difficult to control. The flowers are typically only 1½ to 2 inches across and can be seen from May through July, and they have an odor that resembles sage. It grows in most soil conditions.

The oxeye daisy is great for attracting ladybugs, parasitic wasps, and tachinid flies.

Queen Anne's Lace (Daucus carota)

This wildflower is also known as wild carrot. The plant grows up to 4-feet tall with long, fern-like leaves but it is the flowers that makes this plant well known. The plant's flowers are tiny, white, and set into a lacy, flat-topped rosette. Each flower has a  purple center and shows up from May to October. It lives for two years, flowering in the second year. The large taproot is an edible carrot. Be careful because the foliage can cause skin irritations.

Queen Anne's lace attracts predatory insects like the green lacewing, which eats aphids. The flower nectar attracts bumble bees and honey bees, various birds, and the swallowtail butterfly.

Stinging Nettles (Urtica dioica)

Many people consider stinging nettles a weed. However,
considering that the plant
is rich in iron and nitrogen,
you should consider planting
this in your garden – if only
to add to your compost pile.
The plant usually grows from
3- to 7-feet tall by the end of

summer and dies back over winter. The stems and leaves are hairy, and the
flowers are small and either green or brown.

The nettle excretes nitrogen, silica, iron, protein, and formic acid, giving
strength and flavor to any crops growing close to it. If you need to pull the
nettles, then add them to the compost. They make good companions to
potatoes and horseradish plants. They are particularly helpful at stopping
mold on tomatoes. The flowers attract bees.

Yarrow (Achillea millefolium)

Yarrow is among the hardiest of the perennials and is considered a wildflower, weed, and an herb, depending on where you live. Both tall and
dwarf varieties exist. The most common plants produce bright yellow flowers and there are some with red, pink, and white blooms. They are striking
to look at and flower from summer to until frost hits. They can be grown
from seed into the garden, or started indoors to transplant out when the
soil has warmed. They prefer full sun and well-drained soil. They tolerate
dry spells. Thin the plants to 1 foot apart, and the plants can be separated
into several plants in the fall.

Yarrow is a good companion for vegetables, in particular cucumbers and corn. The plants also increase the essential oil content and aroma of herbs when planted close by. They attract beneficial insects like ladybugs and predatory wasps and repel bad insects. You can add yarrow leaves to the compost to speed up the decomposition process. Good companion plants include campanula, blanket flower, catnip, hardy geranium, Shasta daisy, and speedwell.

O ver time, the term "bulb" has become a generic term encompassing corms, tubers, rhizomes, and roots that are similar or resembling a tuber in nature and includes fall, spring, or flower bulb categories. A **corm** is a swollen, underground plant stem; a **tuber** is a thickened portion of an underground stem; and a **rhizome** is a horizontal plant stem with shoots above ground and roots below. The bulbs store food that will be used in the spring. Spring bulbs are planted in spring for blooms in late summer or early fall. However, fall bulbs are planted in the fall and will bloom in the spring.

The general rule of thumb for bulbs is to plant them four to six weeks before the first frost in your area. They are usually planted in border gardens along walkways, in front of a house, or around trees. All bulbs prefer a sunny exposure and a well-drained soil.

Asiatic Lilies (Lilium asiatic)

There are many beautiful lilies available for local gardeners at most nursery centers, and one of the prettiest varieties is the Asiatic lily. They are available in an amazing array of colors like yellow, orange, pink, red, white, and multi-colored varieties. These plants grow from 2 to 4 feet tall and will bloom in the early part of summer for a couple of weeks.

Good companion plants for these lilies include coreopsis, dianthus, campanula, Shasta daisies, peonies, hibiscus, daylilies, poker plant, and Black-eyed Susan.

Amaryllis (Amaryllis)

The amaryllis is also known as Dutch or South African amaryllis. The flowers bloom in late spring for about a month and come in red, pink, white, as well as bi-color variations. The plants grow from 2 to 3 feet tall and require a full-sun location. Plant the bulbs 8 inches deep and 6 to 12 inches apart. They prefer to be kept in small clumps of two or three bulbs together in one hill.

Good companions for the amaryllis include alyssum, daylilies, iris, peonies, cotoneaster, coreopsis, baby's breath, weigela, aster, poker plant, and the Japanese maple.

Anemone (Anemone)

Anemones are also known as Easter flower, Pasque flower, thimbleweed, snowdrop anemone, and windflower. There are a huge variety of these plants, both spring and fall bloomers, in a wide color range. This plant is usually considered a flower but it is an old medicinal herb as well. The tubers are planted in the fall approximately 5 inches deep in a full-sun location. They will tolerate a certain amount of drought.

Good companion plants for anemones include alyssum, Japanese maple, iris, daylily, peonies, cotoneaster, spirea, weigela, hosta, iris, bleeding heart, and rhododendron.

Crocus (Crocus)

There are many different crocus varieties on the market
today, some are spring flowering, and others are summer
or even fall flowering. They
bloom in most colors and
all require similar gardening
conditions. Plant the bulbs
in full sun or slight shade

and they will grow approximately 6 inches tall. For spring-flowering bulbs,
plant in the fall and for fall-flowering bulbs, plant in the summer.

Crocuses are a great companion to most plants but in particular with forsythia, winter jasmine, periwinkle, and japonica or witch hazel.

Daffodils (Narcissus)

Daffodils are an early- to late-spring flowering bulb producing yellow,
white, and yellow with white flowers. They like a full-sun location and
should be planted in the fall several inches apart. These bulbs need to be
planted 8 inches deep and will grow close to 10 inches above ground. They
do tolerate some drought conditions.

Good companion plants for daffodils include japonica, forsythia, winter
jasmine, weigela, and rhododendrons.

Dahlias (Dahlia)

Dahlias are all about variety. The plants come in almost every size, offering
small to huge dinner-plate sized flowers that come in an amazing range of
colors including orange, salmon, bronze, apricot, yellow, red, and many

shades of purple. Regardless of the variety, dahlias are an easy plant to grow. They can be started from seed or purchased as established tubular roots. These plants are perennial in warmer climates but the roots will need to be dug up and stored inside for the winter and replanted in the spring in climates where there are hard frosts. They like a full-sun location in a rich soil. They are heavy feeders and would benefit from compost and fertilizer throughout the year. Space tubers approximately 1½ to 2 feet apart for the larger varieties.

Dahlias, besides attracting birds and bees into the garden, are known to repel nematodes. Artemisia is a great companion for dahlias as slugs are attracted to the dahlias but are repelled by Artemisia.

Daylily (Hemerocallis)

Daylilies can be found every-where and with so many unique color combinations for the flowers, there is one to make every gardener happy. There are early flowering and late flowering varieties and daylilies come in different sizes and offer different fra-  grances. They are an easy plant to grow and one that requires little to no maintenance. They do prefer partial-shade and are tolerant of most soil conditions. They work great as a border or for planting in large quantities.

Companion plants for daylilies include amaryllis, Asiatic lilies, iris, ornamental onion, Persian buttercup, snowdrops, spring starflower, and tulips.

Four O'Clocks (Mirabilis)

Four o'clocks are another old-fashioned favorite, with Mirabilis jalapa being one of the most common. They are often considered an annual but are a perennial. Like dahlias, they have a tuber root system and should be dug up and stored over winter. They  are a special plant in that they bloom in the mid-afternoon (hence the name) and stay open overnight then close in the early morning. They are also known as Marvels of Peru. They are more commonly grown from seed and germinate quickly. They will grow up to 2 to 4 feet high. Sow directly into the garden before the last frost and thin the seedlings to 2 feet apart. They like a full-sun location and love a rich soil.

The four o'clocks attract Japanese beetles but the foliage is poison to them, killing them off quickly. They are also poisonous to people and animals so be careful.

Gladiolas (Gladiolus)

There are more than 250 members of the Gladiolus genus. Gladiolus are also known as glads and sword lilies. They are a well-loved garden bulb coming in almost every color imaginable. They are planted in spring for summer and fall flowering, and can be left in the ground if your region does not have harsh winters – if it does, dig up the corms and store them over winter to replant in the spring. There are dwarf plants that will barely reach 1 foot tall and there are giants that will exceed 5 feet. The gladiolas like an average soil and do well in sun or partial shade. They do need good drainage but other than that, they are extremely easy and rewarding to grow.

Do not plant gladiolas close to strawberries, peas, and beans as they are bad companions. They are happy next to other bulbs like iris and daffodils.

Hyacinths (Hyacinthus)

Hyacinths are also known as Dutch, common, and garden hyacinth. Use only firm, healthy-looking bulbs. They are normally planted in the cool weather of fall. The bulbs need cold weather to force them into the dormant period that they will grow from in the spring. If you live in a warm climate, common practice is to put the bulbs into the refrigerator for three weeks instead of outside. The reason for placing the bulbs in the fridge is the temperature is more stable there than outdoors where temperatures may be more inconsistent. Pick a location that offers full sun and good drainage. The bulbs go into a small hole approximately 5 inches down and about 6 inches apart. Place the bulb with the pointed end down.

Hyacinths are good companions to most garden plants, particularly other bulbs like daffodils and tulips. They are particularly good companions to pansies and black walnut trees (one of the few plants that can grow next to this tree). They are poor companions for carnations. If you plant hyacinths where carnation have grown in the past, the hyacinths will die. The same goes for carnations – they will die if planted where hyacinths have grown.

Iris (Iris)

There are many iris varieties to choose from, offering many colors and shades. The bulbs are usually planted in the fall for early spring flowers that will last for close to two weeks. Dwarf varieties grow to 6 inches tall and the taller varieties will top 4 feet. The bulbs are planted 5 inches deep in a full-sun location and will tolerate some afternoon shade. They will tolerate some drought conditions and cannot be left sitting in water or the bulbs will rot. They are easy to grow throughout most of the United States and Canada.

Good companions for the iris include forsythia, japonica, winter jasmine, daylilies, and periwinkle. They make good companions for amaryllis, anemones, gladiolas, ornamental onion, Persian buttercup, tulips, peony, hardy geranium, and the blanket flower as well as most other bulbs.

Liatris (Liatris)

Liatris is also known by the names of blazing star, gay-feather, and by the lesser known names of colic root and button snake root. Liatris is another easy to grow perennial that can be grown from seeds or rhizomes. These plants are available at nursery centers. The plants prefer full sun but will do fine in partial shade and most soil conditions. If you are growing them from seed, be aware they will not flower until the second year. The plants should be spaced 1 foot apart and will need to be divided and separated at the end after a few years. They will not do well in a soggy soil as the roots will rot. The plants can grow up to 5 feet tall and will bloom in the summer with tall spikes of purplish flowers opening from the top down. The leaves will turn bronze in the fall depending on the variety.

Liatris is known to attract parasitic wasps, hoverflies, butterflies, and hummingbird moths. They are a striking addition to any garden, giving a great vertical accent.

Lily of the Valley (Convallaria majalis)

This plant is considered a weed by many for its ability to spread throughout a garden. It is also known as Our Lady's Tears, May lily, May bells, and ladder-to-heaven. The plants are easy to grow and are usually started from nursery stock. They like a full-sun location or partial-shade and require a well-drained soil. Set the plants 1 foot apart. Once established, the plant forms rhizomes and new shoots that form new plants. These plants stay in the ground and need a cold winter to flourish. It blooms early in spring and over the years, they will become a dense groundcover.

All parts of the lily of the valley are poisonous so keep away from children and animals. The plant is a good companion to other spring bulbs while in the ground. However, if you put lily of the valley flowers in the same vase with other flowers, they will both wilt. Good companions include forsythia, hosta, periwinkle, ivy, winter jasmine, anemones, ferns, cotoneaster, and weigela.

Ornamental Onion (Allium)

There is a huge variety of ornamental onion plants but the *Allium cristophii* and Allium *giganteum* make wonderful border plants. The ornamental onion is a distinctive plant with 3-foot high plants topped normally with round puffball flowers. The bulbs are planted in the fall for early summer flowers that will last for several weeks. Plant the bulbs 1 foot apart and 8 inches deep. They like a full-sun location but will tolerate partial-shade and it tolerates some drought.

Good companions for the ornamental onion include Asiatic lilies, in particular yellow and white, coreopsis, dianthus, iris, peonies, baby's breath, daylilies, cornflower, foxglove, mullein, and the red hot poker plant. It does well around most bulbs.

Paperwhites (Narcissus papyraceus))

Paperwhites are also known as narcissus. They are a warm weather climate bulb as they flower in early winter for close to 3 months. The plants grow close to 1½ feet tall and the flowers, available in yellow or white, are known for their rich fragrance. The bulbs are planted in October to November in a full-sun location and warm soil. They are easy to care for once established.

They are good companions to forsythia, winter jasmine, japonica, and periwinkle.

Persian Buttercup (Ranunculus asiaticus)

This flower is also known as ranunculus. This flower is semi-hardy and will flower early in the season. It is typically planted in the fall, and in zone 7 it will need to be mulched; if grown in zones 8 and 9 no mulch is needed. The plant produces masses of flowers in an array of colors including white, pink, red, yellow, gold, orange, and various mixed colors. It needs full sun but will tolerate drought conditions.

Good companions for the Persian buttercup include alyssum, aster, coreopsis, hosta, iris, sedum, rhododendron, daylilies, spirea, and weigela.

Snowdrops (Galanthus)

Snowdrops are planted in the fall for early spring flowering. The plants grow only 6 inches high and produce small, delicate, white flowers. They thrive in any rock garden or bed. They require minimal shade and will do well with either full sunlight or partial  shade. The Giant snowdrop variety, *Galanthus elwesii,* grows to 10 inches tall and will flower at the beginning of the year with large flowers.

Good companions for snowdrops are forsythia, daylilies, japonica, winter jasmine, and periwinkle. Snowdrops do well with most other bulbs.

Star of Bethlehem (Ornithogalum umbellatum)

This plant is also known as Nap at Noon, Snowdrop, and Eleven-o'clock Lady. The star of Bethlehem is a small plant that produces tiny white flowers. It is planted in the fall for late spring flowers or early summer flowers when it will bloom for close to a month. It likes a full-sun location but will do fine with light shade. It is tolerant of drought conditions but will need water for the growing season. A word of warning: the plant can become invasive.

The star of Bethlehem is a good companion to anemones, japonica, ferns, hosta, primula, phlox, and rhododendrons.

Spring Starflower (Ipheion uniflorum)

Spring starflower is another bulb that is planted in the fall for a beautiful display in mid-spring. It will bloom for just over a month. The plant stays small, rarely topping 4 inches in height. It will produce a beautiful display of light blue flowers. The plant likes full sun, but if you are only able to offer this plant partial shade, make sure it receives morning sun. It needs to be planted 5 inches deep and will tolerate some drought conditions.

Good companions for the spring starflower include alyssum, campanula, coreopsis, dianthus, daylilies, and rock cress.

Striped Squill (Puschkinia libanotica)

Striped squill is a fall planted bulb that produces tiny bluish-white flowers come the following April, depending on growing conditions in your area. The plants grow 4 to 6 inches tall and will bloom for close to a month. They do well in most of the United States, particularly if mulch is used. They like full-sun to partial-shade conditions, preferring to have morning sun if possible. They tolerate drought conditions.

Good companions for the striped squill are forsythia, periwinkle, winter jasmine, and barberry.

Summer Snowflake (Leucojum aestivum)

The summer snowflake is also known as snowbell and dewdrop. It is a fall-planted bulb that flowers in mid-spring for several weeks. The plant grows more than 1 foot tall and has small flowers with tiny green markings. It is a great ground cover. The bulbs are planted 5 inches deep in a partial-shade location. It tolerates drought conditions well.

Good companions for the summer snowflake include anemone, ferns, phlox, primula, ranunculus, columbine, bleeding heart, Lenten rose, and Japanese flowering maple.

Tulip (Tulipa)

Tulips are loved the world over. This easy-to-grow plant comes in so many colors and styles there is one for everyone. They are a fall-planted bulb for late spring flowers. The plants can grow 6 inches tall for dwarf plants to 2 feet for regular plants. They are easy to look after. The bulbs are planted 8 inches in the ground and should be placed in a location with full sunlight or an area that offers partial shade with morning sunlight. It will tolerate some summer drought. The bulbs will rot if they get too wet.

There are several companion plants for tulips including most other bulbs and alyssum, coreopsis, dianthus, daylilies, iris, peonies, showy mullein, rock cress, and baby's breath. Tulips inhibit the growth of wheat, so do not plant the two together.

CASE STUDY: AMY PADGETT

Writer and rose specialist
amy@amypadgett.com or amy@amycorwin.com
www.amypadgett.com

Amy Padgett, who writes fiction under the name Amy Corwin, is an heir-loom or Old Garden Roses specialist. A member of the Wilmington Cape Fear Rose Society for years, she also been active in the New Bern Rose Show where she won top awards including Dowager Queen and Victorian

Rose awards and several 1st place awards for English (David Austin) roses. Her garden is enrolled in the National Wildlife Federation's Backyard Wildlife Habitat Program, ensuring that her gardens provide water, shelter, and food for all creatures without the use of pesticides or other sprays.

"I love nontraditional companion planting as I do not spray my roses. Practice has shown me that the following combinations work:

- Heirloom roses are often pale pink to rich mauve, examples include 'Sydonie' or 'Baronne Prevost,' and they are stunning mixed with 'Filius Blue' or 'Tri-Color Variegata' peppers. Herbs we have paired with these pale roses include borage, chives, chervil, thyme, parsley, sage, and basil. We also have some lovely sprawling rosemary that serves wonderfully in corner positions next to rocks or bricks.

- Newer rose varieties that have more intense colors can be beautifully mixed with hot colored peppers such as the ornamental 'Medusa' variety. These modern roses also can benefit from pairing with marigolds and pyrethrum as those plants purportedly have mild insect-repelling characteristics.

- Of course, many bulbs look gorgeous with roses, including daffodils and lilies. The lilies are nice as they often bloom just when the roses are taking a rest between bloom cycles.

- Some of our most beautiful pairings have included the fragrant, pale pink rose 'Souvenir de la Malmaison' paired with 'Tri-color Variegata' peppers that have gorgeous leaves streaked with white and purple. The leaves perfectly complement the pale roses. The lush, salmon-colored David Austin rose, 'Lilian Austin,' paired with the pepper 'Medusa' and interspersed with 'Snowball' marigolds work well.

- Because we start a lot of seeds, sometimes it comes down to finding an empty spot in the garden, and sometimes those accidental pairings turn out the best. An example of this was when we planted borage and a horehound herb near our rich pink 'Sydonie' rose. The blue of the borage, silvery-green horehound leaves, and pink rose books just seemed to work. Some years we've planted masses of marigolds and pyrethrum edging the more modern roses, particularly yellow or salmon-tinged roses. Those are excellent in the fall and really brighten up the garden.

- For easy care, many of our beds are interspersed with daylilies and other bulbs as they require less maintenance. Not to mention that daylily flowers are excellent stuffed with cream cheese mixed with chives!

- Make sure your companions have similar soil and water requirements or make sure you can accommodate targeted watering. For example, roses like a lot of water while many herbs prefer dry environments. You can still grow them together, but one way to manage it is to place the rose to the back of the garden and gradually raise the garden level toward the front and edge it with rocks or bricks. You can then place dry-loving plants near the edge where the ground level is slightly (maybe only an inch) higher. Water will drain toward the back where the rose will appreciate it, and the herbs will flourish in a drier, hotter location toward the front.

- We have not seen any difference between beds with pest-controlling plants and those that don't have them. We've tried pyrethrum and marigolds among others. The plants themselves don't suffer from a lot of pests, but they do not seem to significantly discourage pests on companion plants. We did reduce Japanese beetles by using milky spore but we have not found any plants that will naturally keep them off the roses in July. Nothing stops the thrips except sprays, which we don't use.

There is almost always a way to make combinations work, so don't give up if you have your heart fixed on a specific pairing of plants. Be creative and express your own interests. Don't be afraid to try something different because the great thing about gardens is that they are easy to change. If you don't like the effect you've created with a pairing, you can always separate the plants and try a different pairing. It's very difficult to ruin a garden so don't be afraid to experiment."

· CHAPTER 12 ·

Shrubs, Bushes, and Vines

S hrubs are often confused with trees and other smaller plants. However, they can be identified by their several woody stems. The plants that climb, twist, or travel along the ground or up various structures, including other trees and shrubs, are called vines. Vines are missing the strong rigid stem or trunk that can take the plant up to sunlight. They have tendrils, holdfasts, or twining stems that give them a means to climb up to sunlight. Shrubs rarely grow bigger than 15 feet and there is no real limit on the size of vines. Even with these differences, they can be confusing to sort out as some bushes like the honeysuckle also have climbing varieties. Berry bushes are technically considered shrubs but are often in a class all their own. *You can find berries in Chapter 13 covering fruit.* Then there are vines that cover the ground and can form dense shrubbery-looking lumps, such as poison ivy. There are also smaller tree varieties that are included as shrubs such as sumacs.

Many shrubs flower early in spring, like the honeysuckle. Then by summer, the shrubs are already producing berries and other fruits that can last well into fall where they provide a necessary food source for various wildlife. The foliage of some of these shrubs will also change color in the fall, like sumacs, providing some of the most brilliant fall color possible for gardens, extending the season of delight.

Companion planting with these types of plants means looking at the wild-life they attract, the shade they can provide, as well as aspects like the color, size, and shape of the plant as to how well it will fit into the garden.

Akebia Vine (Akebia quinata)

The akebia is a lesser-known, fast-growing vine that is also called the choc-olate vine due to its purple or white flowers that can smell like chocolate, vanilla, or spices. The plant blooms in mid-spring. It can grow to 30 and 40 feet, making it an excellent cover for arbors, trellises, and fences. The plant does need cross-pollination in order to produce fruit. It can be invasive and might need aggressive pruning to keep it contained.

The akebia is attractive to bees, butterflies, and birds that together with its unique fragrance, make it an excellent plant for the garden. It makes a good companion plant to the clematis.

Azalea (Rhododendron)

The azalea is also related to the rhododendron. This evergreen shrub prefers a well-drained soil and a sunny to partial-shade location. The plant prefers mulch and/or peat moss around its base and the roots will actually rot in soil that is too moist. The plant needs protection from strong winds. These shrubs are hardy and long lived and top the list of best garden shrubs. Aza-leas, depending on variety, can grow from 2 to 6 feet high and will produce flowers in May in a wide array of colors depending on variety.

The azalea and rhododendron bushes are great for attracting birds. Hum-mingbirds are particularly fond of this plant. Do not plant near black wal-nut trees.

Bittersweet Vine (Celastrus orbiculatus)

Bittersweet is a fast-growing, climbing vine that produces yellow to orange fruits with red seeds. These make the plant a favorite for fall crafts. The vine is easy to grow and hardy. It will do well in most locations and most soil conditions. You will need to purchase both a male and a female to produce fruit as the male plant produces enough pollen for up to eight female plants, which produces the berries. The plants are difficult to tell apart until they are mature. There are two common varieties available so look for the American bittersweet as the Oriental bittersweet is considered an invasive pest. The plant can reach 60 feet and will bloom in May and June. Plant where it can climb around arbors, trellis, and fences, but preferably not other larger trees as it can grow too tight and cripple the tree.

In the fall, the plant will bring many birds and animals into the garden. It is popular with bees, birds, squirrels, rabbits, chipmunks, and toads to name just a few and will shelter many of these same animals over winter.

Bog Rosemary (Andromeda polifolia)

Bog rosemary loves being in moist soil and peat moss. It is an evergreen shrub that grows remarkably fast. It is perfect for rock gardens in full sun or partial shade. The shrub will grow from 1 to 2 feet high and could spread 3 feet wide. It produces profuse quantities of delicate white to pink flowers in May. It also offers unusual foliage in a soft blue-green color.

The bog rosemary, in the right location, will bring the pollinators into the garden in droves, making it an excellent companion plant for any flowering plants.

Butterfly Bush (Buddlei davidii)

The butterfly bush is a unique shrub to grow. The plant likes full sun but prefers a moist and well-drained soil; however, it is tolerant of most conditions. It will grow 6 to 7 feet wide and from 5 to 10 feet high. There are more than 20 different varieties, all producing flowers of different arrays of purple, blue, pink, lavender, magenta, and white. Some of the varieties have variegated leaves, dark leaves, blue-green leaves, and even silver-gray leaves, giving every gardener choice for overall effect. The flowers are produced on arching branches and can extend for 10 inches.

The plant is well named as it will attract many butterflies to your garden. It will also bring in other pollinators like bees.

Buttonbush (Cephalanthus occidentalis)

This is another easy to grow shrub that grows in most areas of the United States. This plant likes to stand in water, and needs moist to wet soil at the minimum as it will not do well in dry soils. It is perfect if you have a large water feature or a boggy area that holds moisture. It will grow 6 to 10 feet tall. In late spring to summer, the plant produces very fragrant, creamy white flowers that appear in clusters and will become brownish ball-like fruits filled with seeds in fall. Be aware the foliage is poisonous to livestock.

The plant is well loved by pollinators like bees and will attract butterflies and various wildlife. The deer will come in to eat the leaves and twigs and the buttonbush seeds are well loved by ducks and geese. Song birds are known to build nests in the shrubs and small animals will use it for shelter. It is also a good plant for shorelines as it helps to control erosion and can handle floods.

Boxwood (Buxus)

This shrub has been a popular choice for generations. It is a non-flowering evergreen that can be pruned to any desired shape. If left to grow on its own, some varieties can reach up to 20 feet. There are dwarf varieties that work great as a border, edging, or to define areas of your garden or line pathways. It has a bright green color all year long, making it a great foundation for the rest of the garden. The shrub will tolerate some drought conditions and will grow in dry soil but will do better in loamy or sandy soils. It prefers full-sun to partial-sun locations.

The boxwood, besides being a great companion plant from an ornamental perspective with the ability to be shaped as desired, is also deer resistant. The boxwood is also supposed to repel the Japanese beetle.

Clematis (Clematis)

Clematis is a climbing vine that produces unique-looking flowers, depending on variety, in the spring and fall or throughout the summer. There are varieties that offer blooms of almost every color including reds, purples, pink, white, striped, and blended  colors, as well as solid colors. The clematis requires a structure to climb like a trellis or tree and it likes a full-sun location in well-drained soil. Space the plants 2 feet apart.

Good companion plants for the clematis include aster, bee balm, purple coneflower, tall bearded iris, Shasta daisy, other clematis, ground covers, and climbing roses. If you choose different varieties of clematis and plant them together, you will have a showy display all growing season. They also attract hummingbirds.

Cotoneaster (Cotoneaster)

Cotoneaster is a perfect ground cover shrub that has glossy green leaves all summer and then turns to a beautiful red in fall. There are red berries throughout summer and fall. The plant likes full sun but will tolerate partial shade. It also does better in well-drained soils. The type of plant makes it ideal for rock gardens, covering large ugly spaces. The cranberry cotoneaster will grow to only 3 feet tall with pink flowers it the spring. At the other end of the scale is the bearberry cotoneaster, which can reach 14 to 18 feet high, producing white flowers in spring.

It is a great plant for stabilizing unstable hillsides and for erosion control. It is well known for attracting pollinators like birds.

Devil's Walking Stick (Aralia spinosa)

Devil's walking stick is also known as Hercules' club. This deciduous shrub offers a moderate growth rate, dense foliage, and both flowers and fruit. Hardy throughout most of North America, the shrub can reach from 10 to 20 feet in height. There are many thorns on the branches so be careful when working around it. The new foliage comes in bronze and changes to yellow and red-orange in the fall. The plant flowers in summer with clusters of small white flowers and then produces clusters of purple black berries. The plant will tolerate a wide range of growing conditions but prefers sun to partial shade and a well-drained location.

The Devil's walking stick is a good companion to plants you want to protect from small animals due to its heavy thorns. The flowers attract bees and tiger swallowtail butterflies, and the fruit attracts many different birds.

Deutzia (Deutzia)

Deutzia will grow in both moist or dry conditions but prefers a well-drained soil in a full-sun to partial-shade location. The plant is great for a hedge and will flower starting in May. There are many great varieties and the Chardonnay Pearls Deutzia is one of the most fragrant. It has lime-yellow foliage and produces pearl-like buds that open to star-shaped flowers in springtime. Like most of the deutzia varieties, it is a compact bush that will grow 2 to 3 feet high and should be spaced at least 2 feet apart. The shrubs like a full-sun location in well-drained soil.

Most of the deutzia shrubs are deer resistant. The fragrant flowers will attract butterflies and pollinators to your garden.

Dutchman's Pipe Vine (Aristolochia durior)

This vine is a bold statement for any garden with its large, 6- to 10-inch, heart-shaped leaves and height of 30 feet. The plant likes a full-sun to light-shade location with well-drained soil and some structure to climb as it will twine around the nearest object. It will grow rapidly once established. It is grown mostly for the unique foliage but it will produce mahogany- and cream-colored flowers in late spring. The flowers have a unique fragrance as well.

The plant is a good companion for plants requiring dense shade. The flowers will attract birds and butterflies, in particular the swallowtail butterfly.

Fothergilla (Fothergilla major)

Fothergilla is often called bottlebrush (Callistemon) but these two plants are quite different. Fothergilla is a nice addition to a garden. The shrub grows approximately 3 feet high and needs to be spaced 3 to 4 feet apart. The plant likes a full-sun to partial-shade location in a moist but well-drained soil. It will produce spring flowers, usually white, sticking out straight from a center stem like a bottle brush. There are several varieties available, including Blue Shadow that has silvery blue foliage turning to yellows, oranges, and reds by fall.

The bottlebrush, as it prefers a slightly acidic soil, makes a good companion to the rhododendrons and azalea bushes. It will also attract birds.

Glossy Abelia (Abelia x grandiflora)

Abelia is a beautiful, hardy shrub that provides profuse blooms with intense fragrance. It is a great alternative to the lilac bush. It grows from 6 to 9 feet high and should be spaced 10 feet apart. This shrub does better with a full-sun to a partial-shade location. The blooms arrive in late spring in a soft pink or white if you choose *Abelia chinensis*. An additional attraction of the *A. x grandiflora* shrub is that the glossy green foliage turns orange-red in fall. The plant can be pruned and shaped easily. It will grow in a wide variety of soil conditions and is happy without much care. The *Abelia mosanensis* is a lovely fragrant variety.

Abelia is deer resistant and is one of the best for attracting birds while offering seasonal interest throughout the year.

Japanese Barberry (Berberis thunbergii)

Japanese barberry, also known as Thunberg's barberry and red barberry, is an excellent flowering shrub for your garden. It will tolerate drought and can grow well in drier soil. It needs a well-drained, loamy soil in a full-sun to partial-shade location. The purple variety will turn green in the shade. It prefers a more acidic location that has a pH level of 7.7. It is considered allergy free and pest tolerant. The bush can grow, depending on the variety you choose, from 3 to 9 feet high. They generally produce yellow flowers on very thorny stems. Some, like the Japanese barberry, will turn a reddish-purple in the fall.

Barberry is a good companion plant for the garden as it will attract pollinators like birds. The thorns also make it a good barrier plant.

Honeysuckle (Lonicera)

Honeysuckle is a popular plant found in many gardens across North America with the Japanese honeysuckle *(Lonicera Japonica)* being one of the most common. The plant grows quickly and comes as a shrub or a vine that can grow up tree trunks or other shrubs so plant close to trellises or fences for support. It is most often grown for its sweet-smelling flowers that are followed by small black berries. The plant blooms from April through to July. The flowers come in white and in shades of red, orange, and yellow. Plant in a full-sun location where it will have a chance to fulfill its 25 feet of growth.

The honeysuckle is a great companion plant for any garden as its fragrance will attract butterflies, pollinators, and birds, especially hummingbirds. Insects drink the nectar and the birds eat the berries, plus deer have been known to eat the plants. Small animals may use the plant as shelter.

Hydrangea (Hydrangea)

Hydrangeas are easy-grow-  ing, flowering shrubs. They will grow from 6 to 8 feet high and need to be spaced at least 6 feet apart. Some variet- ies prefer shade and there are a few that like sunny spots, so it is important to pick the right variety for the garden location. The flower colors vary widely from white to blue to burgundy, pinks, and purples. There are shrub, tree, and climbing varieties like the *Hydrangea petiolaris* that can go to 50 feet. Some of the plants are highly prized for their foliage, like the oakleaf hydrangea *(Hydrangea quercifolia)*, which produces wine, orange, and deep mahogany colors in the fall.

With the oakleaf hydrangea in particular, song and game birds, as well as mammals, eat the seeds. The flowering hydrangea is a good shade plant to bring in pollinators and fill shady corners. The tropical hydrangea produces fragrant red and pink blooms. The bush attracts bees and butterflies.

Ivy (Hedera)

English ivy *(Hedera helix)* plants are evergreen vines. They can grow hori- zontal along the ground or climb up fences, rocks, and any other structures like trees. The plants do well in partial-shade to full-sun locations in well- drained soil. They can bear greenish flowers but are grown for their foliage. They are considered an invasive plant by many but they are a good choice for shady areas like under trees. Another favorite to consider is Boston ivy *(Parthenocissus tricupspidata)*.

Ivy is a great groundcover, covering large unsightly areas and choking out weeds. It can also be used for erosion control or to cover large walls, unsightly sheds, fences, and more. Ivy is known to attract tachinid flies and birds. Boston ivy is known to attract bees.

Lilac (Syringa vulgaris)

Lilacs are an old-fashioned shrub that never goes out of style. The shrubs are low maintenance and will grow in a variety of locations and soil conditions. They can be planted on their own or together to form a hedge. They do like well-drained soil so plant where they will not sit in water. They will benefit from mulch but because new shoots will come up, keep the mulch only a few inches thick. Lilacs bloom for only few weeks at time so it helps to have both early and later flowering varieties planted together for continuous blooms. The colors of blooms vary slightly but most common are white, lavender, blue, pink, and purple. Flowers come in both single and double petal varieties as well. Some lilacs can grow as high as 30 feet and there are dwarf varieties barely reaching 3 feet. As there are more than 1,000 varieties, there is sure to be a variety for every garden.

Lilacs are a good companion to many garden flowers and vegetables. They can function as a windbreak for those plants needing shelter and shade for plants that do not like too much sun. Lilacs do not do well close to black walnut trees.

Porcelain Berry Vine (Ampelopsis brevipedunculata)

This vine is easy to grow, flowers quickly, and sets fruits easily. The plant needs a full-sun location but will grow in a variety of soil conditions, provided it is well-drained. Mulch around the base helps to prevent the weeds from taking over until the plant is well established. The vine will need structural support, making it another good plant for trellises or covering up old fences. Cut it back in the fall to keep it under control. There are dark green leaf and variegated leaf varieties. It is fast growing and is considered invasive by some. If you plant it, cut it to the ground in late winter to avoid it taking over. It can reach 20 feet in length. After flowering, it will produce clusters of green, purple, and blue fruits.

The plant is known to attract bees and butterflies. The profusion of fruit at the end of the season brings in many different types of birds.

Rhododendron (Rhododendron)

Rhododendrons are a common sight across the country. With their big bright flowers they make a great addition to any garden. They love an acidic soil and will grow best in partial-shade. They prefer a peat moss base and must have a well-drained location.  There are many varieties available today offering different colored blooms including pinks, reds, whites, lavenders, and purples. They do not like windy locations.

Rhododendrons, particularly the Carolina and purple varieties, are known to attract birds, especially hummingbirds. Good companions for the rhododendron are astilbe, pieris, and viburnum. Do not plant close to a black walnut tree.

Roses (Rosa)

Roses are a traditional and well-loved plant. Roses can be bushes, trees, or climbers. There are many kinds of roses with a wide variety of blooms available, covering most shades of colors. Rose colors hold a special meaning, such as red for love, pink for appreciation, and yellow roses symbolize joy and friendship. Regardless of the type of rose, they all like similar growing conditions. Roses like a well-drained soil with a neutral pH and will also tolerate a slightly alkaline soil. They like a full-sun location.

There have been complete books written on roses and one common companion planting theme is that they grow well with garlic because the rose's roots pick up the exudations from the garlic, making the plant less attractive to some insects like green flies and aphids. But there are also many other plants that make great companions to roses, like parsley that works to keep green flies away. Marigolds and tansy are also effective as pest repellants. Nasturtiums make a great trap crop by attracting the insects to it and therefore away from the roses. Chives and other members of the allium family are said to increase the perfume of the roses, ward off aphids, and help to prevent black spots. Herbs are also great companions, such as thyme, which are said to ward off Japanese beetles and aphids. Lavender and catmint are helpful for keeping rabbits away. Four o' clocks and larkspur are said to kill Japanese beetles. Planting yarrow will help attract in ladybugs, which in turn feast on aphids.

Rose-of-Sharon (Hibiscus syriacus)

This flowering shrub can grow up to 10 feet tall and spread at least half that height. There are a few varieties that are shorter. Some varieties produce single flowers and others offer double flowers, meaning flowers that have extra petals or flowers within flowers. The shrubs will bloom in later summer long past when most other flowering shrubs have finished their blooming cycle. There is a wide range of flower colors including white, red, blue, and lavender. This member of the hibiscus family loves heat and is even drought tolerant once established. Plant in a full-sun location in well-drained soil.

Rose-of-Sharon is known to attract hummingbirds. It will also attract other birds and butterflies.

Santolina (Santolina)

This plant is also known as cotton lavender, gray lavender, lavender cotton and gray santolina, petite cypress, holy herb, and ground cypress. There are several dozen varieties of santolina and it belongs to the aster family. This small evergreen shrub grows to approximately 1½ to 2 feet tall. The plants need to be spaced about 1 foot apart. It is generally grown for its aromatic silver-gray evergreen foliage. It does produce clusters of bright yellow, ball-like flowers in mid- to late spring. It makes a great border or edging plant. Once the flowering is done, prune the plant back to promote bushiness.

Santolina is a good companion for roses and can be used as a groundcover to keep weeds down. Rabbits do not like santolina and the plant is known to deter some insects like moths. As a dried plant, it is mixed with lavender for a mothball replacement in drawers and closets.

Scotch Broom (Cytisus scoparius)

This deciduous shrub is also known as Scottish broom, English Broom, and common Broom. The shrub can reach as high as 10 feet and will expand to close to 6 feet wide. It is an upright, rounded shrub that likes a sunny location and prefers dry soil conditions in poor soil. It will flower in late spring on old growth. The flowers vary depending on type and can include red, pink, and gold flowers. The foliage is bright to medium green and stays this color over winter.

The plant is known to attract birds of all kinds.

Silver Lace Vine (Polygonum aubertii)

The silver lace vine is a vigorous climber that will easily cover 25 feet in one growing season. If your winters are harsh, the plant will die back and may only grow 15 to 20 feet the following year. In summer, the vine produces tiny fragrant white blooms that cover most of the plant and stay throughout the bulk of the growing season. The vine does well in most locations except total shade. The plant is also tolerant of most soil conditions but prefers well-drained soil. Once established, it is drought tolerant. They have a strong root system that will take over the space around them so plant them 4 feet from other plants. Choose a location with firm support before planting.

The silver lace vine, besides providing fast coverage of old fences and ugly corners in a garden, works well to provide shade for the garden. It also attracts hoverflies.

Spice Bush (Lindera benzoin)

The spice bush is a small shrub that grows approximately 6 feet tall. It grows wild across much of the United States and is often mistaken for witch hazel. The leaves start off dark green but turn yellow in the fall. The leaves give off a pleasant aroma when they are crushed. This shrub is one of the first to flower in the spring and it produces small yellow blooms in March and April. After flowering, small red berries are produced. The plant grows in most locations and most soil conditions, making it an easy option for the back corners of a yard where nothing else grows well.

The fruit of the spice bush attracts various birds like robins, Eastern King-birds, and Northern Bobwhite. The spicebush is ideal for a butterfly garden as it attracts many of them, in particular the Spicebush Swallowtail and the Eastern Tiger Swallowtail. It is also known for attracting wildlife as deer like to eat the leaves and twigs. It also makes a good shelter for small mammals. The spice bush is a good companion plant for elderberry.

Strawberry Bush (Euonymus americanus)

This shrub is also known as Bursting-heart, Hearts a'Bustin, and Brook Euonymus. The strawberry plant will grow from 4 to 6 feet tall and will need to be spaced a couple of feet apart from each other. They like a light-shade to a full-shade location in well-drained soil. It is drought tolerant once established and its evergreen foliage is a blue-green. It is a fairly innocuous looking plant but grows nicely in difficult locations where many other plants will not. The bush flowers in mid-spring through early summer when it produces pale yellow to yellow-green flowers. However, it is in the fall when the plant really shows well as it becomes covered in a globular fruit starting in August and the fruit ripens until it turns the color of fuchsia raspberries. In fall, the husk opens to show five stunning bright red berries hanging by a fine stem.

The strawberry is a big attraction for the various birds including wood thrushes, Eastern bluebirds, Yellow-rumped Warblers, and Northern Mockingbirds. The leaves and twigs are poisonous for cows so do not plant close to livestock.

Sumac (Rhus)

There are many sumac varieties, with some like the smooth sumac *(Rhus glabra)* growing 10 feet high and the winged sumac *(Rhus copallinum)* reaching upwards of 30 feet. The sumac generally does not live more than a few years, and it is common in open woods and fields. It prefers dry soil and makes a great thicket when grown close together. There are poisonous varieties that can cause a skin rash, but there are non-poisonous sumac varieties that offer a stunning autumn display of color. The poisonous varieties have hanging white berries and the non-poisonous have red berries that grow upright.

Besides bringing in stunning autumn color, the sumac is well noted for its ability to attract birds of all kinds, including Mourning Dove, Eastern Bluebird, Northern Cardinal, Brown Thrasher, Dark-eyed Junco, and Purple Finch. Rabbits will eat the bark and white-tailed deer will eat the leaves and stems if available. The shrub can also offer shelter for many small animals.

Sweet Pepper Bush (Clethra alnifolia)

This deciduous shrub is also known as Anne Bidwell and summersweet. There is another common variety called the mountain pepper bush or cinnamon bark clethra *(Clethra accuminata)*. These bushes can grow up to 12 feet tall. They like a sunny to partial-shade location and like a moist soil. The mountain pepper bush prefers a well-drained soil whereas the sweet pepperbush will tolerate flooding and wet soils. The shrubs will flower in early summer when it produces long stalks of white flowers. Some varieties produce pink flowers. The flowers are also fragrant. The mountain pepper bush also has a red cinnamon-colored bark.

The shrub is a good plant for any garden or lawn. It is known to attract bees, butterflies, and hummingbirds. The seeds produced after flowering bring in the birds again.

Trumpet Vine (Campsis radicans)

The trumpet vine is also known as the trumpet creeper, hummingbird vine, and Cow Itch. This woody vine can reach 30 feet in height with the main stem going 7 inches thick. The vine is well-known for producing stunning bright red flowers that are approximately 3 inches long. The vine can grow up trellises, fences, and walls but if there is nothing around to climb, it will stay as a small shrub but this is rare. The vine blooms from early summer through to September. The trumpet vine is often mistaken for a close relative called the cross vine. The cross vines are slightly shorter with smaller flowers. The trumpet vine prefers a full-sun location but will tolerate partial-shade. They require regular watering during the growing season. The vines will also reseed easily so care needs to be taken that the vine does not take over as it can become invasive. Some people can get a rash similar to poison ivy from the vine.

The trumpet vine is one of the most important nectar sources for the ruby-throated hummingbird. There are very few critters that can reach the nectar inside the long flowers and hummingbirds and bumblebees are two of them. They are required to pollinate the flowers. Many animals use the trumpet vine as a shelter as well, including the American Goldfinch, the Great Crested Flycatcher, and the Common Yellowthroat.

Viburnum (Viburnum)

Viburnum flowering shrubs have been a popular choice for gardeners for years. With more than 150 varieties to choose from, there is a perfect choice available for everyone. Some grow well in sun, others in shade; some grow as shrubs, others as trees. There are varieties that like wet soil and some that prefer dry. Most viburnum varieties are happy in the sun and will adjust to partial-shade. As a general rule, they like alkaline to neutral soils but check with your local nursery center. These shrubs actually belong to the honeysuckle family and most are hardy and pest resistant. Viburnums are great as a single bush or when planted together as a hedge. They do flower in white or pink with blooms that resemble snowball flower. There are a couple of self-pollinating varieties but most will need another variety to produce fruit.

Viburnums are a great choice if you are looking to increase the bird presence in your garden. Birds and small animals alike enjoy the small fruits. Viburnum is one of the best shrubs for attracting butterflies.

Virginia Creeper (Parthenocissus quinquefolia)

This fast-growing vine is a common sight in gardens as a groundcover. It can quickly grow out of control and needs to be pruned regularly. It does grow well in shade, making it valuable to cover dirt under trees and in dark corners. It can grow up to 50 feet in length and will grow sideways or climb. It will grow in most locations and soil conditions. The leaves are green with a red blush and in the fall, the leaves become a deep red. The vine produce greenish-yellow clusters in June through to the end of summer. The fruits are tiny black berries.

The berries of the Virginia creeper bring in the birds, including the Eastern Bluebird, Northern Cardinal, chickadees, and woodpeckers. The vine also attracts other mammals such as mice, chipmunks, squirrels, and deer.

Virginia Rose (Rosa virginiana)

The Virginia rose is also known as common wild rose or prairie rose. It is a woody shrub that is part of the rose family and is considered an invasive weed in much of North America. It can grow up to 6 feet in height and will produce pink flowers in summer and can grow just about anywhere. Be prepared to keep its growth regulated or it will take over your garden.

The Virginia rose is an excellent choice for your garden if you want to encourage wildlife because it is an important food source for many critters. It attracts pollinators like bumble bees and honey bees. It is the fleshy bulb or rose hip that is left behind once the flower dies that makes the plant so valuable. These hips are large and will stay on the plant throughout the fall and winter. They are a food source for many birds including American Robin, Northern Mockingbird, Cedar Waxwing, Eastern Bluebird, American Goldfinch, Northern Cardinal, and even the Song Sparrow. Skunks and mice eat them as well. The leaves also attract butterflies including Mourning Cloak and Red-spotted Purple butterflies. The heavy brush provides shelter for other animals and birds as well.

Weigela (Weigela)

Weigela is another old-fashioned favorite. It is easy to grow, requires little maintenance, and flowers in a variety of colors. The shrub prefers a full-sun location and will adapt to most soil conditions. Some of the weigela varieties will grow up to 8 feet high and 8 feet wide so read the label on the plant before choosing the best location. The shrub appreciates a layer of mulch around the base once planted. In late spring through summer, the weigela produces trumpet-like flowers in pink, red, white, and purple. There are variegated and purplish foliage varieties available.

Weigela flowers are known as a favorite nectar source for hummingbirds, and in the fall, the birds come for the seeds.

Wisteria   (Wisteria)

This hardy vine offers thousands of clusters of pendulum-shaped flowers. The Chinese and Japanese varieties will bloom in white, pink, lilac, and purple and are slightly frost hardy. They are both strong growers and are often considered invasive so be prepared to prune the vines to keep them in control. The American variety is less aggressive and less frost hardy, but it blooms lavender and mauve once in spring and again in September. Purchase the largest plant you can afford as the larger

the plant, the sooner it will flower. Wisteria can be grown from seed – if you have a dozen years to wait for it to bloom. Wisteria does best in a full-sun location but can tolerate some shade in a neutral to slightly acidic soil (6 to 7 pH). The plant will need a strong structure to climb and it will become very heavy as it gets older so consider planting wisteria close to pergolas and wooden arbors.

Wisteria is a scented shrub that attracts insects as well as the predators that consume them. Two main birds that love the wisteria are flycatchers and warblers. The dense foliage offers cover for nesting birds. Wisteria also attracts pollinators like bees as well as butterflies.

Witch Hazel (Hamamelis)

Witch hazel is unique in that it flowers in winter, making it one of the few flowering shrubs offering winter color. The common witch hazel blooms in late fall and the variety called Vernal witch hazel blooms in early spring. They usually grows to 15 feet but can mature up to 30 feet long. It grows wild in many forests but has become popular as a landscape plant. Depending on the species, the small, party streamer-looking flowers bloom in yellow, gold, orange, and red with the *H. japonica* variety offering a purple tone. Most of the varieties offer a nice spicy scent. The foliage also turns from dark green to yellow with a blush of red and purple come fall. The shrub prefers shade but will adapt to some sun. They are tolerant of most soil conditions but do prefer a moist, well-drained soil.

As it is a shade-loving plant, witch hazel does well growing underneath large trees and is often found under hickories, American elm, poplar, pine, and red maple trees. The bush provides shelter for birds and small animals and the seeds are food for chipmunks, squirrels, rabbits, as well as attracts in many birds.

Yucca (Yucca)

Yucca plants are hardy throughout most of the United States. They will grow close to 10 feet in height. They have woody stems and beautiful spiky, sword-shaped leaves. They are available with variegated or solid colored leaves including red to pink shades. Yuccas are available in many variety of shapes and sizes with the differences being in the length of the stem and their flowering ability. Plant in full-sun in well-drained soil. They should be no closer than 1½ feet apart for small varieties and 4 feet apart for larger varieties. Their sword-shaped leaves are sharp. The plants do well even when virtually ignored. They will bloom, shooting up a stalk of huge white, bell-like flowers in the summer

The yucca is great as a centerpiece in a garden or a border. The flower stalk with its 4-inch white flowers tinged in red or purple attracts hummingbirds.

G rowing fruit is a rewarding process. They are a long-term project and you should carefully plan their placement. The fruit trees like apples, peaches, cherry, and plum all produce a spectacular display when they flower and should be considered into the design of your garden. They make excellent shade trees as well. The smaller fruits like blueberries can be treated as a flowering shrub and will fit in with forsythias and spireas. Grapes do not need to be kept in a vegetable garden and will give a spectacular display if they are hanging from a covered walkway or arbor. It is a great way to cover up an old fence or beautify a corner of a patio in need of uplift.

Few gardeners have room to set aside an area to serve as an orchard and therefore your tree's location in the backyard needs to be well thought out first. These plants can attain unexpected heights, so make sure you allow ample room for your tree to grow. Make sure the ground is well worked over with compost and manure. All trees need a well-draining soil as they do not like to sit in water. The soil should be loose and not hard-packed clay so the roots can grow rapidly, establishing support for the growing tree. Wait for the soil to settle before planting. For most of the United States and

Canada, it is recommended to plant fruit trees in the springs; in the South and Southwest, it is possible to plant in the fall or early winter.

Before placing the tree in the hole, be sure to fill it with water and let it to drain completely. This soaks the ground around where the roots will be growing, but be sure to not plant the tree in any standing water or the roots may rot. After planting the fruit trees, surround the trunk with a layer of mulch to preserve moisture and provide nutrients over time.

Fruit trees are discussed within this chapter but the information is directed at those gardeners with fruit trees already growing in their garden or yard. If you are going to plant fruit trees, be sure to speak with the experts at your nursery center to choose the best variety for the location you have available. There are many dwarf varieties you can include if space in your garden is limited.

Apple Trees

There are both early- and late-blooming apple varieties. A general rule is to plant two together for pollination purposes. If you want the apples to appear even earlier for your variety, plant feverfew and dandelions around the base of the tree because  they will attract bees and other major pollinators to your tree's blossoms.

Good companion planting practice is to plant nitrogen fixers at the base of the tree like beans, clover (mow before flowering to keep it in control), and peas, which will climb up the tree. Another good companion for apple trees is chives; although it takes three years, it will eventually prevent scab on the tree. Borage helps bring in the bees, adds trace minerals to the soil, and has the ability to increase the tree's resistance to pests and plant disease. Nasturtiums will climb up the trunk and help to repel codling moths. Foxglove is supposed to protect the tree from disease while helping the fruit last longer once picked. Wallflower and apples both grow better when together. Other good companions include onion, marigold, alyssum, pansy, garlic, and sweet woodruff. Do not plant potatoes close to the apple trees as they become more susceptible to blight when close to apple trees. Bad companions include walnut trees and hawthorn.

Apricot

Apricot trees are great for back yard gardeners. They are all self-pollinating but can still benefit from being planted in pairs if you have room. They can be pruned nicely to make them easy to pick and the fruit is always sweet. Like the apple tree, they do better with nitrogen-fixing plants like beans, peas, and clover planted at the base of the tree. If you plant clumps of basil, tansy, or wormwood around the base of the trees, they will reduce the number of fruit flies considerably. These herbs have a strong scent that flies do not like so they will deter the flies from the fruit. Nasturtiums make another good companion plant for the same reason. Other good companion plants include asparagus, pansy, borage, chives, and garlic.

Bad companions include tomatoes because the roots of the apricot and tomato do not react well when close by. As well, keep oats and potatoes away from apricot trees.

Blackberries

Plant blackberries in a full-sun location in well-drained soil. They will tolerate some shade but will produce more fruit in the sun. Dig over the bed, and make sure it is slightly acidic – anywhere from 5.5 to 7 pH. Plant early in the spring approximately 4 feet apart with the rows 10 feet apart. Cut the bushes back to 6 inches above the ground and water well. Apply a thick mulch and leave to grow. During the time they are producing fruit, keep them well watered.

Tansy is great at repelling flies and ants, although you may want to plant in containers as it will take over quickly. If you keep several pots of tansy around your berry patch, the blackberries will grow faster and bigger. Consider planting mulberries, elderberries, or chokecherries close by to lure the birds away from the blackberries. Do not plant raspberries close to the blackberries to avoid cross pollination.

Blueberries

Blueberries are easy to grow throughout most of North America. They do need an acidic soil around a pH of 4 to 5. There are several varieties to choose from – some early- and some late-producing, as well as some that are low-growing and others that
are high-growing bushes; you should be able to find one that suits your garden and your location. Blueberries are self-pollinating but they will grow more and produce larger berries if you plant two different varieties to cross pollinate. Prepare the soil well with pine needles to make the ground more acidic, and add peat moss and compost to help prepare a rich base. Plant in a full-sun location; however, they will tolerate some shade but will produce less fruit. Set them approximately 4 feet apart in rows that are at least 6 feet apart. Do not let them sit in water.

Blueberries, because they need acidic soil, do well close to pine and oak trees.

Cherry

Cherry trees are a great fruit tree for your back yard. With the cultivation of so many varieties, there is a cherry for everyone. Sour cherries are self-fruiting and have no pollination issues if there is only one tree. They are a relatively easy tree to take care of, only requiring nutrients in the spring and pruning after the picking season is over.

Good companion plants for the cherry tree include garlic, onion, tansy, and nasturtiums to keep the pests away. The garlic is known to help repel rabbits, aphids, spider mites, apple scab, borers, peach leaf disease, Japanese beetles, spider mites, ants, cabbage looper, and cabbage maggots. Potatoes are prone to blight if planted in the vicinity of cherry trees. Wheat will also do poorly if planted close to cherry trees.

Elderberry

The elderberry shrub can easily reach 16 feet. The bush does prefer a moist soil so plant with peat moss or in a hollow where it can hold the moisture. The plant will bloom in May and June, producing clusters of small white flowers. The elderberry flower resembles the Queen Anne's lace flowers. After flowering, the shrub will produce edible, small, black berries that make lovely jelly, preserves, and wine. One of the newest varieties, the Black Lace elderberry, offers maple-like lace foliage

that provides a stunning display of dark red to black foliage and produces pink flowers.

The elderberry is often planted just to attract wildlife, making it an excellent companion plant for any garden. The flowers attract butterflies. Many birds eat the berries including the Eastern Bluebird, Blue Jay, Eastern Kingbird, European Starling, Brown Thrashers, Cedar waxwings, woodpeckers, Tufted Titmouse, and robins. Mice also enjoy the seeds. Rabbits and woodchucks are known to eat the bark while deer will eat the leaves and twigs.

Grapes

There are so many varieties of grapes available for such different purposes that you need to consult with your nursery professional for the right one. Some are self-seeding so you only need one plant for a high yield, while others require more plants for  cross-pollination. Once you have the varieties you want, be sure to plant in full-sun with well-drained soil with a pH around 5.5. Grapes benefit from southern exposure. Plant in loose, loamy soil that has been well dug over. They need compost and mulch to grow well, and they will also need a trellis or some kind of climbing support. They can be trained to grow across most fence-like structures such as arbors. Also, consider the purple-leaf grape, which is popular for its purple foliage, that turns hot red in fall. It produces small quantities of fruit.

Good companion plants for grapes include basil, beans, oregano, geranium, clover, peas, and blackberries. Hyssop will increase the vine's yield. Planting clover will set the nitrogen in the soil, but you should mow it flat before it goes to flower to keep it in control. Chives will help repel aphids. Other companion ideas include planting the vines under elm and mulberry trees. Bad companions include radishes, cabbage plants, and cypress spurge. Legumes work well for interplanting.

Melons

The term melon here applies to honeydew, cantaloupe, muskmelon, and watermelons. Melons will grow in most of the United States, although you may need to protect them if a frost warning comes and the fruit is almost ripe. The plants need full sun and they can be started from seed if you are in a warmer climate or may wish to purchase started plants from nurseries if you live in a shorter growing season area. Give them a location that is protected from wind and plant in hills after the last frost. Plant them 4 feet apart or only 2 feet apart if they are a bush variety.

Melons are good companions to radishes, pumpkin, peanuts, sunflower, squash, and corn. Nasturtium will help to deter bugs and beetles, and oregano provides general pest protection. Marigold helps to deters beetles. Potatoes are bad companions for this plant.

Passion Flower

The passion flower is an exotic-looking plant for any garden and comes as both a shrub or vine. The plants can be started from seeds but are much easier to grow if you purchase young nursery stock. If choosing seeds, you will need to start them

indoors where they will need a close eye on them so they do not totally dry out. After the last frost, transplant into the garden where the plant can climb, such as near a trellis or lattice. Unless you live in a very hot area, plant the passion flower in a full-sun location, otherwise a partial-shade location works well. They do well in most types of soil but prefer a light to sandy location. Passion flowers have delicate root systems so be careful when removing them from the pot. They will need regular watering as they can grow an inch a day and will use up fluids quickly; however, do not let the plant sit in water as the roots will rot. Once established, the plant will take off and bloom during the summer. The flowers come in a variety of colors including pink, lavender, red, white, and yellow shades. There are now several self-pollinating varieties as well. The oval fruit will ripen approximately 70 days after pollination.

The passion flower is known for attracting in pollinators like bees and wasps. It is also a great plant for bringing in butterflies and hummingbirds.

Peach

Peach trees attract birds and insects with their blossoms first and the sweet fruit later. Ants can be a problem, however. Plant basil at the base of the tree to stave off fruit flies. Use the strong scent of garlic and onions to keep other pests away. Tansy is  another great addition around the tree as it repels most insects, including the peach-top moth and fruit flies. Nasturtium, pansies, alyssum, and marigolds make good flowers to plant at the base of the tree as well. The nasturtium will climb the trunk and help repel coddling moths.

Nectarines are peaches and will pollinate peaches if planted nearby and peach trees will increase the crops of the nectarine trees.

Good companion plants include horseradish, nasturtium, pansies, alyssum, marigolds, grapes, southernwood, and strawberries. Other good companions for peach trees include peas, clover, and beans as nitrogen fixers. Some herbs to plant at the base include borage to attract bees and add trace minerals to the soil, chamomile, and comfrey, which adds minerals to the soil at the end of their life cycle. Garlic is always good to have close by as it is known to repel many insects including borers, aphids, ants, cabbage loopers, and cabbage maggots, as well as stave off peach curl disease. Poor companions include potato, tomato, and raspberries.

Pear

Pears are a hardy fruit tree that it is easy to grow. They do like a nitrogen-rich soil so add in manure and compost for a healthy producing tree. Try to produce an earlier crop by planting dandelions and feverfew around the base of the plant because they will bring in major pollinators earlier to the tree for an earlier crop. Pear trees require little fertilization except nitrogen, so make sure you plant at least one nitrogen fixer, such as clover, beans, or peas, at the base of the tree. Plant garlic to repel many pests including borers, aphids, ants, cabbage maggots, and cabbage looper. Garlic has been thought to stave off peach curl disease as well.

Good companions for pear trees include borage, which brings in the pollinators, adds trace minerals to the soil, as well as increases the tree's resistance to pests and disease. Nasturtium helps repel coddling moths. Plant foxglove to protect the tree from disease. Other good companions include onion, marigold, alyssum, pansy, garlic, and sweet woodruff. Pear trees do particularly well when planted close to currants.

Bad companion for pear trees are potatoes and grass because the roots give off an excretion that stops the roots of the pear tree from growing.

Plums

Plum trees are common back yard sight. They are an abundant producer and there is a variety available for most North American climates. They also benefit from many of the same companion planting tips of the apple tree. Basil wards off fruit flies and garlic and onion work to keep many of the other pests away. Garlic helps repel scab, peach leaf curl, ants, aphids, borers, Japanese beetles, spider mites, cabbage loopers, rabbits, and cabbage maggots. Tansy helps deter most insects including fruit flies. To help the nutrient level of the soil for the plum roots, plant nitrogen fixers like peas, clover, and beans and several plants that will add nutrients to the soil like borage, chamomile, and comfrey.

Good companion plants include horseradish, nasturtium, pansies, alyssum, marigolds, grapes, southernwood, and strawberries. Apricots make poor companions for this plant.

Quince

The flowering quince is another beautiful plant that is often grown for its ornamental qualities over the fruit it produces. The shrub grows 6 to 10 feet high and approximately the same width. The foliage starts as a bronze-red then turns to dark, glossy, green color. The plant likes a full or partial-sun but can grow well in partial-shade only it will produce less flowers. The plant is tough and hardy and will grow throughout most of the United States. In the fall, the shrub will produce red, pink, or white flowers followed by 2-inch, edible, apple-shaped fruit.

This shrub makes a great ornamental focal point, and as it does fine in shade, it can be planted under tall trees. Companion plants for the flowering quince include forsythia, day lilies, and irises as both will do better when together. The plant is known for attracting birds, especially hummingbirds.

Raspberries

There are summer- and ever-bearing raspberries. Summer bearing mean the raspberries will produce berries in the summer whereas ever-bearing means the raspberries produce for a longer period of time. Most raspberries require soil that is close to  neutral with a pH of 6.5. The summer-bearing variety will produce fruit in early summer then stop producing fruit and put all their energy into new plant growth. The ever-bearing varieties will produce berries in spring and fall. Purchase the raspberry plants (canes) and plant in acidic soil late in spring after the last frost. Plant in a sunny location several feet apart. Cut the canes back to 6 inches high. Do not plant purple raspberries together with black raspberries; they have to be at least 600 feet apart or the varieties can cross pollinate.

A good companion for the raspberry bushes is tansy as it is great for repelling insects and will also help the bushes grow faster with better yields. Other good companions include turnips, yarrow, garlic, wormwood, and lavender. Bad companions include blackberries and Logan berries. Raspberries are bad companions for potatoes, making the potatoes more susceptible to blight.

Strawberries

There are June-bearing and ever-bearing strawberry varieties available for home gardens. These are the common garden plants and are not to be confused with the strawberry bush from the euonymus family. Strawberries need a site that has full sun, warms up early, and allows good drainage. Plant the strawberry plants in a slightly acidic soil (around 6 pH) deep enough that just the crown shows above ground. Plant them 18 inches apart in rows that are 3 to 4 feet apart. They do well if hilled with compost or mulch.

Good companions for strawberries include beans, lettuce, spinach, onions, sage, and marigolds. Borage will help strengthen the plant's resistance to insects and disease as well as bring in the honeybees. White hellebore will control sawflies. Thyme is perfect as a border as it deters worms. Pyrethrum will also keep many of the insects away. Bad companions include cabbage, broccoli, Brussels sprouts, cauliflower, kohlrabi, and gladiolas.

· CONCLUSION ·

Now that you are armed with the knowledge presented in these chapters, it is time to put the book down and get your hands dirty. Gardening — especially when using companion planting techniques— is a cathartic process full of learning and joy. Approach your garden as dynamic project, one that is always changing and growing as the plants develop. Be sure to leave yourself a place that allows for new plants as there will always be a new one you just have to have when you go to nursery centers.

Be generous. Divide, separate, and share your plants with your neighbors and friends and they will return the favor, giving your garden an ever-changing landscape. Gardeners have a lot in common, and almost all of them are happy to share their secrets, making them a great resource as you learn the intricacies of your own space. Try different companion combinations and keep track of your results. As you learn what works well and where, tell others so that they may try companion gardening as well. May people are already trying out many of the suggestions in this book and many would like to – they just do not know about it yet. Companion gardening is not a well-researched topic in gardening, so you can be a pioneer in this gardening venture.

Be daring. The garden is a creative expression and can be wild and joyous or contained and refined. Try different plant combinations, experiment with what works in one corner over on a different corner, add in something new and see what happens to your plants. Your garden is an expression of who you are, just as your home is. In addition, just as you may want to get new furniture every couple of years, or move what you have around the house, expect to have a similar penchant for your garden. Your gardening needs and ideas will change over time; be adaptable and realize that most of the plants are adaptable too.

Be delighted. Most importantly, remember to enjoy your garden. Take time to walk around every morning — a habit you will quickly get into, like most gardeners, to see what is in bloom, and what is about to bloom. Gardens are wonderful places to sit and enjoy a cup of coffee or to take a laptop and work for a few hours. Make the garden an extension of your living space. Remember, this is your piece of land to do what you wish — make it real and make it yours to enjoy.

Online Information Resources

- USDA Natural Resources Conservation Service – this Web site allows you to search the database by either scientific name or the common name of various plants as well as by location. **http://plants.usda.gov/checklist.html**

- The Virginia Tech Department of Forest Resources and Environmental Conservation offers a database that allows you to search for information on various trees. You can search by the location or by hardiness zone. **www.cnr.vt.edu/dendro/dendrology/factsheets.cfm**

- The online version of the Audubon Field Guide series is available at **http://enature.com**. This is an excellent resource for looking up various information on most plants.

- Texas A & M University and Bioinformatics Working Group have complied a vascular plant image library that offers photos of most North American plants **http://botany.csdl.tamu.edu/FLORA/gallery.htm**

- The University of Wisconsin also offers an excellent resource with their Wisconsin State Herbarium specimen database at **www.botany.wisc.edu/wisflora/**

- This Web site lets you to search the University of Connecticut Plant Database for various trees, shrubs, and vines that you might be researching **www.hort.uconn.edu/fmi/xsl/search.xsl**

- North Carolina State University provides information on various plants as well as information about what plants will attract butterflies. **www.ces.ncsu.edu/depts/hort/consumer/factsheets/**

- An easy-to-understand garden insectary from Eartheasy.com is available at **www.eartheasy.com/grow_garden_insectary.htm**

Resources for Frost Dates and Hardiness Zones

- The U.S. National Arboretum has a hyperlinked map showing the hardiness zones across North America at **www.usna.usda.gov/Hardzone/ushzmap.html**

- For plant hardiness zones in Canada specifically, Agriculture and Agri-Food Canada offer a series of maps at **http://sis.agr.gc.ca/cansis/nsdb/climate/hardiness/intro.html**

- The Old Farmer's Almanac offers charts showing the last and first frost dates by area In the United States at **www.almanac.com/content/frost-chart-united-states** and for Canadian locations at **www.almanac.com/content/frost-chart-canada**

Online Resources for Nursery Stocks and Seeds

There are many good sources available on the Internet to purchase gardening supplies. Some that are the easiest to use include:

- Gardeners Network – this site offers bulbs, flowers, nursery stock as well as being a go-to place for information on growing various plants **www.gardenersnet.com/flower.htm**

- Territorial Seeds – this is another great online supplier of seeds, plants, and insects. **www.territorialseed.com/**

- Diane's Flower Seeds – Diane Linsley runs two Web sites; one for her seeds and the other for her daylilies. She prides herself on the quality of her product, the rare perennials, heirloom flower and tomato seeds **www.dianeseeds.com/Index.html**

- GardeningPlaces.com — this site offers a directory of online seed catalogues. On the home page, you can choose the type of online catalogues you want to look at **www.gardeningplaces.com/index.htm**

- Heirloom Vegetable Gardener's Assistant — this site offers an excellent listing of heirloom seed companies at **www.halcyon.com/tmend/links.htm**

- Some other favorites for buying seeds include:
  - Burpee seeds and plants at **www.burpee.com**
  - Stokes Seeds at **www.stokeseeds.com**
  - Henry Field's Seed & Nursery Co. at **www.henryfields.ca**
  - Vesey's Seeds offers both a U.S. Web site at **www.veseys.com** and Canadian Web site at **www.veseys.com/ca/en**
  - Richters for seeds and plants at **www.richters.com**

Recommended Reading

Here are few other book titles on companion gardening to consider:

- Carr, Anna, *Good Neighbors: Companion Planting for Gardeners,* Emmaus, PA: Rodale Press 1995.

- Cunningham, Sally Jean, *Great Garden Companions, A Companion-Planting System for a Beautiful, Chemical-free Vegetable Garden,* Emmaus, Pennsylvania: Rodale Press 1998.

- Little, Brenda, *Secrets of Companion Planting: Plants that Help, Plants that Hurt,* Sandy, Utah: Silverleaf Press 2008.

- Lord, Tony, *Encyclopedia of Planting Combinations,* Buffalo, New York: Firefly Books (USA) Inc. 2008.

- Phillips, Ellen, *Rodale's Illustrated Encyclopedia of Perennials,* Emmaus, Pennsylvania: Rodale Press 1993.

- Riotte, Louise, *Carrots Love Tomatoes: Secrets of Companion Planting for Successful Gardening,* North Adams, MA: Storey Publishing Ltd. 1998.

- Riotte, Louse, *Roses Love Garlic,* North Adams, MA: Storey Publications 1998.

· GLOSSARY ·

Aerobic decomposition: the process of decomposing in the presence of oxygen

Annuals: a plant that completes its life cycle in one year or less

Bolt: go to seed quickly

Brown garden materials: compost materials that are high in carbon and typically brown in color, including dry leaves and twigs

Companion planting: the practice of planting two or more plants together to enhance the growth and quality of nearby plants; to provide maximum ground cover; and, when possible, to improve the soil

Compost tea: a mixture that results from steeping compost in a large bucket of water, essentially providing a diluted, liquid form of compost you can spray over gardens and plant beds

Container gardening: the process of growing plants in pots or containers instead of in the ground; the advantage to this system is gardeners can easily move plants if they are not growing well or plants can be grown indoors

Corm: a swollen, underground plant stem

Cottage garden: an informal, light-hearted garden that contains perennials, herbs, and rosebushes; there are often fences, trellises, arbors, or seating areas that will give a vertical aspect to the garden without detracting from it

Country garden: a form of garden that is a mix between the mixed border garden and the cottage garden style; it may incorporate trellises, arches, perennials, hedges, trees, and elements that are both formal and informal

Cover crop: a crop planted to improve the function of a primary plant

Crop plants: plants that are grown primarily for human and animal feed

Crop rotation: relocating crops to a different part of the garden every year

Cut-and-come-again salads: salad greens that do not need to reach maturity before harvesting and can be cut to grow again

Dampening off: when young seedlings suddenly die, most likely from rot

Deadheading: the process of plucking dead blooms off flowers; also called pinching off

Digging a plant under: the practice of leaving a plant in the ground and turning the dirt and soil over, chopping the plant and roots as you do so

Division: the process of separating a plant into several smaller versions of the original to keep the plant healthy

Dolly: a small platform with wheels used to move heavy objects

Dwarf trees: versions of trees that have been kept artificially small through horticultural practice

Floret: a tiny grouping of flowers centered together on a series petal-like bracts

Flowering shrubs: shrubs grown primarily for their flowery show

Formal garden: a garden that features defined shape and structure, often featuring clearly outlined beds and strong, geometric shapes

Frost heaves: when the freezing and thawing process plants go through causes the soil to expand and contract, which can break roots and force plants out of the ground

Fruit bushes/trees: trees and/or shrubs that bear edible fruit

Full-shade garden: a garden when no direct sunlight reaches the ground at any time of the day

Full-sun garden: a garden that can grow in the hottest and driest conditions; fruit trees, vines, and shrubs grow well in this type of environment

Garden insectory: a type of garden designed to attract or harbor beneficial insects

Grafting: attaching a plant from a differing type of fruit or tree onto another tree

Grasses: plants that have jointed stems, leaves, and produce seed-like grain

Green garden materials: compost materials that are high in nitrogen, including grass clippings and annuals pulled from the garden

Green manure: a form of organic compost that benefits a garden

Hardening off: the process used to acclimate seedlings to an outdoor environment; it usually entails setting seedlings outdoors during the day and bringing them in at night until they are used to the temperature

Hardiness: the temperature range in which a plant will survive

Hardiness zones: the different zones, as determined by the USDA, where various trees, shrubs, and flowers will most likely survive

Hardscape: aspects of a garden that do not grow; for example, driveways, walkways, and fountains

Herbaceous border gardens: a form of garden that is backed by a high stone wall or a picket fence and features summer perennials of various heights and foliage varieties

Herbaceous plants: plants that their tops die down while the roots or bulbs remain alive

Herbs: small, seed-bearing plants that are most noted for their aromatic, medicinal, healthful, and cooking qualities

Intercropping: another term for companion planting

Lawn dressing: a 1- to 3-inch layer of compost that is added on top of existing grass

Level interactions: planting tall plants with short plants to provide shade and structure

Light shade: a garden's lighting condition where filtered sunlight comes through the leaves of trees, still allowing some light to hit the plants beneath the tree

Loamy: a form of soil that is a mixture of sand, clay, and organic matter; this is an ideal form of soil

Microclimate: a mini-climate or a small, specific place found within a larger climate area; this results from different types of exposures to the elements

Minimalist garden: a garden that features a clean, crisp look and incorporates clean lines, simple spaces, and are often used in conjunction with contemporary architecture

Mixed border garden: a simple form of garden that include perennials, annuals, and bulbs

Monoculture: when only one plant is used in a garden

Naturalized garden: a garden that strives to recreate a balance that is often seen in nature; this garden welcomes wildlife and seeds and bulbs are scattered throughout the bed, allowing nature to scatter the plants instead of planting them in rows

Nitrogen fixation: when plants such as peas, beans, and clover excrete excess nitrogen into the soil, allowing other plants to absorb the nitrogen

Nut bushes: bushes grown for the nuts they produce

Ornamental shrubs: these shrubs are grown purely for looks

Overwinter: surviving the winter season

Perennials: plants that live longer than one year

Polyculture: a method of planting species of plants together for mutual benefit, usually in agricultural situations

Prairie garden: a mix of perennials and grasses that are grown together

Rhizome: a horizontal plant stem with shoots above ground and roots below ground

Run to seed: when a plant matures too quickly and produces seeds more quickly than they can be eaten

Scorching: when leaves burn and dry up because of too little water

Seeding: sowing seeds of plants you want to appear in spring and summer

Side dressing: fertilizing mid-way through a growing season

Soaker hose: a hose with small holes throughout the tubing that allows the hose to equally distribute water among plants

Taproot: one long, single root

Thinning: pulling out plants that are growing too close together and moving them to different areas of the garden

Trap cropping: using a specific plant in a garden to trap or attract a pest, keeping it away from another plant in the garden

Tuber: a thickened portion of an underground stem

Vegetable: plants that are edible or part of the plant is edible

Vertical gardening: using plants that will climb taller than standard plants so gathering vegetables, fruit, or herbs is done at a higher level

Wildflower packets: a wide variety of plant seeds mixed together and used to throw into fields to achieve a natural look

Winter burn: damage that winter temperatures cause

Woodlands garden: a garden style that typically incorporates a canopy of trees, a layer of shrubs, and the woodland floor

· BIBLIOGRAPHY ·

Adams, Sheena, "Using wood ash in the garden," Garden Wise, **www.gardenwiseonline.ca/gw/ sustainable-gardening/2006/11/01/using-wood-ash-garden**, accessed January 12, 2010.

"Adam's Needle," Dayton Nurseries, **www.daytonnursery.com/Encyclopedia/Trees_Shrubs/ Yucca.htm**, accessed January 30, 2010.

"Balloon Flower," Dayton Nurseries, **www.daytonnursery.com/Encyclopedia/Perennials/Platy-codon.htm**, accessed January 23, 2010.

Baltz, Dottie, "Companion Planting," **www.gardensandcrafts.com/CompanionPlanting.pdf**, accessed December 20, 2009.

Beaulieu, David, "Companion Planting," **http://landscaping.about.com/cs/soilsfertilizers/a/ companion_plant.htm**, accessed January 14, 2010.

Beaulieu, David, "English Ivy Plants," **http://landscaping.about.com/od/groundcovervines1/p/ english_ivy.htm**, accessed February 10, 2010.

Beaulieu, David, "How to Kill Grass," **http://landscaping.about.com/od/alternativestograss/a/ how_kill_grass.htm**, accessed January 14, 2010.

Beaulieu, David, "Poison Sumac: Exception, Not the Rule," **http://landscaping.about.com/cs/ landscapecolor/a/sumac_2.htm**, accessed February 10, 2010.

Beaulieu, David, "Rose of Sharon Bush," **http://landscaping.about.com/od/shrubsbushes/p/ rose_of_sharon.htm**, accessed February 10, 2010.

"Beneficial Insects," basic-info-4-organic-fertilizers.com, **www.basic-info-4-organic-fertilizers. com/beneficialinsects.html**, accessed January 12, 2010.

"Bleeding Heart," Dayton Nurseries, **www.daytonnursery.com/Encyclopedia/Perennials/Dicen-tra.htm**, accessed February 23, 2010.

"Blueberries," Dayton Nurseries, **www.daytonnursery.com/Encyclopedia/Fruits/Blueberry.htm**, accessed January 30, 2010.

Brown, Ellen, "Growing Blueberries," Thriftyfun, **www.thriftyfun.com/tf31995840.tip.html**, accessed January 28, 2010.

"Burning Bush," Dayton Nurseries, **www.daytonnursery.com/Encyclopedia/Trees_Shrubs/ Euonymous.htm**, accessed January 30, 2010.

"Buttonbush," Dayton Nurseries, **www.daytonnursery.com/Encyclopedia/Trees_Shrubs/ Cephalanthus.htm**, accessed January 30, 2010.

"Buttonbush," Study of Northern Virginia Ecology, **www.fcps.edu/islandcreekes/ecology/buttonbush.htm**, accessed January 24, 2010.

Chalker-Scott, Linda, "The Myth of Companion Plantings," Puyallup Research and Extension Center, Washington State University, **www.puyallup.wsu.edu/~Linda%20Chalker-Scott/Horticultural%20Myths_files/Myths/Companion%20plants.pdf**, accessed January 12, 2010.

Cheever, Jenney, "Companion Plants for Fruit Trees," Life 123, **www.life123.com/home-garden/ trees-shrubs/fruit-trees/companion-plants.shtml**, accessed January 30, 2010.

Chernega, Carol, "Cotton Lavender," English Garden Site of Bella Online, **www.bellaonline. com/articles/art25463.asp**, accessed January 17, 2010.

"Chrysanthemum," Gardenguides.com, **www.gardenguides.com/149-chrysanthemum-chrysanthemum-garden-basics-flower-perennial.html**, accessed December 22, 2009.

"Clematis Vine," Dayton Nurseries, **www.daytonnursery.com/Encyclopedia/Vines/Clematis. htm**, accessed January 28, 2010.

"Climbing Bittersweet," Study of Northern Virginia Ecology, **www.fcps.edu/islandcreekes/ecology/climbing_bittersweet.htm**, accessed January 28, 2010.

Cohen, Dan, "Iowa's Shrubs and Vines," Iowa Association of Naturalists **www.extension.iastate. edu/Publications/IAN307.pdf**, accessed February 19, 2010.

"Common Elderberry," Study of Northern Virginia Ecology, **www.fcps.edu/islandcreekes/ecology/common_elderberry.htm**, accessed January 27, 2010.

"Companion Planting," **www.dgsgardening.btinternet.co.uk/companion.htm**, accessed January 12, 2010.

"Companion Planting," Golden Harvest Organics, **www.ghorganics.com/page2.html**, accessed February 1, 2010.

"Companion Planting," Sustainable Gardening Australia, **www.sgaonline.org.au/?p=207**, accessed February 22, 2010.

"Companion Planting; Bedfellows in the Garden," Our Garden Gang, **http://ourgardengang. tripod.com/companions.htm#att**, accessed January 12, 2010.

"Companion Planting: How to get your vegetables growing even better," The Vegetable Patch, **www.thevegetablepatch.com/companion.htm**, accessed January 12, 2010.

"Companion Plants: Insect-Repellant Plants – Beneficial Insects," Rex Research, **www.rexresearch.com/agro/comp1.htm**, accessed February 23, 2010.

"Composting Instructions: How to Compost at Home," Composting Instructions, **http://compostinstructions.com/how-to-use-compost-in-your-yard-and-garden**, accessed January 10, 2010.

"Cotoneaster," Dayton Nurseries, **www.daytonnursery.com/Encyclopedia/Trees_Shrubs/Cotoneaster.htm**, accessed January 30, 2010.

"Creeping Phlox," Dayton Nurseries, **www.daytonnursery.com/Encyclopedia/Perennials/Phlox%20subulata.htm**, accessed February 23, 2010.

Cunningham, Sally Jean, *Great Garden Companions, A Companion-Planting System for a Beautiful, Chemical-free Vegetable Garden,* Emmaus, Pennsylvania: Rodale Press. 1978

Davis, Dee, "Pear Tree Companion planting," eHow.com, **www.ehow.com/way_5801730_pear-tree-companion-planting.html**, accessed March 15, 2010.

"Daylily," Dayton Nurseries, **www.daytonnursery.com/Encyclopedia/Perennials/Hemerocallis.htm**, accessed January 28, 2010.

"Deutzia," Dayton Nurseries, **www.daytonnursery.com/Encyclopedia/Trees_Shrubs/Deutzia.htm**, accessed January 30, 2010.

"Digs, Dwellings, and Dens," Wild About Gardening, **www.wildaboutgardening.org/en/dig_dwell_den/section2/index.htm#l4**, accessed January 11, 2010.

"Dutchman's Pipe," Dayton Nurseries, **www.daytonnursery.com/Encyclopedia/Vines/Aristolochia.htm**, accessed January 28, 2010.

"English Ivy," Dayton Nurseries, **www.daytonnursery.com/Encyclopedia/Ground_Cover/Hedera.htm**, accessed January 28, 2010.

Erney, Diana, "Long live the Three Sisters," Organic Gardening, November 1996. p. 37-40. Retrieved Dec. 21, 2009

Evans, Erv, "American Elderberry," North Carolina State University, **www.ces.ncsu.edu/depts/hort/consumer/factsheets/shrubs/sambucus_canadensis.html**, accessed January 24, 2010

Evans, Erv, "Attracting Birds: Shrubs," North Carolina State University, **www.ces.ncsu.edu/depts/hort/consumer/factsheets/birds/text/bird_shrubs.html**, accessed January 24, 2010.

Evan's Erv, "Attracting Birds: Vines," North Carolina State University, **www.ces.ncsu.edu/depts/hort/consumer/factsheets/birds/text/bird_vines.html**, accessed February 1, 2010.

Evans, Erv, "Attracting Hummingbirds: Shrubs," North Carolina State University, **www.ces.ncsu.edu/depts/hort/consumer/factsheets/birds/text/hbird_shrubs.html**, accessed January 24, 2010.

Evans, Erv, "Blackhawa viburnum," North Carolina State University, **www.ces.ncsu.edu/depts/hort/consumer/factsheets/shrubs/viburnum_prunifolium.html**, accessed January 24, 2010.

Evans, Erv, "Boston Ivy; Japanese creeper," North Carolina State University, **www.ces.ncsu.edu/depts/hort/consumer/factsheets/vines/parthenocissus_tri.html**, accessed January 24, 2010.

Evans, Erv, "Butterfly bush," North Carolina State University, **www.ces.ncsu.edu/depts/hort/consumer/factsheets/shrubs/buddleia_davidii.html**, accessed January 24, 2010.

Evans, Erv, "Cinnamonbark clethra: Mountain pepperbush," North Carolina State University, www.ces.ncsu.edu/depts/hort/consumer/factsheets/shrubs/clethra_acuminata.html, accessed January 24, 2010.

Evans, Erv, "Dutchman's Pipe," North Carolina State University, **www.ces.ncsu.edu/depts/hort/consumer/factsheets/vines/aristolochia_durior.html**, accessed January 24, 2010.

Evans, Erv, "English Ivy," North Carolina State University, **www.ces.ncsu.edu/depts/hort/consumer/factsheets/vines/hedera_helix.html**, accessed January 28, 2010.

Evans, Erv, "Hercules' club/Devil's walking stick," North Carolina State University, **www.ces.ncsu.edu/depts/hort/consumer/factsheets/shrubs/aralia_spinosa.html**, accessed January 24, 2010.

Evans, Erv, "Japanese honeysuckle," North Carolina State University, **www.ces.ncsu.edu/depts/hort/consumer/factsheets/vines/lonicera_japonica.html**, accessed January 24, 2010.

Evans, Erv, "Maple leaf viburnum," North Carolina State University, **www.ces.ncsu.edu/depts/hort/consumer/factsheets/shrubs/viburnum_acerifolium.html**, accessed January 24, 2010.

Evans, Erv, "Oakleaf hydrangea," North Carolina State University, **www.ces.ncsu.edu/depts/hort/consumer/factsheets/shrubs/hydrangea_quercifolia.html**, accessed January 24, 2010.

Evans, Erv, "Oriental bittersweet," North Carolina State University, **www.ces.ncsu.edu/depts/hort/consumer/factsheets/vines/celastrus_orbiculatus.html**, accessed January 26, 2010.

Evans, Erv, "Rose-of-Sharon; Shrub althea," North Carolina State University, **www.ces.ncsu.edu/depts/hort/consumer/factsheets/shrubs/hibiscus_syriacus.html**, accessed January 24, 2010.

Evans, Erv, "Scottish broom," North Carolina State University, **www.ces.ncsu.edu/depts/hort/consumer/factsheets/shrubs/cytisus_scoparius.html**, accessed January 24, 2010.

Evans, Erv, "Siebold viburnum," North Carolina State University, **www.ces.ncsu.edu/depts/hort/consumer/factsheets/shrubs/viburnum_sieboldii.html**, accessed January 24, 2010

Evans, Erv, "Spice bush," North Carolina State University, **www.ces.ncsu.edu/depts/hort/consumer/factsheets/shrubs/lindera_benzoin.html**, accessed January 24, 2010.

Evans, Erv, "Summersweet; Sweet pepperbush; Clethra," North Carolina State University, **www.ces.ncsu.edu/depts/hort/consumer/factsheets/shrubs/clethra_alnifolia.html**, accessed January 24, 2010.

Evans, Erv, "Trumpet creeper; Trumpet vine," North Carolina State University, **www.ces.ncsu.edu/depts/hort/consumer/factsheets/vines/campsis_radicans.html**, accessed January 28, 2010.

Evans, Erv, "Trumpet honeysuckle; Coral honeysuckle," North Carolina State University, **www.ces.ncsu.edu/depts/hort/consumer/factsheets/vines/lonicera_sempervirens.html**, accessed January 28, 2010.

Evans, Erv, "Virginia creeper," North Carolina State University, **www.ces.ncsu.edu/depts/hort/consumer/factsheets/vines/parthenocissus_quinque.html**, accessed January 24, 2010.

Evans, Erv, "Virginia rose," North Carolina State University, **www.ces.ncsu.edu/depts/hort/consumer/factsheets/native/rosa_virginiana.html**, accessed January 24, 2010.

"False Spirea/Feather Flower," Dayton Nurseries, **www.daytonnursery.com/Encyclopedia/Perennials/Astilbe.htm**, accessed February 23, 2010.

Flanigan, Lorraine, "Mulching 101," Canadian Gardening, **www.canadiangardening.com/howto/gardening-basics/mulching-101/a/22278**, accessed January 11, 2010.

"Forsythia," Dayton Nurseries, **www.daytonnursery.com/Encyclopedia/Trees_Shrubs/Forsythia.htm**, accessed January 30, 2010.

"Fothergilla," Dayton Nurseries, **www.daytonnursery.com/Encyclopedia/Trees_Shrubs/Fothergilla.htm**, accessed January 30, 2010.

"Golden Privett," Dayton Nurseries, **www.daytonnursery.com/Encyclopedia/Trees_Shrubs/Ligustrum.htm**, accessed January 30, 2010.

"Growing Superb Gardens and Plants," **http://gardenhobbies.com/flower/chrysanthemum.html,** accessed December 22, 2009.

Haase, Janette, *From Seed to Table – A Practical Guide to Eating and Growing Green,* London, Ontario: Insomniac Press, 2009.

7Hill, Stuart B., "Companion plants," Ecological Agriculture Projects, **http://eap.mcgill.ca/publications/EAP55.htm**, accessed January 4, 2010.

"Honeysuckle Vine," Dayton Nurseries, **www.daytonnursery.com/Encyclopedia/Vines/Lonicera.htm**, accessed January 28, 2010.

"Hosta," Dayton Nurseries, **www.daytonnursery.com/Encyclopedia/Perennials/Hosta.htm**, accessed February 23, 2010.

"How to Grow Achillea Perennial Flower Plants," The Gardener's Network, **www.gardenersnet.com/flower/achillea.htm**, accessed January 20, 2010.

"How to Grow and Care for Alyssum Flowers," The Gardener's Network, **www.gardenersnet.com/flower/alyssum.htm**, accessed January 20, 2010.

"How to Grow and care for Amaranth Flower," The Gardener's Network, **www.gardenersnet.com/flower/amaranth.htm**, accessed January 20, 2010.

"How to Grow and Care for Amaryllis Flowers," The Gardener's Network, **www.gardenersnet.com/flower/amaryllis.htm**, accessed January 11, 2010.

"How to Grow and Care for Aster Flowers," The Gardener's Network, **www.gardenersnet.com/flower/aster.htm**, accessed January 11, 2010.

"How to Grow and Care for Azalea Bushes," The Gardener's Network, **www.gardenersnet.com/tree/azalea.htm**, accessed January 20, 2010.

"How to Grow and Care for Bachelor Buttons," The Gardener's Network, **www.gardenersnet.com/flower/bachelor.htm**, accessed January 20, 2010.

"How to Grow and Care for Blanketflower," The Gardener's Network, **www.gardenersnet.com/flower/blanketflower.htm**, accessed January 20, 2010.

"How to Grow and Care for Calendula Flowers," The Gardener's Network, **www.gardenersnet.com/flower/calendula.htm**, accessed January 20, 2010.

"How to Grow and Care for Cosmos Flowers," The Gardener's Network, **www.gardenersnet.com/flower/cosmos.htm**, accessed January 20, 2010.

"How to Grow and Care for Cypress Vine," The Gardener's Network, **www.gardenersnet.com/flower/cypressvine.htm**, accessed February 1, 2010.

"How to Grow and Care for Lilac Bushes," The Gardener's Network, **www.gardenersnet.com/flower/lilac.htm**, accessed February 1, 2010.

"How to Grow and Care for Rhododendrons," The Gardener's Network, **www.gardenersnet.com/ tree/rhododendron.htm**, accessed January 20, 2010.

"How to Grow and Care for Rock Cress Plant," The Gardener's Network, **www.gardenersnet. com/flower/rockcress.htm**, accessed January 20, 2010.

"How to Grow and Care for Trumpet Flowers," The Gardener's Network, **www.gardenersnet. com/flower/trumpetflowervine.htm**, accessed February 1, 2010.

"How to Grow Blazing Star, Liatris Flowering Plants," The Gardener's Network, **www.gardeners-net.com/bulbs/blazingstarliatris.htm**, accessed January 17, 2010.

"How to Grow Chrysanthemums," The Gardener's Network, **www.gardenersnet.com/flower/ mums**.htm, accessed January 20, 2010.

"How to Grow Coreopsis Flowers," The Gardener's Network, **www.gardenersnet.com/flower/ coreopsis.htm**, accessed January 20, 2010.

"How to Grow Daffodil Flowering Bulbs," The Gardener's Network, **www.gardenersnet.com/ flower/daffodil.htm**, accessed January 17, 2010.

"How to Grow Dahlia Flower Plants," The Gardener's Network, **www.gardenersnet.com/flower/ dahlia.htm**, accessed January 20, 2010.

"How to Grow Four O'Clock Flowers," The Gardener's Network, **www.gardenersnet.com/ flower/fouroclock.htm**, accessed January 20, 2010.

"How to Grow Foxglove Flowers," The Gardener's Network, **www.gardenersnet.com/flower/ foxglove.htm**, accessed January 20 ,2010.

"How to Grow Delphinium Flowers," The Gardener's Network, **www.gardenersnet.com/flower/ delphinium.htm**, accessed January 20, 2010.

"How to Grow Geraniums," The Gardener's Network, **www.gardenersnet.com/flower/geranium. htm**, accessed January 20, 2010.

"How to Grow Gladiolus Flowers," The Gardener's Network, **www.gardenersnet.com/bulbs/ gladiolus.htm**, accessed January 14, 2010.

"How to Grow Grapes," eHow, **www.ehow.com/how_172717_grow-grapes.html**, accessed January 24, 2010.

"How to Grow Hyacinth Flowering Bulbs," The Gardener's Network, **www.gardenersnet.com/ flower/hyacinth.htm**, accessed January 17, 2010.

"How to Grow Larkspur Flowers," The Gardener's Network, **www.gardenersnet.com/flower/ larkspur.htm**, accessed January 20, 2010.

"How to Grow Marigold Plants," The Gardener's Network, **www.gardenersnet.com/flower/mari-gold.htm**, accessed January 20, 2010.

"How to Grow Nasturtium Plants," The Gardener's Network, **www.gardenersnet.com/flower/ nasturt.htm**, accessed January 20, 2010.

"How to Grow Petunias," The Gardener's Network, **www.gardenersnet.com/flower/petunia. htm**, accessed January 20, 2010.

"How to Grow Raspberries," eHow, **www.ehow.com/how_2100127_grow-raspberries.html**, accessed January 25, 2010.

"How to Grow Rhubarb," eHow, **www.ehow.com/how_2006_grow-rhubarb.html**, accessed February 23, 2010.

"How to Grow Snow Crocus," The Gardener's Network, **www.gardenersnet.com/bulbs/crocus. htm**, accessed January 12, 2010.

"How to Grow Strawberries," eHow, **www.ehow.com/how_2000_grow-strawberries.html**, accessed February 10, 2010.

"How to Grow Sunflower Plants," The Gardener's Network, **www.gardenersnet.com/vegetable/ sunflowr.htm**, accessed January 20, 2010.

"How to Grow Sweet Pea Flower Plants," The Gardener's Network, **www.gardenersnet.com/ flower/sweetpea.htm**, accessed January 20, 2010.

"How to Grow Tansy Flowers," The Gardener's Network, **www.gardenersnet.com/flower/tansy. htm**, accessed January 20, 2010.

"How to Grow Tithonia Mexican Sunflower Plants," The Gardener's Network, **www.gardeners-net.com/flower/tithonia.htm**, accessed January 20, 2010.

"How to Grow Tulips, King of the Flowering Bulbs," The Gardener's Network, **www.gardeners-net.com/bulbs/tulips.htm**, accessed January 17, 2010.

"How to Grow Vinca or Periwinkle Plants," The Gardener's Network, **www.gardenersnet.com/ flower/vincaperiwinkle.htm**, accessed January 20, 2010.

"How to Grow Zinnia Flowers," The Gardener's Network, **www.gardenersnet.com/flower/zin-nia.htm**, accessed January 20, 2010.

"How to Mulch," How Stuff Works, **http://home.howstuffworks.com/how-to-mulch.htm**, accessed January 11, 2010.

"How to use Flowering Quince in Your Landscape," Do It Yourself, **www.doityourself.com/stry/ how-to-use-a-flowering-quince-in-your-landscape**, accessed February 10, 2010.

Hunter, Lorraine, "Witch hazel: A Tree that Blooms in Winter," Canadian Gardening, **www. canadiangardening.com/plants/trees-and-shrubs/witch-hazel-a-tree-that-blooms-in-winter/a/1344**, accessed February 14, 2010.

Iannoti, Marie, "Garden Maintenance – Pinching, Deadheading, and Cutting Back," **About.com, http://gardening.about.com/od/gardenprimer/ss/GardenMaint_9.htm**, accessed January 12, 2010.

Iannoti, Marie, "Growing Blueberries," About.com, **http://gardening.about.com/od/berries/a/ Blueberries.htm**, accessed March 15, 2010.

Iannoti, Marie, "Perennial Gardening – How to Divide Perennial Plants," About.com, **http://gar-dening.about.com/od/perennials/ss/DividingSBS_10.htm**, accessed January 12, 2010.

Iannoti, Marie, "Shrubs for Seasonal Interest, Attracting Birds, and All Around Beauty," About. com, **http://gardening.about.com/od/treeshrubs/ig/Top-Shrubs-for-the-Home-Garden**, accessed February 15, 2010.

Iannoti, Marie, "Viburnums," About.com, **http://gardening.about.com/od/treesshrubs/a/ Viburnums.htm**, accessed February 15, 2010.

"Japanese Honeysuckle," Study of Northern Virginia Ecology, **www.fcps.edu/islandcreekcs/ccology/japanese_honeysuckle.htm**, accessed January 28, 2010.

"Japanese Hydrangea Vine," Dayton Nurseries, **www.daytonnursery.com/Encyclopedia/Vines/ Schizophragma.htm**, accessed January 28, 2010.

"Japanese Spirea," Dayton Nurseries, **www.daytonnursery.com/Encyclopedia/Trees_Shrubs/ Spiraea.htm**, accessed 1/30/10.

Lerner, B. Rosie, "Annual Versus Perennial Flowers," **www.hort.purdue.edu/ext/annper.html**, accessed January 28, 2010.

Little, Brenda, *Secrets of Companion Planting: Plants that help, Plants that Hurt,* Sandy, Utah: Silverleaf Press 2008.

"Lily of the Valley," Dayton Nurseries, **www.daytonnursery.com/Encyclopedia/Perennials/Convallaria.htm**, accessed January 28, 2010.

"List of Companion Plants," **http://en.wikipedia.org/wiki/List_of_companion_plants**, accessed December 1, 2009.

Lord, Tony, *Encyclopedia of Planting Combinations,* Buffalo, New York: Firefly Books (US) Inc. 2008.

McIntosh, Jamie, "Get Rid of Squirrels in the Garden," Suite101, **http://organicgardens. suite101.com/article.cfm/get_rid_of_squirrels_in_the_garden%20january%2010.10**, accessed January 10, 2010.

McMillan, Stuart, "Predator Profile: Minute Pirate Bug," The Canadian Organic Grower, **www. cog.ca/documents/PredatorProfileSU07.pdf**, accessed January 12, 2010.

Musial, Peggy, "Mulch Types: Advantages vs. Disadvantages: Cover all the bases when choosing right mulch," *Orlando Sentinel,* August, 17, 2002 **www.gomulch.com/index.cfm/name-sentinel**, accessed January 12, 2010.

"Natural Pest Control," Grinning Planet, **www.grinningplanet.com/2005/04-26/beneficial-insect-natural-pest-control-article.htm**, accessed January 12, 2010.

Newman, Lauri, "Fruit Trees and Family Friends: Beneficial Plant Neighbors Make Balanced Ecosystems," The Free Library.com, **www.thefreelibrary.com/Fruit+trees+and+family+friends:+ beneficial+plant+neighbors+make...-a0170927545**, accessed March 15, 2010.

"Ornamental Elderberry," Dayton Nurseries, **www.daytonnursery.com/Encyclopedia/Trees_ Shrubs/Sambucus.htm**, accessed January 30, 2010.

"Paperwhite Narcissus Flowering Bulbs," The Gardener's Network, **www.gardenersnet.com/ bulbs/paperwhite.htm**, accessed January 17, 2010.

"Passion Fruit," California Rare Fruit Growers, **www.crfg.org/pubs/ff/passionfruit.html**, accessed February 2, 2010.

"Peony," Dayton Nurseries, **www.daytonnursery.com/Encyclopedia/Perennials/Paeonia%20 suffruticosa.htm**, accessed February 23, 2010.

"Perennial Plants," **http://en.wikipedia.org/wiki/Perennial_plant**, accessed December 1, 2009.

Phillips, Ellen *Rodale's Illustrated encyclopedia of Perennials,* Emmaus, Pennsylvania: Rodale Press 1993.

"Pinks/Carnations," Dayton Nurseries, **www.daytonnursery.com/Encyclopedia/Perennials/Dianthus.htm**, accessed February 23, 2010.

"Plains Coreopsis," **http://en.wikipedia.org/wiki/Plains_coreopsis**, accessed December 22, 2009.

"PlantFiles: Tropical Hydrangea, Pink-Ball," Dave's Garden, **http://davesgarden.com/guides/pf/go/54587**, accessed January 28, 2010.

"Porcelain Berry Vine," Dayton Nurseries, **www.daytonnursery.com/Encyclopedia/Vines/Ampelopsis.htm**, accessed January 28, 2010.

"Privet," **http://en.wikipedia.org/wiki/Privet**, accessed December 1, 2009.

"Purple Leaf Akebia," Dayton Nurseries, **www.daytonnursery.com/Encyclopedia/Vines/Akebia.htm**, accessed January 28, 2010.

Pyle, Robert Michael, *National Audubon Society Field Guide to North American Butterflies.* New York: Alfred A. Knopf, 1981.

"Pyrethrum," **http://en.wikipedia.org/wiki/Pyrethrum**, accessed December 1, 2009.

"Queen Anne's Lace," The Gardener's Network, **www.gardenersnet.com/flower/queenann.htm**, accessed January 20, 2010.

Rice, Graham, *All-in-one Garden: Grow Vegetables, Fruit, Herbs, and Flowers in the Same Space,* New York, New York: Sterling Publishing Company Ltd. 2006.

Riotte, Louise, *Carrots Love Tomatoes; Secrets of Companion Planting for Successful Gardening,* North Adams, MA: Storey Publishing Ltd. 1998

Sanders, April, "How to Deter Rabbits From a Garden," eHow, **www.ehow.com/how_4443152_deter-rabbits-from-garden.html**, accessed January 10, 2010

"Silver Lace Vine," Dayton Nurseries, **www.daytonnursery.com/Encyclopedia/Vines/Polygonum.htm**, accessed January 28, 2010.

"Smoke Bush," Dayton Nurseries, **www.daytonnursery.com/Encyclopedia/Trees_Shrubs/Cotinus.htm**, accessed January 30, 2010.

"Smooth Sumac," Study of Northern Virginia Ecology, **www.fcps.edu/islandcreekes/ecology/smooth_sumac.htm**, accessed January 28, 2010.

"Snow on the Mountain," Dayton Nurseries, **www.daytonnursery.com/Encyclopedia/Perennials/Aegopodium.htm**, accessed January 28, 2010.

"Solomon's Seal," Dayton Nurseries, **www.daytonnursery.com/Encyclopedia/Perennials/Polygonatum.htm**, accessed February 23, 2010.

"Spicebush," Study of Northern Virginia Ecology, **www.fcps.edu/islandcreekes/ecology/spicebush.htm**, accessed January 28, 2010.

"Spiderwort," Dayton Nurseries, **www.daytonnursery.com/Encyclopedia/Perennials/Tradescantia.htm**, accessed February 23, 2010.

"Spotted Dead Nettle," Dayton Nurseries, **www.daytonnursery.com/Encyclopedia/Perennials/Lamium.htm**, accessed January 28, 2010.

Stewart, Angus, "Fact Sheet: Weed Tea Fertilizer," Gardening Australia, **www.abc.net.au/gardening/stories/s2267268.htm**, accessed January 12, 2010.

"Strawberry Bush," Hilton Pond Center for Piedmont Natural History, **www.hiltonpond.org/ThisWeek030915.html**, accessed January 14, 2010.

"Tansy," **http://en.wikipedia.org/wiki/Tansy**, accessed April 11, 2010.

"The Best Perennial Vines for Your Garden," *Better Homes and Gardens,* **www.bhg.com/gardening/trees-shrubs-vines/vines/best-perennial-vines/?page=1**, accessed February 4, 2010.

"Trumpet Creeper," Study of Northern Virginia Ecology, **www.fcps.edu/islandcreekes/ecology/trumpet_creeper.htm**, accessed January 28, 2010.

"Trumpet Vine," Dayton Nurseries, **www.daytonnursery.com/Encyclopedia/Vines/Campsis.htm**, accessed January 28, 2010.

Uyterhoeven, Sonia, "In Good Company: Companion Planting for Roses," About.com: Gardening, **http://gardening.about.com/od/rose1/a/Rose_Companions.htm**, accessed February 23, 2010.

"Virgina Creeper," Study of Northern Virginia Ecology, **www.fcps.edu/islandcreekes/ecology/virginia_creeper.htm**, accessed January 28, 2010.

"Virgina Rose," Study of Northern Virginia Ecology, **www.fcps.edu/islandcreekes/ecology/virginia_rose.htm**, accessed January 28, 2010,

Weinmann, Todd, "Companion Planting," North Dakota State University, **www.ext.nodak.edu/county/cass/horticulture/vegetables/companion.htm**, accessed January 15, 2010.

"Wisteria Vine," Dayton Nurseries, **www.daytonnursery.com/Encyclopedia/Vines/Wisteria.htm**, accessed January 28, 2010.

"Witch Hazel," Study of Northern Virginia Ecology, **www.fcps.edu/islandcreekes/ecology/witch_hazel.htm**, accessed January 28, 2010.

"Why Garden for Wildlife?" Royal Society for the Protection of Birds, **www.rspbliverpool.org.uk/Helpgardening.htm**, accessed February 10, 2010.

Wooten, George, "The Herbal Database" Docstoc.com, **www.docstoc.com/docs/7415207/The-Herbal-Database---A-Listing-of-Herbs-Spices-and-Medicinal-Plants-and-Some-Clues-to-Their-Uses/**, accessed April 7, 2010.

· AUTHOR BIOGRAPHY ·

As a certified technical writer, editor, and researcher, Dale has a passion for the written word and for all subjects, new and old. She's been writing for more than a decade in nonfiction, fiction, poetry, and screenplays. Her published books cover topics including gardening, resume writing, and even the mortgage industry. She enjoys writing nonfiction because it keeps her brain grounded in this world, while her mind has a tendency to drift off creating other worlds for her fiction. A single mother of four, she successfully manages her full-time writing career around parental responsibilities and still squeezes in time to write new manuscripts each year. Learn more about her at **www.dalemayer.com**.

· INDEX ·